Who are
The Progressives
Now?

Who are the Progressives Now?

An Account of an Educational Confrontation

MAURICE ASH

With

Kenneth Barnes, Isabel Cabot, H. A. T. & L. A. Child,
Liam Hudson, Royston Lambert, D. Pidgeon,
L. C. Schiller, D. W. Winnicott and Michael Young

A Dartington Hall Study

ROUTLEDGE & KEGAN PAUL
LONDON

First published in 1969
by Routledge & Kegan Paul Limited
Broadway House, 68–74 Carter Lane
London, E.C.4

Printed in Great Britain by
Richard Clay (The Chaucer Press), Ltd.,
Bungay, Suffolk

© *The Trustees of Dartington Hall, 1969*

SBN 7100 6401 2

Contents

PART ONE

PART TWO

v

Those Present at
the Dartington Colloquy April 1965

From the Independent Progressive Schools

KENNETH BARNES *Head, Wennington School, Yorks*
HU AND LOIS CHILD *Joint Heads, Dartington Hall School*
E. FITCH *History Master, Dartington Hall School*
N. KING HARRIS *Head, St. Christopher School, Letchworth*
MISS JUNE OTTAWAY *English Mistress, Dartington Hall School*
MRS. ELEANOR URBAN (the late) *Head, Monkton Wylde School*

From the State Educational System

MRS. H. R. CHETWYND *Head, Woodberry Down Comprehensive School, London*
DR. D. COOK *Devon Education Authority*
MISS RUTH FOSTER *Formerly H.M.I., now Deputy principal, Dartington College of Arts*
MISS E. M. INGRAM *Primary School Head*
W. ELMSLIE PHILIP (the late) *Chief Education Officer, Devon*
ROY POTTER *Devon Education Authority*
L. C. SCHILLER *Formerly H.M.I.*
PETER SNAPE *Head, King Edward VI School, Totnes*
C. H. ZOEFTIG *Battersea Training College*

From Universities and Research Institutes:

ALAN BRIMER *University of Bristol, Institute of Education*
MISS D. E. M. GARDNER *University of London, Institute of Education*
DR. J. L. HENDERSON *University of London, Institute of Education*
MISS MARJORIE HOURD *Department of Education, Exeter University*

Introduction

It is a temptation to be resisted, to suppose that Progressive Education continues the search for Paradise Lost. Primaeval innocence has indeed been the inspiration of much noble and cloudy philosophy, which has placed upon children the burden of a symbol. Progressive Education takes the child's view, it is true, and the pursuit that ensues if this view is faithfully followed (as in a few places it has been) can lead on to dangerous ground. Sometimes, therefore, fresh stock has to be taken. Yet if this pursuit does not lead us—nor ever could—to Paradise Lost, and if sometimes it even ends in the sadness of false hopes, nevertheless in every generation fresh spirits will entrust themselves to it and want to savour no alternative experience. There is something perennial here and perhaps something profound, that dares to question the conventions even of thought—even the more so, that it should reject those false ideals sometimes wished on it by well-meaning friends.

At Dartington, Devon, during three days of the spring of 1965, a Colloquy was held on this subject. A Colloquy? Rather, a confrontation! For what began as an intended meeting of minds between two groups each considering themselves to be educational progressives ended in an irreconcilability of attitudes that was distressing, perplexing and ominous. Between the representatives of the classical idea of Progressive Education and those of the advance guard of progress in the modern educational movement, common ground was hard indeed to find, and constructive agreements were nil. In this, after all, the Dartington Colloquy was but a microcosm; the issues hidden in its disagreements are reproduced in the world at large. To report them, therefore, may add a mite of explanation to much that troubles us.

The report that follows, however, is idiosyncratic—necessarily so. A transcript of what in itself was often a confusing discussion would, after all, be doubtfully illuminating. Rather, an attempt must be made to appropriate the many valuable things that were said—spoken, many of them, from deep experience and wide practice—to fit some theme which, can it but be made explicit, hopefully will have the understanding of the authors of those comments. It is a precarious exercise, not to be judged —such are the risks involved—till it is quite ended. But it is an exercise worth attempting because the goodwill present on all sides at Dartington, the desire to come together, was patent— and its frustration was perplexing. If the reason for this can be found, it would seem justifiable to try to put the bits together again.

The book contains extracts from the background papers prepared for the Dartington Colloquy. These are both of intrinsic interest and should help as reference marks in dealing with the report on the Colloquy itself. (For this latter purpose, at the same time, it is hoped that these papers will not be found essential and that the report will to an adequate degree prove self-explanatory.) The book further contains an appendix by Isobel Cabot, reporting some research she has carried out on children's creativity as a function of their type of schooling. This is included here (if any excuse is needed for so doing) because, after all, this book is not intended simply to be a report, but to be a vehicle for carrying forward, with an urgency which much of the time it must be at pains to conceal, the debate about the significance of Progressive Education. Isobel Cabot's contribution is an addendum to just such a purpose and constitutes a challenge (it claims to be nothing more) to others to continue this debate.

Part One

by

MAURICE ASH

I

The Ingredients of Conflict

'I'd like to come in here, to make the point that the progressive school is a protected environment.'

Professor Harry Rée, sharing his feelings with several others in the room, was finding something amiss in the idiom of Progressive Education, in which he had long enough been lectured.

A progressive school [he went on] almost inevitably is a protected environment. And aren't those of you in progressive schools suffering in all sorts of ways from this conflict, this artificiality? You don't want to be a protected environment and yet you have to be. Many of your children perhaps need this protected environment. But it's not only protective from possibly harmful personal relationships; it's also protective against, for instance, the impositions of our supposedly terrifying curricula requirements—which I think you exaggerate, if I may say so.

You may say that we in the State system don't know about progressive schools. Perhaps we don't. But I do think that for your part you've got almost the *Boys' Own Paper* image of what goes on in State schools. One does stop the routine of a lesson in a State school, you know, if one gets an interesting point, and one says, 'To Hell with the curriculum.'

Another conflict you inflict on yourselves, and one you haven't mentioned, is that you're protective in keeping the children and the school away from immediate and

immense social problems. We have an enormous advantage
in being right up against these in ordinary day schools.

I think the whole gentleness of your schools could
healthily be upset by contact with a little of what, with
hesitation, I would call 'reality'. One does get the impression that you're producing an awful lot of well-
adjusted people (in a sense), but they are well adjusted to a
warm community, and when they leave they tend to marry
similar people, naturally, and perhaps they do evolve for
themselves, socially, another warm community around
them. But they are not in their own lives deeply concerned
with immediate social injustices, such as we know of in the
State system; and even if we don't always succeed in
making our pupils aware of these, yet we are able to
achieve quite a lot in this connection.

I just wonder how many products of progressive schools
have really involved themselves in social injustices as a
result of their experiences at school. I know you have
Voluntary Service ideas in Quaker schools, Oxfam and so
on, and these are much concerned with social justice at a
distance. But how many of you do know what's going on in
the next street?

This accusation against the independent progressive schools,
of isolation from social reality, was a constant burden of the
discussions at the Dartington Colloquy. It typified, in a nut-
shell, the disagreement that festered between two groups, each
thinking of themselves as educationally progressive.

The independent progressives were politely asked whether,
for instance, their children were made aware of the sick, the
bed-ridden, the under-privileged of their neighbourhoods. The
politeness merely covered a certain incredulity that experience
of this kind of reality was of any concern to Progressive Education as such. Such questioning, moreover, extended beyond the
rebuke implied in it, to something more disdainful. Elmslie
Philip, for instance, commented:

Turning to the contribution the progressive schools
might make to the State system of education, what have
you got to offer to justify the use of scarce public funds?
What have you got that the national system hasn't got? or

won't have shortly? I find it awfully difficult to puzzle out what it is.'

A quizzical attitude was likewise adopted by Dr. Cook.

I don't know [he said] how many schools there are that call themselves 'progressive' schools, how many children there are in them, but I suspect it's a very, very small proportion of the children of this country. I do feel that the progressive schools seem now to be on the defensive: perhaps they feel themselves at the cross-roads. I have a feeling there is a sense of insecurity about them: that they are too self-conscious about their non-conformity. And I am certain they are hopelessly ignorant about what goes on in the State system. I am shocked by this. I am shocked to have heard things said here which imply, for example, that headteachers are virtually imprisoned.

Occasionally, in the draft advertisements for staff sent for my approval by Heads, I come across one with the phrase, 'This is a progressive school.' I find myself always crossing that sentence out, because it usually comes from a school that is hopelessly reactionary. I wonder, indeed, whether the progressive schools are as progressive as they think they are. I would still like to hear more about what it is that makes them feel different. (I suspect it is largely the choice of parents that they have.)

What I think may be happening to you, if I may venture to suggest it, is that you are arriving at the position the Church schools arrived at at the beginning of this century. They did their pioneering and then, by compromises, they came into the State system. I wonder whether the time hasn't come when you should begin to think about coming into the State system?

Little direct response was made to these reproachful suggestions by those present from progressive schools at the Dartington Colloquy. King Harris could testify that St. Christopher School, at least, had a Social Service group. But in general there was a gulf here that only silence could fill. Should children bear these social responsibilities? Could they be expected to do so honestly—the responsibilities surely not being

theirs? Why should they be asked to share them? to accept the
guilt? If these questions went unasked it was because the
answers would have come from the other side of the gulf of
understanding, not recognizing the grounds of the questions
themselves. Society and Society's problems none the less exist,
do they not?

What meeting place, indeed, do such different preoccupa-
tions allow?

It was certainly true that the progressive schools were on the
defensive. Is there, then, something new abroad in education,
a new and all-conquering progressivism? Or has there, simply,
been an inner loss of self-confidence in Progressive Education
as such. This is what a report on the Dartington Colloquy must
seek to unravel. There was reflected there the thrusting, confident bustle of today's educational concourse, relative to whose
immediate problems the movement for Progressive Education
appears an insignificant backwater: protected, precious, unreal; no longer the vanguard of achievement, but rather a
curiosity, something apart. And yet, despite this surprising
reversal of roles, there remained a stubborn conviction among
the progressive schools that they should not succumb: that, no
matter how enlightened or liberal the orthodox educational
system might be, nor how perfect the society it either served or
determined (the distinction seems not to matter), yet the progressive schools still do not belong with it. This stubbornness,
indeed, was clearly born of something other than injured pride,
or vested interest, or resentment of one kind or another. It was
born, rather, of a separate discourse about 'education'.

King Harris at one point expressed this attitude as follows:

> I indeed have a feeling at the back of my mind that
> what we have been saying up to now may sound frightfully
> precious: that we can go through the various things we've
> been talking about—what the progressive schools have to
> offer—and that every one of these can be found in some
> State school; and that we should be told that even in the
> State secondary schools, in which people have been saying
> these things don't yet exist, in fact they do exist and exist
> in a far wider range than many of us believe. This dis-
> cussion doesn't leave me frightfully happy. Yet I do believe

there is something intangible, such as we haven't yet put our finger on, in the progressive schools.

I believe this, because although when somebody asks me, 'What is it that the progressive schools have?' I can't make a list (as we have been attempting to do here) of anything that I can honestly say doesn't exist at all in the State schools, yet from staff, pupils and parents who have had experience of both kinds of school I know that there is something real, and something very different, and something great and something important to be found in the progressive school. But I don't feel we've yet put our finger on it.

Christian Schiller made the same point, but did so by carrying the war into the other camp. In expressing his contempt for the new-style progressivism, he said:

We shall not change things by doing little bits of research. That is going to get us precisely nowhere at all. We have got to have something just as revolutionary as was A. S. Neill forty years ago. I remember him perfectly well. He was a madman—and we have got to have somebody who is prepared to be a madman.

That is the way you always begin.

Let us take English! All over the place we are seeing that boys and girls of six, seven, eight, nine, ten and so on can write creatively. Nobody thought they could: they can. How is it you get, here and there, this quite free-and-easy creative writing? Whatever it is, you always find that it hasn't anything to do with the curriculum, conventionally speaking.

We want the whole thing started up again by someone who is prepared to be a madman.

As a programme for rallying adherents to the standard of a new movement in Progressive Education, the foregoing obviously leaves something to be desired. Its spirit, nevertheless, is unmistakable. However, a more cautious and studious approach to the enervating search for definition was expressed by Alan Brimer.

'I have been depressed on some occasions during this

B

Seminar,' he said, 'by the extent to which people have felt the
need to justify themselves in ways that are not conceptually
definable.' He went on to suggest that in a progressive school
'what one got the sense of, was that here you had a perpetuating
community, one where the people in it were aware of the good
relationships they had established, aware of a certain right-
mindedness which they had fed into one another; and I would
suggest it is chasing something quite undefinable to try to conceptualize the characteristics of the progressive school'.

This chase of the indefinable, nevertheless, is precisely
characteristic of situations of conceptual confusion, of inner loss
of direction. Such a situation is not resolved by hoping that it
does not exist. The luxury of not worrying over concepts is
reserved for calmer situations, where things are taken for
granted and the on-going momentum of events is all-sufficient:
or for situations where, effectively, the topic is dead. But at the
Dartington Colloquy there was a general and anxious striving
after an understanding of progressivism in education, such as
belied any thought of the topic being dead but, rather, simply
betrayed the state of confusion about it.

Edward Blishen, in one of his remarks, intimated the validity
of many people's concern to find again the meaning of Progressive Education. He said:

> King Harris has said he couldn't lay his finger on what is
> special about progressive schools. Doesn't one of their
> obvious differences from ordinary schools lie in the way in
> which immense thought is concentrated on them: in the
> way in which everybody concerned is stimulated by a
> strongly held outlook? You find there but a small element
> of the everyday rough-and-ready. I mean, they are in a
> sense the aristocrats of the educational scene. Everybody
> concerned in them subscribes to their general flow of
> activity.

What Edward Blishen appears here to be saying is, simply,
that Progressive Education exists (and therefore merits discussion) because sufficient numbers of persons are determined
that it shall exist. Indeed, in this and many other comments
(and even by the mere attendance, at no small personal in-
convenience, of a diversity of persons at the Colloquy) the

spirit of Progressive Education showed, for all its lack of definitive utterance, its power over people still to move them. Nor is this power dissolved by the admitted diversity of the movement. Hu Child had noted the fact of this diversity when he said:

> Because the origins of Progressive Education come from a pretty wide diversity of thought, and a great diversity of personalities, there is a great deal of diversity, thought and personalities in the schools themselves. There is a very wide spectrum in all they do, in their attitude to religion, to work, to discipline, to games, to almost anything. No one progressive school is just like another, and quite a lot of them are poles apart. Therefore, I think it is a little dangerous to generalize with too much facility about progressive schools as a whole.

This diversity must be acknowledged. No weakening of the case for Progressive Education is, however, implied by this acknowledgement. Nor, conversely, does such an acknowledgement allow of any private, arbitrary or esoteric practice to be indulged in in the name of Progressive Education. All concepts, it seems safe to say, are the outcome of a diversity of particular experiences. In a sense, the diversity but confirms the general. Arising from this, one must be on one's guard against seeking for the ideal, as something that resolves an undeniable diversity. The ideal progressive school is indeed an unreality—far more so than is an 'indefinable' concept like Progressive Education, but concerning which people conduct a continuing debate. The diversity of Progressive Education—as of any other social form —has to be accepted; indeed, it is the proof of the concept's significance. Rather, we are here confronted with one of those always fascinating moments when we become aware that words are changing their meanings. (One has only to think of that long moment when the words 'public school' changed their meaning.) Such moments are endemic to our comprehension of society; they are the setting of our unending language-games.

At Dartington Miss Gardner outlined some of the processes through which changes of this sort can occur, in particular as they relate to innovations in education.

I've got a theory [she said] that you go through three waves in education. First, are the pioneers, who say, 'What has gone on is not good enough and we have got to do something better for our children.' They are prepared to stand up to opposition, to be very awkward, not to be smiled upon at all because they know, in the depth of them, they must do something better.

Now in this country, under the State school system, Authority does no worse than say, 'I think you will find it won't work, my dear'—which is about as far as any Inspector will ever go, and very rightly, to our glory! You finally win your case and the powers-that-be, instead of saying, 'I think it won't work you know; you'd better give it up', begin saying, 'It does work', and sending other teachers to the school because it is working. You then become popular.

You then enter Stage two, when you attract towards yourself certain half-baked adherents who can, for a time, do far more harm to you than the enemy ever did. You get to the point where the half-baked adherents say, 'This is what we have always stood for'—and then for a time you feel you have lost your cause. Everyone says you have got to go back to the past, things are not working.

Now, most of you don't go back; you don't kill truth. What you do is you get rid of a lot of these trappings, and the essence of what was based on real truth, what the pioneers knew, gradually gets assimilated, and you move into Stage three.

I think we went through all this, then, from the days when we broke away from trying to keep all children together, all learning things at the same pace when the teacher told them to. At first only the pioneers said, 'We don't care if you have got fifty or sixty children; children can't learn at the same pace. We are going to grade the apparatus to them. It's no good people telling us it won't work. It's got to. We are going to give them work that they can succeed in, instead of failing in. Children are going to be happier.'

They made their case and they did it. You then got half-baked adherents very nearly throwing it over by putting in the most fantastic lot of apparatus—the shops were quick enough to produce it because they made a lot of money by it—apparatus that wasn't understood by the children at all, and all the tickets got into the wrong boxes; you seemed to spend half your time sorting them out. And everyone said, 'Oh for those good old days when teachers did a bit! I want to hear someone standing in front of the class and addressing it in ringing terms!'

One Training College supervisor said to me—her back was breaking with stooping over desks to see that children were at the right stage in their apparatus—'It looks as if everybody had gone mad, and the colleges turned into cardboard factories.' Everyone said, 'We will have to go back to class teaching. This has failed.' But we never did.

Never again have little infants been supposed to go all at exactly the same pace, the bright ones being held back with weights on their ankles, as it were, and the duller ones goaded and pushed along. We learnt to get rid of the meaningless apparatus. We learnt to gear things much more to the purposes of children—and we went ahead. All these stories of going back leave me cold; and the idea that these dead, formal places will mysteriously do something better for a difficult child, I feel profoundly sceptical about, not on any theory but on experience.

The Progressive Education movement could be said to have gone through several evolutionary phases like those described by Miss Gardner. Undoubtedly it has been weakened, diluted, by the disintegrative forces to which it has been subjected, as other schools have assimilated some of its 'apparatus'. Such counter-reactions as the movement has been able to muster have obviously not fully restored its momentum; some of the steam has gone out of it. In consequence, it is in danger of being left with the trappings of a cult, with mere appearances—a situation well calculated to cause irritation to those not members of that cult. Such irritation was undoubtedly felt at the Dartington Colloquy.

In fact, however, the air at Dartington was not heavy with the erstwhile clichés of Progressive Education. There was no talk of 'child-centredness', and though there were certain bland assertions of the need to pave the way for society's 'redemption', or to prepare for its 'evolution', the resentments against it were largely brought to the discussion ready-made from the controversies in the greater world beyond. The proponents of Progressive Education were, as has been said, on the defensive; on the whole, they were reserving their case. However, their established position benefited from at least one spirited rationalization in its defence. This came from Kenneth Barnes, and significantly he took his stand on the key issue of personal relations and the seemingly all-important contribution to be made to these by Progressive Education.

In the first place, Kenneth Barnes was tempted to dissociate himself from the conceptual debate:

I think it is unfortunate [he said] that we are forced to justify the term 'progressive'. It is not a label I welcome, and I doubt whether we can find a definition of it to satisfy us all. The most we can do, perhaps, is to say what each of us is trying to do.

I myself am interested in a particular task, although it is a very broad one. I am concerned with how the relationship between one child and another, or between a child and an adult, can become a creative one, one from which something new begins, from which originality and initiative spring. I think this is characteristic of many of the teachers I find in the progressive movement. If we have made any kind of a discovery, this is it.

I don't know if we have set out consciously to look for this; but if you take the detailed record of the subsequent history of the movement's pupils you will see an astonishing record of originality. It is simply amazing to see how many of them have broken into new fields of thought or action in some way or other, become leaders or pioneers in that particular field. I am not merely concerned, as I might be if I were just working from statistics, with originality that can be measured in a technological, or literary, or artistic field. I am thinking also of originality and creativity in personal relationships.

This completely undermines the dichotomy between individual and society, which is about thirty or forty years out of date. We no longer talk in those terms. Today, we think of a child not as an individual who requires individual attention simply in order to justify his education but as a person growing up and becoming himself from his relationships; a person, personally related to the community, contributing to this community and growing with it and through it.

The great difficulty in life, the great difficulty in marriage, in fact the great difficulty throughout the whole of society, is to tolerate and to understand and to perceive what other people's temperaments are, and how they can be lived with creatively. I would say that if there is any kind of brief description of what one is trying to do in a progressive school of this sort it is to search into personal relationships in this way. That comes first, and to hell with the curriculum if it gets in the way!

So much, then, for the direct defence at the Dartington Colloquy of the established positions of the Progressive Education movement. Kenneth Barnes' contentions must be returned to; yet even had others present aided more energetically his conduct of this defence, their efforts, considering the direction from which new assaults against it were launched by the other style of progressive present, would have been largely irrelevant. The general platform from which these assaults were launched was one which questioned the complacency, the self-satisfaction, of the progressive schools. At least, complacency is the guise in which whole-hearted conviction appears to those nowadays armed with the dissecting-knife of quantitative analysis.

Empirical investigation in education was born long after Progressive Education; to that extent, the former rather than the latter is what is new in education. Undoubtedly, a certain usurpation is taking place. The lack of knowledge that there is about what actually happens in Progressive Education—deeper, the possibility that knowledge, conventionally speaking, is unobtainable about this activity: that it is of the character of faith—is galling to the new educational scientist. For he, too, wishes to practise and preach: is imperceptibly drawn into the educational arena itself, if only in order to make new experiments (but what experiments should he choose?). He, too, by investigating becomes involved, but involved necessarily in a piecemeal way. In this manner, your new educational empiricist is compelled implicitly to accept the mass of current orthodoxy and to be concerned, rather, with variations to it: concerned, therefore, largely with the efficiency of the system as a processing machine. The end product is what provides the criterion of assessment; and the end product is the citizen, the child as a more or less satisfactory, integrated citizen.

Perhaps this is but a description of an entirely proper, indeed inescapable, procedure, to which there is no alternative in an age in which measurable criteria are surely indispensable. And yet, conceptually a person remains a person no matter how he has been processed. As such, he acknowledges a certain autonomy. And an education posited on this notion, concerned with inward development, would not be dependent on the accumulation of sociological information: would not also, above all, be prone to the danger of being adjusted to whatsoever criteria were most susceptible of measurement.

Maybe, at this stage in this Report these are premature comments. But at the Dartington Colloquy the most massive assault on the Progressive Educational position derived from ideas that hold to the world's perfectibility: ideas assuming the manipulability of man by rational controls, controls based on the discovery of the laws governing his actions: hence—since as atomic units we each must be equally subject to such laws—an egalitarian world, one whose perfection is a self-fulfilling prophecy. Indeed, as if it were the Devil in its midst, this system of thought rejects anything so uncontrollable and unpredictable as the human personality. Yet it is noteworthy that progressive schools, significantly and in deep contrast to their contemporary scientific critics, have traditionally been tinged with religion: generally, not the religion of any dogma or cult, but the religion that stems from the humility known to a person alone, and from an awareness of human insignificance.

Naturally, if citizenship provides (overtly or implicitly) the educational criterion, the society to which the citizen belongs will itself come under the scrutiny of the educators. And, as has been said, if this scrutiny is of the social-empiricist kind an egalitarian society is most likely to provide the goal—indeed, it must provide the goal—if the socio-empiricist analysis is to justify itself. Education thus becomes the tool of social policy. This, in fact, was the immensely strong tide against which the progressive schools at the Dartington Colloquy found themselves erecting barriers of resistance. For obvious reasons, the instrument of the new progressivist wave was seen as the educational system of the State. Very sincerely, the proposition was put from several sides that the State had taken over the torch of Progressive Education—and, moreover, that in the darkness of a hostile world only the State could be entrusted with this burden.

Not unexpectedly, it was the Comprehensive School that was put forward as the vehicle of the new Progressive Education. The Comprehensive School, because it renounces the system of selectivity—and at least modestly reforms the curriculum that attaches to selectivity—within the unifying framework of the School, accepts all children as equally important. (As we shall see, this is only by a verbal confusion to be equated with considering each child as a person.) Indirectly—not by virtue of being 'comprehensive' so much as because 'comprehensiveness' was attracting more resources from the State towards education in general—the new progressivism was seen as providing the material opportunities that helped liberate the individual potentialities of children. Again, the attractiveness of the comprehensive schools, by emboldening parents to participate in the educational system, was invading the bureaucratic tyranny. The very size of these schools, moreover, was ensuring a spectrum of provision for individual capacities such as hitherto only the progressive schools, and then by very expensive staffing ratios, had been able to consider. The comprehensive schools were bound to be concerned with all the society of their neighbourhoods; thus, like the progressive schools, they were not concerned with the preservation or establishment of social strata.

They were also perforce co-educational, and their extra-curricular life extended beyond working hours and beyond the school's boundaries. They had, perhaps because of the invasion by the neighbourhood of the school, achieved a degree of informality in staff–pupil relationships that bore comparison with the progressive schools themselves. They were, also, stimulating and lively places where new ideas were readily tried out and where experiment was welcomed. They were, in brief, the natural heirs to Progressive Education.

Points like the foregoing constituted the main platform of the case for the redundancy of the independent progressive schools. However, a deeper questioning of the traditional progressive case itself was also entered upon. In its milder form this questioning centred upon the paradox of impersonal treatment as an aid to a child's development. Peter Snape, for instance, hinted at this possibility as a reflection of the virtues of comprehensive schooling.

I think [he said] the situation is completely changed now that we have this common secondary school, because, by its very nature, it is bound to stress the education of the individual child. If you are working in a boys' Grammar School or in an independent Public School your task is quite clear from the parents' point of view; it is to produce a certain type of boy, in the Victorian sense, to produce a certain type of boy for society. You select on entry those boys or girls who will fulfil this role. If, however, you throw out that selection method and say, 'We are taking all the children of the neighbourhood', obviously we cannot stand only for one type of child; we must stand for as many types of children as we have children on the roll. So, straight away, you are forced into the position of concentrating on the individual needs of the child.

I think this is 'progressive' in the sense that progressive schools mean. I think, also, because of the varying kinds of children there are, this means that your curriculum will be very much wider and there will be stress on the aesthetic elements. I think, too, that parents' involvement is coming near, because most of us have always believed this important. In fact, this is the only way you can run these schools efficiently.

So I think you have a new situation in the State system which, by its very nature, must embody progressive ideas.

More directly, Elmslie Philip expressed this paradox of the necessary impersonality of a contemporary progressivism.

Concerning this question of numbers, [he said] educationalists who wanted to translate these things into fact—the care of the individual and so on—had to go about it in a paradoxical way. In order to produce the conditions for individual education within the limitations of the public sphere, you must have a mass of children. This is the great paradox. Of course, you split the community down into more manageable units—and very successfully this has been done. But the large schools you must have are, anyway, on balance worth it, because of the possibilities they give for individual education.

Clearly, this reasoning is not posited on the idea of personal relationships as Kenneth Barnes, for instance, understands it. It is, rather, individual capacity that, in the circumstances envisaged, will be fostered. (The distinction between the individual—as a unit of some whole—and the person—as an autonomous entity—is basic to this educational analysis.) The unresolved question here, however, is the extent to which the development of individual capacities may be a means of assuring personal development—and to what extent the latter may be inhibited by failure to provide for the former. The paradox in question, in fact, is not in principle really so extraordinary. But, conversely, a much more positive questioning of the traditional progressive position was developed at the Dartington Colloquy. This took the form, initially, of refuting the progressive schools' exclusive claims to hold a 'corner' in human relationships.

Contentions were made, with some supporting evidence, that especially for scientists rich personal relationships are of secondary importance to work. Furthermore, even when rich personal relationships were attained—as admittedly they seemed to be in progressive schools, whose easy relationships could create in a visitor the sense of arriving on another planet—there was no assurance whatsoever that these would ensue in greater achievements of any material kind. Rather, the achievement of skills tended to be positively discounted in such places, while a certain softness at the centre characterized those who had been there, a softness only compensated for by their continuing tendency to gather together in exclusive coteries.

Such people, moreover, seemed even to lack ordinary, un-ambiguous sexual appetites and to avoid close personal involve-ments of that kind. Indeed, it was suggested, it is not people who have been nurtured, as in progressive schools they are, but only those who somehow have been harrowed who are capable of profound emotional relationships. Hence, progressive schools are at best irrelevant to the development of those personal relationships out of which achievement in general springs—if indeed it does so spring.

Of course, Progressive Education has long been inured to the common-place accusation that it but affords children a recipe for their happy idleness. Our kind of civilization pro-vides a natural soil for this criticism: our attitude to 'work' and its fetishistic importance: our association of labour with un-happiness, together with the notion of purgation through suffering. Criticism of this kind might crudely be classed with the 'prize-fighter syndrome': the notion that it is out of poverty that champions materialize. At the Dartington Colloquy, how-ever, a far more sophisticated analysis was advanced to suggest that behind the smoke of popular disapproval of 'undisciplined' education there might be a real fire. So long, indeed, as society and the achievements recognized by society sufficiently com-prehend the cosmology of education—and, after all, must there not be something fixed against which to measure ourselves?— this doubt about the freedoms of Progressive Education will always find expression. For if suffering proves socially beneficial to the child it becomes the obligation of the school as the agent of society to impose a measure of suffering upon the child. This is a loan to the child of the world's currency, so to speak, out of which he will learn—as otherwise he could not—to make re-payment with interest through his work. It is of no account to this thesis that suffering may be innate to us: that if it is merely with the role of suffering we are concerned this does not have to be imposed; we are born to it—and to no happiness that idleness can bring. This proposition apart, however, there remains an over-riding doubt as to whether, in order to re-pudiate a monopoly of personal relationships sometimes claimed for Progressive Education, it is expedient to invoke an equally speculative theory of social determinism. Both may be wrong.

Apologists for orthodox education, however, are particularly open to the temptation to advance deterministic propositions. Dealing as orthodox education very much does, in external disciplines to produce behaviour that meets the approbation of some social yardstick of conduct, it is prone to accept theories of cause and effect. Now, to say the least, causal relationships in social analysis are doubtfully susceptible to the definition of laws. More certainly, they are of use as a means of elucidating the characteristics of whatsoever they are deemed to relate, one to another. For this reason, apologists for orthodox education claiming to produce the best 'results' are in effect using those results to select that form of education which ostensibly produces them. And when the results are brought under question —e.g. as to whether orthodox education does not produce dull, unimaginative, uncreative quasi-adults—the causative process (in this case that of suffering) can quite plausibly be given a twist. In fact, however, this twist serves merely to expand the terms characterizing the effect, such as to allow the causal agent—orthodox education itself—to remain unchanged. This is possible because social criteria are here the constant reference of conduct and it is still possible to account for 'creativity' within a framework of successful social change. Now none of this is to question the validity of orthodox education itself, within its own terms of reference. It is, rather, simply to suggest that it were perhaps better for that form of education not to be justified in terms of the doubtful validity of 'objective' criteria. A further warning to this effect lies in the perhaps paradoxical observation that the notion of childhood's happy innocence is important precisely to idealistic social philosophy. It is this strain of philosophy for which the elimination of conflict and the ultimate abolition of labour is so fundamental: the Marxist restoration, by sophisticated, scientistic processes, of Rousseau's Natural Man. Society's redemption of Man, as discovered in his pre-social state—what tyrannies, large and small, have not been committed in its name!

Of course, at the Dartington Colloquy these claims of orthodoxy did not go unchallenged by those present from progressive schools. The latter's case at least is illuminated by some of the responses that were made. Lois Child, for instance, was one who baulked at the standard criticism of the permissiveness of progressive schools, yet tried to be constructive in her reply.

> We are told [she said] we can either, as progressive school-teachers, make our children contented, or make them brainworkers, but we are not likely to do both. Happiness breeds idleness, and in a progressive school we are in fact committed, unashamedly, to giving children as much happiness as we are capable of. We are, apparently, committed to producing idle, happy children.
> Progressive schools have always made their entry a much broader one, in intelligence terms, than either Grammar Schools or the more popular Public School. In this connection, it is possible that in our schools the medium scorer may be suffering from our present reliance on intelligence tests. We do a great deal for him in a progressive school that I think would not be so likely to be done for him elsewhere. At Dartington, for example, this child would have the widest choice of programme, which he chooses for himself, certainly by the age of fourteen. His specialism would have every encouragement. But it may be that because his I.Q. label is not particularly academic, this success in his limited field is regarded as a kind of compensation for him, not as a source of excellence. The findings of research suggest we should do something much more positive about this kind of child and that the standard we should exact from him in his own field is a matter of very great importance.

Lois Child's further remarks were more ironic:

> There has been reference to the case of Darwin. Now for Darwin there was no science to do at Shrewsbury; further, in his biography he writes, 'During my whole life I have been singularly incapable of mastering any language.' He left school—where he was happy!—and dabbled in medicine for two years at Edinburgh. He then changed to Cambridge and dabbled in theology. Then his autobiography suddenly lights up! 'No pursuit at Cambridge was followed with nearly so much eagerness, or gave me

so much pleasure, as collecting beetles.' I think our critics are wise to remind us of Darwin!

We have heard it asserted that excellence in any field means dedication to work on a scale that is bound to devalue the side of life which is concerned with social and personal contacts. The opinion is that putting work before love need not be thought of as a sign of neurosis; it is a mode of life which is suitable to some—a superfluity of interest in ideas rather than in people. The implication is, of course, that such a driven person would find no support in a school which puts the social life of children in such strong relief as a progressive school does. In fact, however, this self-motivated worker has everything in his favour in such a school. He will have his right to undisturbed stretches of free time recognized. He won't be driven to the games field, or to a compulsory subject, or to an entertainment, or even to a compulsory art-room or music-room. He won't be exposed to any of the contrivances of keeping school-children together and out of mischief, such as constitutes so much of boarding-school life. He'll find conditions that will enable him to work—perhaps even too hard. Above all, the individual mode of life will be respected. He won't be censured if he is not a good mixer—not because we don't believe in good mixers but because any mode of life which is creative is cherished in these schools.

Our critics are bound to conclude that the progressive school is unlikely to foster potentially original people. For, they say, all will come to naught unless such children are to some degree exposed to unhappiness: not the unhappiness which all children must face, but a contrived unhappiness, an unhappiness that appears from teachers who misunderstand them, are unfriendly to them, and from a school where subtle dangers and savageries exist. The fact is the converse: that in a progressive school the adult gets very little sense that his task is just to breed contentment. It is not the child's contentment that challenges him: it is the nature of the child's discontent. The child hasn't yet reached that state of balance about love and work (in Freud's terms); and all we are concerned with is to help him with his disbalance. This 'either/or' of happiness or work is accepted by neither adult nor children as a norm, but as the central educational problem.

Kenneth Barnes was even more emphatic in refuting the notion that progressive schools were posited on the happiness of the child. He said:

> This concept that the progressive school is a place that aims to be happy—it doesn't! If a parent comes to me and days, 'I want my child to be happy', I say, 'Take your child somewhere else! I can't guarantee it.' A progressive school (if we are going to accept that label) is an ebullient place, a place where the energy comes to the surface. But that energy comes to the surface often very painfully. It's turbulent—and good heavens, don't we know how we're exhausted by the emotions and the difficulties, the personal difficulties, that come to the surface in a situation in which inhibitions are lifted!
>
> One of our girls, in the course of her teacher training, had to do a little bit of research; so she thought she would write round to a selection of the progressive schools and to a number of conventional schools to find out whether the children were contented or discontented. Nearly all the children in the progressive schools said they were 'discontented' and all those in the conventional schools said they were 'contented'. A good deal of desire, urgency, comes to the surface in our schools and cannot at the time be satisfied. The child is having to cope with reality himself, and it is a very painful process. It has very much to do with the tragic element always potentially present in human life, with having to face pain and suffering and the inevitability of it. I am quite sure there is just as much pain and suffering in our kind of school, but it's about something real, instead of something artificially inflicted.

Obviously, by now, we are in the presence of a misunderstanding classical in its proportions. People are at cross-purposes; different 'progressives' are talking about different things. The suspicion therefore is surely planted, that a deep reconsideration of terms may be required of progressives of every kind. As always with such reconsiderations, surprising new evaluations may then freshly emerge. One can, however, hazard the preliminary suggestion that this misunderstanding stems from whether the view being taken by the disputants is external or internal to what we embody as 'man'. The ensuing discourse will be different, even if the same words—like 'progressive'—may be used. Of this, however, the reconciliation remains still obscure. Whatever the causes, there were other illustrations at the Dartington Colloquy of how deep and painful, and sometimes how ironic, the misunderstanding was. For instance, it was actually contended that the progressive schools had in some cases succeeded where the Public School had failed: they had achieved the sexless society, the sublimation of sex! They had managed this because of their deeply ingrained puritanism, a puritanism that by a subtle conspiracy had overcome normal lust, indoctrinating its victims with hallucinations of an uncomplicated innocence, such as resulted in the most anaemic of relationships between the sexes. Indeed, there is some historical support for such a view. As Kenneth Barnes had written in his background paper:

> . . . I have heard, in the early days of co-educational boarding-schools, that if the boys and girls fell in love it was regarded as 'silly', and attempts were made to inhibit any such manifestations by the scorn implied in that word. It has been suggested that this policy of repressing sexuality in the co-educational situation produced frigidity in some of the girls involved. I hope there is no co-educational school in which such a policy persists.

It should be admitted that there has been a puritan strain in Progressive Education. (Not to recognize this, nowadays, would be to store up trouble.) Yet this strain, in its pure state, was more protestant than puritan. The stress which this form of education places upon the person surely is protestant in character. It may be that the personal restraint, the very apartness, of the protestant ethos has close ties with the rigours of a puritan society. If so, progressive schools should heed the warning, that in these times any such translation as this of their belief in personality may find itself incompatible with the world surrounding these schools.

Of still greater gall to the old-style progressive at the Dartington

c

Colloquy, however, was the pervasive belief of some others present, that by a well-meant concession to the independent progressive schools a niche could be found for them in the State system as recipients of one kind or another of difficult children. The principle was put forward, for instance, that in so far as the progressive schools claimed certain results by virtue of the 'total' character of the environment they offered, deprived rather than privileged children should reap the benefits. The suggestion was not, of course, that the progressive schools would make useful dumping-grounds for the drop-outs of the orthodox system. Rather, the implication was that the progressive schools were marginal to education: that they might be conceded certain special properties, properties that would be abnormal in a properly run society—e.g. one in which no parents were separated, or neurotic—but that, pending the materialization of such a society, the progressive schools could be tolerated. Since to the old-style progressives their form of education was nothing if not universal in its application to children—was, so to speak, more normal than the norm—this role, which the State might have in mind for the progressive schools, could not have seemed more ominous.

Evidently, then, the chasm is there. Probably, as has already been suggested, it was there from the start, imported into the Colloquy from larger controversies in the world itself. Deep divisions of attitude, divisions which are reflected in our very civilization, are here involved. Such divisions cannot fail to be present, and even be high-lighted, among educators themselves. 'Freedom' is one key notion around which such conflicts generate. Since a minority opinion that will not succumb is important to the majority, if only as clarifying the premises on which it itself stands, and freedom being so obviously important for progressive education, any misconceptions that exist about this notion should for the general good be cleared away. Fortunately, at the Dartington Colloquy certain contributions to this end were made. Eleanor Urban, for instance, touched on this issue, and did so with the self-doubt that should, indeed, accompany it.

Isn't it the question [she said] that some people put the social pressure on at too early an age? and isn't it that we in the progressive movement think that the individual will in fact make a better contribution to society if the child has been allowed to develop and mature without those pressures? He will then, automatically—because human beings are social animals—make a contribution to society.

I do wonder, however, if the contribution of progressive schools at the moment should not take a slightly different direction from the one we originally set out on. For there is a good deal of very foolish and completely unrealistic anarchy going around at the moment, which is individualism run riot—and I'm sure we don't want that.

There is indeed an irony latent here. Progressive Education has, traditionally and implicitly, relied upon society's normal processes, separate from education, to impart to the child a sufficiency of the world's ways. In a time of social breakdown, can this reliance be maintained? Is it possible, even now, that matters are being turned inside out? Can Progressive Education still assume social stability? and, if not, can it remain 'progressive', remain concerned with the person rather than with society? These are sobering questions, to be asked now rather than answered here. Meantime, Miss Gardner had things to say which shed a stronger light upon the idea of freedom as it needs to be understood in connection with Progressive Education.

She said:

As for the half-baked adherents, who don't quite understand progressive education, when they have asked for advice, which they sometimes do, to them I think I would say: 'Try to keep your own minds clear. If a child is longing to learn, to find out, to achieve things in the world around him there is no reason on earth why you shouldn't make positive suggestions out of the depth of your experience. You've got far more than he had.'

It's the art of progressive teaching to see where a child is trying to go, and to open up the paths so that, if he follows them, he may find the answer to his problems. The people who think you just mix up the children and the materials and then hope for the best (and because it is 'freedom' you must never suggest anything) sometimes get children, when once they have come to the end of their own ideas, into a sort of mental vacuum. They can't see how they can go any further, and they feel frustrated. I sometimes think a teacher, conscientiously believing she shouldn't suggest anything, really appears to the child like a mother who won't feed. ('I don't love you enough to give you, right out of my head, the things I know of and the opportunities that I could put in your way.') That's why you get this odd sort of resentment from children if a teacher won't teach, if a teacher isn't prepared to say, 'Now, here are all these things you can do.'

If you are an adult in a progressive school you must be prepared to be rejected. Sometimes you are. You suggest something optimistically, thinking the child is interested, and it isn't and it shows it isn't. You have got to be prepared to take that tranquilly if you really care about teaching in line with children's purposes. But you had much better suggest than leave children in a vacuum. Children, as much as Nature, abhor a vacuum, and if they are not getting anywhere, even in a play-centre, they will turn on each other with hostility and aggression, and will feel very bad about you. There's this very strong creative urge in children, and I don't think you can isolate ideas of discipline and freedom from ideas in learning.

A rich environment with lots of problems to solve is one in which you really can be free because you can be creative. People who think a dull curriculum is all right, as long as children are free about their conduct and their discipline, are only doing half their job. That is what gets things in such a muddle; this is what gets children feeling so hostile. Perhaps your half-baked people think that you just fix up the children and the materials and that involves everything. Progressive ideas half-understood can sometimes allow of licence, becoming not really on the child's side. The child's deepest impulses are not gratified in an atmosphere where no one loves him enough to protect him against his own aggression, or that of other children, or feed him enough ideas for him to be able to feel an enormously worthwhile person because he can do worthwhile things.

Yet, as might be expected, it was from the psychiatrists present, oblique though their comments often were, that the deepest caution came against regarding education in the orthodox sense as an exclusive mode of appraising the growing child. Dr. Winnicott, in particular, had things to say that stemmed from a large experience.

Now I am stuck first of all [he said] with the word 'progressive', as everyone here must be; and I like the idea that there must be a madman somewhere. It seems to me that the word 'progressive' means that. It implies that someone is being awkward, somewhere; and they have got a group around them and they are going to go on being awkward, in such a way that somebody eventually notices that they may not be being awkward because they are awkward. They are trying to socialize their awkwardness—and it turns out to be a new school.

The children going to the school, however, don't say, 'We are progressive pupils'; they think, 'This is what school is.'

What is 'progressive' possibly going to mean in future? What mad people are going to turn up? What awkward people are going to turn up who are going to be progressive? From my point of view, I think you will very easily agree that the word 'progressive' could mean something completely different in the future from what it meant in the past. It just simply means a different kind of awkwardness, appropriate because, to be awkward, you have to realize where society is at the moment and be awkward about it.

I want to choose the idea of the progressive school developing the line of all the different angles of teaching, but in terms of the diagnosis of the child. I do feel there is more to be done about teaching related to the diagnosis of the child—particularly when you consider something specific like the title given for me to speak to: 'Do Progressive Schools Give too Much Freedom to the Child?' How could you possibly answer that question? Too much freedom for which child?

For this reason I have tried to draw attention to a form of diagnosis which is of vital importance to educators and which is not always given due prominence because it doesn't fit in with the scheme of things: (i.e. of sexual psychosis, of psycho-neurosis, of obsessional neurosis, and depression and so on). I mean, deprivation and the reaction to deprivation.

I think this extremely simple concept is not being used fully. By 'deprivation' I don't mean that a child is being subjected to privation, now or at any time. I am implying that, in the history of a child, there was development based on a good provision (of course, development comes from inside, from a maturational process in the child) and development has gone well enough. Then there was a deprivation, sometimes quite sudden, but very often over a period of time, in which the child is already organized and old enough to recognize that things were all right and that then they weren't. This we call a deprivation.

A child then reacts to this and, first of all, becomes in a muddle and has confusional states, and so on, and looks like an ill child—and may be quite easy to manage and teach. Then recovery from this gives the child what you can call 'the anti-social tendency'. He is beginning to gather himself together to become a person and to try to deal with this deprivation thing—because nothing else matters and they can't get on in life until they have got somebody to acknowledge and to try and make up for this deprivation fact. (It is an external factor, you see, unlike psycho-neurosis, where the difficulties arise from conflicts in the inner psychic reality.) This is an external factor, and the child pushes away at it, and until somebody can do something about it they go on doing so. We call that 'the anti-social tendency'.

Of course, it is very simple if all is conscious and somebody really can do something about it. Actually, funnily enough, it often is very near to consciousness, near enough for somebody to do something about it, if only they would give the child long enough to talk. (But that is another matter, because you are not wanting to be taught to be child-psychiatrists.) Nevertheless, here is this anti-social tendency which the child is in the grip of, which deals with quite a lot of fairly unconscious material and makes the child have certain claims. The two directions of claim are: stealing and destruction. (It is much more complex than that, as you know, because bedwetting can come into it and everything, but let's say 'stealing' and 'destruction'.) The stealing has a largely unconscious aim, laying claim on something that belongs to somebody else. In other words, the stealing arises because as the child begins to make good relationships so hope begins to turn up, and stealing turns up as a final symptom.

Of course, people don't understand that, so the child gets into trouble. It isn't nice having your bicycle stolen— however awfully healthy it is for the child to steal—and you have to be two people at once: one person who doesn't like having his bicycle stolen, but the other one who is seeing that at that moment the child is feeling hopeful and is beginning to claim something. This provides tremendous problems of tolerance.

The other direction, roughly speaking, could be taken to be destruction—in which the child is becoming destructive to make society put a grip round him so he can be controlled. This is what he lost; the child in the deprivation area lost the firm control of the family and the father, and had to go into a state of inhibition, premature and pathological self-control, in which the impulses are lost. He is looking for somebody to take a grip on him, so that he will be able to be free to be spontaneous, impulsive and aggressive.

Then if he's controlled he can rediscover his creative impulse and become uninhibited. The awkward thing is that with children of this type we have to remember that if they are suddenly taken and put in a remand home and dealt with very strictly, with all their time filled up, they often become happy and start learning, when before they didn't learn at all. In the previous period they were all haywire and, if you gave them a free atmosphere, they became inhibited and uncreative, restless. (Their personality becomes split up and then they have outbreaks of useless destruction—which is a pity and isn't any use to anyone, you see.)

I think that if this isn't recognized people can start talking about 'control' and 'security' and 'freedom', without realizing that there is a proportion of these children who react in this difficult way to freedom. They can't stand it; and they are really going to force somebody, eventually, to take control of them, because then at any rate they have their moment of personal release. It is destructive, but then at the same time they're near to a creative impulse.

This is just an illustration of the way in which diagnosis is so important—and you're well aware of this already, I know, and anyway it's not very original. But the point is, if a school is supposed to be 'progressive', then, as you all know, everybody tries to send their 'anti-social tendency' children for you to look after. These children are just going to collect together and make it impossible for you to be 'progressive'. If you can get enough of them you turn into an unprogressive remand home, practically; I mean, you become something holding people for the time being, until they grow a little older and somebody else will hold them. It doesn't matter what a child's I.Q. is; if he's in the grip of the 'anti-social tendency' he's not good material for somebody who wants to be 'progressive'. (I'm saying it dogmatically in order to produce discussion.)

Dr. Winnicott continued, essaying a rather more general application of his ideas:

It seems to me there is room for a use of the words 'progressive school' in connection with the attention you might give, if as teaching professionals you had the time to refer to it, to a child's developmental process. Certain children have to make it their main job to get somewhere in their discovery of the self, to the accommodation of the self into this awkward body they've got. They've got to fit in to what their home is like, what their school is like, what society is like. This is their task, and it's a very difficult one for some potentially valuable people, and some of them fail to reach a solution. The words 'progressive school' can easily be extended to cover the giving to this kind of child the opportunity to be in a group which isn't too big, where everything is personal and where opportunity is given for time to work its healing process. (There are great dangers all along the line, but nevertheless time is required.)

Now in most cases the children have done this already; they have got far enough in their early development to feel that they don't have to make a life's job of working out their own identity. I don't know how to separate off the ones who are struggling because they are ill and are liable to have depressions and failures of establishing themselves from the ones who have done it well at the beginning but are simply richly endowed people, who have decided that life is more important than learning a subject. I don't know how to separate these two off, because they look like each other.

I would like to hand round a picture [he proceeded to do so] done this week by a Dartington Hall school-girl of about fourteen. It is rather a nice picture of herself curled up and asleep—at least, not quite asleep; hidden away, waiting, while she is doing all sorts of silly things. And she is terribly grateful, openly, that she has got parents who are willing to wait and see what this will do. It may be nothing, but it may come out and occupy the whole of herself. (You know this so well, you don't need to see a child's drawings. You have seen thousands. But in a consultation setting sometimes these drawings are very telling.) This school is providing this girl with an opportunity for delaying and not having a false solution but waiting to see whether she can accommodate this true self that's hidden away there. In my opinion, there's no doubt that she will make it, but she can't hurry it. She's got to wait and she's got to go through the development stages. (I don't have to remind you how absolutely different a fourteen-year-old is from a sixteen-year-old, and a sixteen from an eighteen. I mean, the extreme changes they go through: just getting from one little bit to the next bit. You know all about that.)

I want to say just one thing. Let's say there are three things you can do with a good object. (That's a psychoanalytic term, 'object'. It no longer means 'object'; it means anything you like, really. It means Dartington, if you like.) There are three things you can do with a good object. One is to preserve it, and the other thing is to destroy it. (Yes, to

destroy it—which is distressing, but still, that's the fundamental thing.) The third thing you can do, which belongs
to health—and it's extremely precarious, the growth towards this—is to use it.

If the object isn't to be preserved—idealized for ever—
then it's to be destroyed. But that's too painful, so clinically
you don't see it. What you see is people (I am talking about
children) mucking up the good object so that it isn't good
any longer; so then it doesn't have to be destroyed, you see.
Now that kind of destruction, that kind of mucking up, is
something that it is no good giving 'freedom' for. They
don't want you to let them muck it up—but they have got
to muck it up, because they can't stand destroying it (and
it is no good preserving, idealizing it). So I am asking you
to have that category in your minds, if you haven't got it
there already. These are categories of destruction that
mean freedom isn't any use.

But freedom is of such great use to the normal individual
—I mean to the healthy child—that it is only in freedom
that they can be destructive, or can be anything at all. It's
in freedom that their creative impulse turns up, which you
can use; and if you can't get to that very precious area of
creative living freedom is of no use to anybody.

I know I have said something very simple in a very
complex way. I must stop myself from saying things even
more complex . . .

and so saying, Dr. Winnicott broke off.

Perhaps naturally and significantly, Dr. Winnicott's remarks
caused more discussion at the Colloquy about treatment for
maladjusted children than about education and freedom. All
too little do these latter concepts lend themselves to a consideration of the individual child. Alan Brimer showed himself
aware of this in what was, in effect, a defence of the idea of
education itself.

I think [he said] that what schools are concerned with is
not so much the process of etiological diagnosis, of determining the circumstances that have brought about a
particular form of behaviour; they are concerned with the
determination of hypotheses for action.

The question is, whether or not in a progressive school freedom consists in the process of withholding action, or whether it is the determination of particular actions which allow greater freedom to the child. I would agree with Dr. Winnicott in the sense that a determination must be made of what kind of setting would give such freedom to the child to act in the way he would wish. But freedom to act is not a process of making a choice in a vacuum. It is a process precisely of making a choice and, therefore, of knowing what choices are available. There are all too many settings where the frame of reference is so unclear that there is no decision for the child to take.

This represents an important challenge. An educationalist is, after all, bound to assert that it is not enough to know what a child is; some decision must also be taken as to what shall be made of him, a decision that must mean he in some respect ceases to be what he 'is'. It is hard even for progressive educators to escape this conclusion—say, simply by arranging the child's environment so as to allow him to 'become', for even this must be accounted a positive decision about the direction of his 'becoming'. Rather, this challenge seems likely, in some way, in due course to concentrate our attention upon the character of the school as such.

Dr. Winnicott for his part, at a later stage of the Colloquy, contented himself with extending his plea for tolerance of the maladjusted child to tolerance of the normally growing child— and intimated that those who could encompass that tolerance had, perhaps, the right to call themselves 'progressive'. He conclusively disclaimed the idea that the progressive school was the school that existed to deal with children of an anti-social tendency. He did this in an oblique way that illustrated his compassion: 'There is always going to be tremendous pressure on us psychiatrists, and we're always looking for somebody to take these cases of ours; and we shall tell lies to get them into places, and we shall go on doing so; and you've got to know that we do that.' Sardonically, perhaps, he ended the discussion on freedom in education as follows:

There isn't, for instance, such a thing as a satisfactory Approved School for girls. I have tried to solve this matter myself by saying there should be a University for the Education of Prostitutes, and make it positive. (I know it's silly, but it's the only solution I can give when I'm asked this question.) This is to say, 'Let's take prostitutes. We know they are going to run off every few weeks and come back again, brought by the police. But while they are with us, let's teach them how to do their work better.'

This might work—but it would be closed down by a Ministry.

What I am trying to say is, the word 'progressive' will, I hope, have to do with the tolerance of the stages of development that the normal and very valuable boys and girls go through in the adolescent phase, in the doldrums of adolescence. These can't hurry; they don't feel anything's real, unless it is absolutely in line with wheresoever they are in their present-day development.

There are going to be, therefore, some illegitimate children. There are going to be some difficulties, and everybody's got to share responsibility for that. Still, this seems to me the bright future for the word 'progressive'; that's what I'm trying to say.

Despite contributions such as these, at every turn in the Dartington Colloquy touchy and sensitive exchanges occurred. For instance, at one stage Eleanor Urban was expressing her doubts about the wisdom of extending to the notion of 'creativity' the importance now becoming demanded of it.

It seems to me rather odd [she said] that at this late stage we should have to think about how to foster creativeness, when of course nearly every child is anyway creative. I mean, just as the acorn, given the right conditions, does become an oak tree, so a child starts to unfold and develop. In a lot of primary schools this is being helped, and if we could but go on in that sort of way at secondary level— instead of halting the process—it seems to me that every single human being will in some way or other be creative—because we just are. I mean, we're just part of life.

Upon this, Dr. Susanna Isaacs took her up.

I see a danger [she said] in Mrs. Urban's point of view: that of idealizing children. I don't think it's quite as simple as making an acorn grow into an oak tree. I think that many children are inclined to labour under the illusion that love is the same thing as contentment. A lot of people would like to believe that; and a lot of children will act just on that assumption. One can call it 'peace at any price'.

In reply to this, Eleanor Urban disclaimed any such intention, and made plain her concern simply with the dangers of distorting the idea of creativity.

I think people tend [she said] to separate ordinary human beings from 'creative' artists or scientists—as if they were something different. Yet a great painter will produce a painting only when he is ready to do so. Again, there were times when Virginia Woolf was very miserable and couldn't write at all; and then she did. I think this applies to everyone's activity. I think we should try to be like life itself and have the flexibility of life—and allow, rather than force, growth. Isn't that what a progressive school is really about?

There are a lot of people who think ours are terrible places, which make people contented so that they never want to do anything. That would be as silly as sticking a dummy into a baby's mouth as soon as it started to cry. I don't think we do that!

Again, in this exchange, there lies an unresolved case of misunderstanding—a misunderstanding which the metaphor of the baby's dummy at best leaves open, but cannot solve. Yet, surprisingly, there was one subject upon which, at the Dartington Colloquy, the new progressives did not overtly reproach the old—the subject closest of all to social considerations: namely, that of the privilege of private education. Of course, it is quite plain that the progressive schools are not concerned to prepare their children for possession of some social perch. Indeed, the parents of these children can be said to be performing an act of courage, of trust in life itself to buoy their children up; and, to that extent, they outface those whose complaint is merely that all children equally are not being prepared for a perch. (By the same token, that the progressive schools cherish their independence is a fact to give pause to the crude thesis about the privilege of private education.) Nevertheless, a certain inarticulated sympathy did exist at Dartington between those representing respectively the progressive schools and the new comprehensive schools of the State system. This sympathy presumably consisted in the shared assumption that a child is no less a child no matter from whence he comes, or what his social environment may be. The divergent conclusions to be drawn from this shared assumption, however, are what make for such sadness: on the one hand, that there should therefore be equality of opportunity in an always undivided society; on the other hand, that a concern for the child is not a concern for an undivided society but is, quite simply, a-social. It would, perhaps, have been better had the nature of this sympathy been articulated. The nature of the fundamental misunderstanding might then more nearly have been approached.

In any case, Kenneth Barnes was at pains to emphasize the, to some, perplexing immunity of the progressive schools from the prevalent social criticism of independent education. This he did by turning the tables upon the conventional argument. Thus, he denied that these schools were in some way a preparation for an ideal world, the world in which all conflict would be resolved. He related this especially to sexual problems.

> One of the things I would emphasize [Kenneth Barnes said] is that I accept conflict as a necessary part of human experience. I don't think it's right that we should make sexual experience easy, and this is one of the ways in which I very seriously part company with A. S. Neill.
>
> I don't think it's wrong that children should have to restrain their sexual impulses and go through a certain amount of suffering and a certain amount of conflict in adolescence. This is only one part of the conflict that we go through in life in general, in coping with our impulses and adjusting them to the community. In the deliberate sex education that we attempt we must have our minds on what actually happens in life, more than on what we would like to happen.
>
> I am now conscious of the way in which, when I first

began to deal with the wide aspects of sex education, I perhaps spent all my time on giving children a picture of marriage as it ought to be, and took too little account of the sexual experience of children as it was likely to be— and as it was certain to be for a proportion of them; and I realized that this attitude was tinged with Pharisaism. All along the line, an education which is primarily concerned with being good and doing the right thing is tinged with Pharisaism. It fails to recognize that there often is a very deep and severe conflict between being good and being warmhearted; and the idealist approach often tends to produce people who are brittle and totally unprepared for the real crises of life. This world, this world that we often hate, that often seems extraordinarily stupid and unreal and artificial, this is the world we were made for.

Conflict between the adult and the child is not necessarily a bad thing. The really bad thing between the adult and the child is the absence of any emotional contact at all. The worst possible thing is to have no contact at all, so that children live in a different and separate world, not accepting us as a part of the real world.

In speaking thus, Kenneth Barnes was, as in honesty bound, even adding to the confusion of the scene. For not only were the old progressives finding themselves at odds with the new progressives at the Dartington Colloquy but among themselves there were undercurrents of unresolved disagreements. Many a proponent of Progressive Education, for instance, would find it hard to renounce the thought that, somehow, that form of education was the precursor of a better world, a world of 'sanity', in which all conflict would be solved. Historically, as Hu Child pointed out, the progressive schools have conducted their affairs on the principle of co-operation rather than of competition (whether of marks or honours). To some, it is probably true to say, this principle has come to assume a key significance, foreshadowing a new kind of world such as only Progressive Education could bring about. To others, it has probably remained of no more importance than as a device for saving the individual child from the social oppressions endemic in orthodox education. Undoubtedly, the representatives of progressive schools at the Dartington Colloquy were handicapped by their own diversity of view in face of the uniform egalitarian attitude of the new progressives. This confusion in their ranks, moreover, is clearly carried over into the wider world, and is made evident in their inability to speak with one voice in face of common dangers. Only a deep conceptual disturbance could account for this. Yet a tenacious spirit keeps these schools alive. At Dartington they probably suffered from a conflict within the conflict. If their own conflict could be resolved, the world might once again become aware of the force that lies perennially within it.

2

In Defence of Progressive Education

The irony of the Dartington Colloquy on Progressive Education consisted in the embattled progressive schools there finding unity, almost their only unifying ground, in their common scepticism of the Comprehensive School—that favoured creation of their tormentors, the new progressives. It was from this scepticism that the progressive schools fought back, and it was this that helped keep alive their belief in themselves.

In itself, criticism of the idea of the Comprehensive School is not a concern of this Report—neither was it, directly, the concern of the Dartington Colloquy. Indirectly, however, such criticism throws light upon the idea of Progressive Education itself, and some of the comments at Dartington—they were by no means confined to people from progressive schools, but came if anything from educational administrators—are illuminating on this subject. Ruth Foster, for instance, was one who, as a means of exploring the meaning of Progressive Education, expressed her doubts about comprehensive schools.

I know the State system [she said] far better than I know the independent progressive schools, although I know a few of these. Now, I don't think I have ever been into any school which would say other than that they cared there for the individual. But, you know, it's the quality of the relationship possible under different circumstances that matters. The quality of the relationship that is possible, say, in a two-teacher primary school is quite different from the quality of relationship possible in even the most progressive State seven-teacher school—let alone twelve-teacher school. The quality of relationship in a Rudolph Steiner school, where there is no Head but a group of staff steering the school—and where certainly they do, as it has been expressed, buy time for their children's development—the quality of relationship in such a school is quite different from that in a large Grammar School.

I doubt whether the kind of problem that Kenneth Barnes has written about in his paper for this Conference (the problem of children's sexual relationships) could be handled at all in very large communities. Whatever the very large community does to break itself down, I do not believe that the quality of relationship can be similar to that of a small one. I believe that one of the contributions of the progressive schools is to be determined not to grow too big.

Mr. Schiller spelt the matter out even more plainly.

One of the chief architects of the Comprehensive School idea [he said] was the late Sir Graham Savage. His argument was this: you must have enough girls and boys in a secondary school to form what is nowadays called a 'grammar stream', so that you can have sufficient staff to give them the proper sixth-form specialist teaching. It's simply a matter of a multiplication sum, therefore, that you must have so large a school.

But this isn't saying, 'What is the sort of school that adolescents find best for them—one hundred, two hundred, three hundred?' not a bit. You make your decision quite apart from that. Now, if that is your point of view I am afraid it is like a cancer. In my view, what you must first face up to is fact: that is, to what is best for these boys and girls at this age. Then you must fit all your other things into it. Nobody has ever argued that it is a good thing to have, say, one or two thousand. Personally, I think it's extremely bad; but it's the very nature of the argument that is the problem. Surely, if you have a progressive school you start with the children and you fit the rest to it? If you are going to deal with human beings scale is all-important. We are, I suppose, about thirty people here, and we conduct this meeting in a certain way. If there were five of us I suppose we would conduct it in a different way; if there were a hundred of us we should again conduct it in a different way. Scale is all-important, and I think we must first think of scale and then arrange all our staff and organization afterwards.

From these and similar remarks there emerges the significant impression of schools constituting administrative *tours de force* (if not actually conceived for that reason). Ineluctably, the very social pressures against which they insulate themselves will be translated into their internal structures—presumably taking the form of a separate world, whose imperatives are peculiarly scholastic. Progressive Education, in fact, cannot be said automatically to inhere in the Comprehensive School, as appears to be believed by some of the latter's proponents. Such a School, indeed, even handicaps itself against being progressive, by reason of the requirement for conformity that administratively it is bound to bring to bear upon each and every child subject to its exigencies. This, of course, is not absolutely to debar any Comprehensive School from being progressive in a way that the progressive schools themselves would recognize. (Nor, of course, is it to deny that the Comprehensive School may have quite other and over-riding virtues.) But the besetting social rationale of orthodox education is evidently not to be evaded simply by a school transposing society's own problems into social problems peculiar to itself. If schools (or education generally) want to simulate a different society from that which actually exists—perhaps, say, giving all types of children an equal opportunity to acquire each kind of social status—admirable as this might be, it is not synonymous (as Progressive Education arguably is) with actual neutrality towards the social matrix. To give all children equal social opportunity is not synonymous with treating each child as a person—and only someone who believes that the social, alone, is real could hold the contrary view.

One aspect of this controversy consists in the advantages of specialization that relate to institutional scale. These advantages are, of course, a strong suit of the Comprehensive School. The question is, however, as to how a child comes to terms with a specialization. Does the child take to book-keeping because book-keeping expresses his attitude to life, is something he has arrived at out of inner conviction? Or does book-keeping impose itself upon the child, as a social skill among a lot of other social skills which society can powerfully demand of him?—an alternative, at least, to learning, say, Latin or Atomic Physics. (How changed indeed the world would be if we chose our jobs, rather than our jobs choosing us! if we in fact were not, as the ultimate phrase goes, 'held up by the shafts'!) It was in this light that Eleanor Urban made a plea for an alternative concept of specialization to that advanced by the Comprehensive School.

> I think [she said] that all those things we have heard are done in Comprehensive Schools could be done in smaller schools if we allowed teachers to offer different things. After all, it is not necessary to be strictly and professionally vocational with workshop training. We, for instance, have some anvils, and children can mess about and learn basically about being a blacksmith. One of our girls is doing jewellery through having messed about with jewellery at school. We do have a whole lot of things like that in a very amateurish way, because I think it is best suited to children to be amateurish.
>
> I don't think that you have to assume that because teachers are Grammar School teachers, and can take their specialist subjects up to University level, that they can't do anything else as well. I think it would be very healthy— and this is something for Teacher Training Colleges—for more teachers to have a chance to be, if amateurishly so, all kinds of other things instead of just ploughing away, year after year, at their specialist subject.

Mr. Schiller also put it plainly.

> Our trouble [he said] is that we are at the moment obsessed with over-specification. We cannot get away from it. We cannot think of boys and girls—adolescents—

growing up as young boys and girls, having time to grow. We are all anxious to say to them, 'Get on to this!', or 'Get on to something else!'

At the deepest level, then, the distrust felt at the Dartington Colloquy by the old-style progressives for the new forms of progressivism rested on the suspicion that these were but benevolent paternalism in a new guise—with the State playing the paternalistic role. As such, this but reconstitutes the perennial situation, which Progressive Education has always been conjured up by rebellious spirits to resist. The benevolence in this instance may be seductive, and the efficiency is sometimes frightening; but to each of these the resistance shown at Dartington by those from the progressive schools was resilient and unmistakable.

An important reinforcement to this attitude ensued from the parody of Progressive Education that took shape from Michael Young's account of the visit he had just paid to Russia. He had noted there many of the appearances of Progressive Education: the shadow of it rather than the substance. This parody does not, of course, strictly apply to our own country's comprehensive schools. (It might, however, apply to that other, somewhat new, kind of independent school in this country— schools that probably would not relish the 'progressive' label— dedicated to social service and established on an ever-ready preparedness for physical rescue.) The Russian example, however, seemed to show in extreme form how Progressive Education becomes deformed if, with the best of intentions, it sets off down the wrong road: that of sub-serving the imperatives of society.

Michael Young spoke as follows:

Last week I went with a group from the Plowden Committee to see primary schools in the Soviet Union— and found, rather to my delight, that there aren't any primary schools in the Soviet Union. (There, as in most European countries, they have all-through schools with no break at eleven or thirteen. The ordinary Russian school is one that goes from the age of seven up to eighteen.) So we were able to look at other sorts of schools. I was especially interested in the new boarding-schools they

have. Naturally, on this subject I am as much an authority
as if I had spent one day at Dartington School!

Last Wednesday I visited boarding-school Number 56
in Moscow. (On the whole, all the schools are known by
numbers, and the children—at least in some cases—are
also identified by numbers placed on their uniforms.)
Boarding-school Number 56, Headmaster Mr. Shervant.
Immediately, I was struck by the superficial similarities
with progressive schools, or some of them, in this country.

First, co-education is universal in the schools of Russia.
In this particular school the boys and the girls lived in the
same houses, segregated on alternate floors. All classes are
co-educational. But what was surprising was that in spite
of their being co-educational, sex, the vibration of sex,
hardly seemed to be in the air at all. It was as though
boys weren't interested in the girls as members of the
opposite sex, and vice versa. This was confirmed for me by
one of the few checks I could make—with an English girl,
daughter of a diplomat, who had recently been to both
English and American schools, and who said it was by far
the most striking difference between these (and particularly
the latter) and her present school.

The second superficial similarity was, no corporal
punishment. Corporal punishment is illegal and, it seemed,
not only illegal but not practised either. Nor were any
other punishments imposed by the staff. 'Free self-
government,' we were told by Mr. Shervant, and again by
every other headmaster and teacher we saw. 'In this school
there is self-government. The children have their own
organs of self-government and they are responsible for
discipline and for dealing with infringements of the rules.'
What are the rules? Well, in this school one rule was that
all children even above the age of fourteen should be in bed
by ten o'clock.

'And do the children observe this rule?'

'Of course not!'

'What time do they have to get to bed?'

'Well, they are usually in bed by eleven o'clock.'

'This seems rather odd, Mr. Shervant. Why, then, don't
you alter the rule to meet the practice?'

'That wouldn't do at all, because if we had the rule at eleven o'clock they wouldn't be in bed until twelve o'clock.'

'Well, what do you do about children who in fact aren't in bed till twelve o'clock?'

'Well, we have to refer this kind of serious infringement to the children's council. The person who infringes this rule can be brought up before the Committee of the Young Pioneers Organization, or the Komsomol Organization, and the Committee will decide what is the appropriate punishment to use.'

Apparently, they only have two possible punishments. The first is reproof—and this is sufficient with children in almost every case. The school seems to use guilt and shame as the driving force. But if reproof doesn't work there is the final, terrifying sanction, which is expulsion: not expulsion from the school, but expulsion from the Young Pioneers Organization. This means you can't then wear your red scarf around your neck. This is something only the bravest children are prepared to contemplate!

The next superficial similarity I found was a reliance upon co-operation. Despite the degree of competition there is, the talk is all about co-operation. 'All our classes,' the headmaster said, and so did the other teachers we saw, 'are unstreamed and not like the classes you have in England.' (They all seemed to know a little bit about English schools.) 'All our classes are of mixed abilities, and we manage it because we succeed in getting the abler children in any class to accept that they have a duty to the weaker children. It is the duty of the abler children to give extra teaching, even in the holidays, to children who are not doing so well.'

In spite, however, of these superficial similarities, there was an extraordinary difference in the general atmosphere. Most important, perhaps, was the feeling that here is a school which is a religious school—perhaps in a way that few people in England would accept as being religious, but a school infused with a kind of religious Communist orthodoxy, with the icon, Lenin, in every single room in the school. (Geography, I found, the school taught in terms

of the places where Lenin had visited. Luckily for the
geography teacher, Lenin had been to many countries in
Europe. London was described as it was in 1903, when
he was there.) Somehow, this was the spirit which seemed
to animate the school.

There was a great emphasis on formal teaching, the sort
of formal teaching that we know exists in schools all over
Africa and the underdeveloped world, but which we have
only in the most extraordinarily backward schools in our
own country. The great emphasis was always on learning
by heart. There was complete inactivity in the classroom,
except that great girls would constantly be bobbing up
from behind their desks in their little black uniforms, with
marks on it to show they were a kind of corporal or something in the Komsomols, saying, if this were an English class:

'Yes, William Shakespeare, when he was a boy he
attended the Grammar School in Stratford-on-a-von.'

'Avon!'

'I am sorry. He attended the Grammar School in
Stratford-on-Avon.'

'What did he learn there?'

'He learnt small Latin and less Greek.'

A parody such as this, then, could not help but catalyse the
distrust felt by the progressive school's representatives at
Dartington for the inducements being dangled before them.
Allied with this distrust, however, there grew an unshakeable
conviction that Progressive Education, as the progressive
schools practised it, mattered, and that it did so for reasons
quite other than those motivating the State-educational progressives. Significantly, if paradoxically, it took a statement of
negative values to open up the world that lay closed to the
philosophy of the new progressives. This came, first, from
Marjorie Hourd, who invoked an idea that was subsequently
used by several others. The idea she invoked was that of John
Keats' striking notion of 'negative capability'. Marjorie Hourd
saw the relationship between teachers and children as one to be
informed by this quality.

You recognize [she said] the phrase 'negative capability',
which comes from Keats. He described any man of charac-

ter as a man with negative capability. Conversely, he had a friend of whom Keats said that he would never get a real idea, just because he was constantly striving after it. Now these comments apply not only to literature (my own subject) but perhaps also to education as a whole.

It is, indeed, another world that opens up before this sort of consideration. It is a world that is recognized perhaps only on the fringes of our Western civilization, though it may seem to occupy the whole of other civilizations—Taoist ones, for example. (It may be that Progressive Education stands as the sentinel of that other world in the midst of our own.) Certainly this ethos could not be more foreign to the bustling compulsion to 'experiment', or to the brash urge upon the progressive schools to propose something 'positive' that they might actually do, or to the busy impulse to perfect the world. But on the other hand, it is a world symbiotic with, for instance, the idea of 'the doldrums of adolescence', as also, generally, with the constructs of the psychoanalysts—those implacable, latter-day Calvinists, for whom not the social environment but the rigour of the psychic endowment of each one of us is what matters. If this attitude, then, has relevance to our own civilization it must surely be in connection with children: that is, with such among us as are not yet societed (which is not the same as saying, are yet 'innocent'). For the interest of the idea is not that it seeks to amend society but that it locates in humanity that which any society, in the functional interests of its own survival, may be compelled to suppress. Only children could remain the repositories of such potentials.

It seems fair to say that this negative quality (of passive expectation) has to do with the personal life. So clear-cut and far-reaching indeed are becoming the repercussions of this different emphasis that clearly this Report can no longer postpone some attempt to clarify the categoric differences between the two kinds of 'progressives' represented at the Dartington Colloquy. That there is a knife-edge which divides, on the one hand, paternalism no matter how benevolent and, on the other, equality of adult with child, cannot be disguised. These are two principles between which there appears to be no reconciliation. Education finds itself at their juncture. It is a juncture which seems likely to bear upon our very notion of reality—and this, perhaps, may help account for the fascination which the idea of education itself holds over us.

The opposites inhering in nearly all the statements quoted in this Report are those of different criteria. Whether one thinks of Harry Rée's desideratum of schools being 'right up against immediate and immense social problems', on the one hand, or Kenneth Barnes' emphasis on the painful inner reality of the child, or Dr. Winnicott's perception of some people's 'awkward-ness' about society no matter where they might find it, on the other, the dichotomy of society and person ran through all the discussion of the Dartington Colloquy. It is, after all, a dicho-tomy that has haunted the movement for Progressive Educa-tion. It resided in Rousseau himself, whose plans for a system of education for the Polish State (let alone his barbarous notions on the education of girls) could not conceivably have stood in greater contradiction to his famous programme for 'Emile'.

This unresolved problem continued, at Dartington, to lie at the heart of the tangle of disagreements. Kenneth Barnes, it will be remembered, dismissed it with his contention that such discussion was 'thirty or forty years out of date' and had been replaced by the concept of 'a person, personally related to the community'—with the implication, here, that social problems would somehow yield to treatment, were but our personal relations healthy. (The resentment of many others over the progressive schools' supposed 'corner' in personal relationships will also significantly be remembered.) Now, with respect to the genius of Kenneth Barnes as an educator, the resolution of the person–society dichotomy has not yet been achieved in any acceptable analytic structure, whether sociological or psycho-logical. No social analysis exists in which social phenomena are convincingly explained in terms of constructs of which persons are the atomic units. And, conversely, such attempts as psycho-logists have rashly made to explain social phenomena (one thinks, even, of Freud's pathetic contribution to the analysis of war) have singularly failed to impress the social scientists. Furthermore, there is, anyway, an alternative and relevant explanation as to why, in Progressive Educational circles, the discussion of this problem should seem 'thirty or forty years out of date'.

Thirty or forty years ago the New Educational Fellowship was at the height of its influence. Binding together as it did the Progressive Education movement in countries all over the world, the N.E.F. could attract enthusiastic thousands to its congresses. In the 'thirties, however, this Movement underwent a transformation—and, in retrospect, it would have been surprising if this had not occurred. Socially speaking, those were perhaps the most searing of years ever endured by our civilization. Among the crowd of others, the N.E.F. no doubt also had to declare where it stood, had to stand up and be counted. The resultant change of approach is conclusively illustrated in the amendment (made in 1932) to the N.E.F.'s 1921 Constitution. The earlier Constitution began as follows:

1. The essential aim of all education is to prepare the child to see and realize in his own life the supremacy of spirit. Whatever other view the educator may take, education should aim at maintaining and increasing spiritual energy in the child.

In 1932 this was amended to read as follows:

1. Education should enable the child to comprehend the complexities of the social and economic life of our times.

Thus pressed by the importunities of society, Progressive Education quietly let go of its sources of inspiration, and so became another forgotten victim of Depression and Fascism. The N.E.F. continues to perform worthy if obscure tasks as an adjunct of U.N.E.S.C.O., but has lost all its power to move men's imaginations. In choosing to fight on the very ground that orthodox education claims as its own—that of preparing children to play their social parts—the progressive movement has had recourse to a pale imitation of the noble but fatuous doctrine of Anarchy: the supposition that, were we all but personally pure of heart, society and its problems would somehow fade away. This supposition in its turn has nurtured trust in the essential goodness of 'human nature', and so in the belief in the primaeval innocence of the child, with a consequent further emasculation of the Progressive Education movement.

It is true that we are here on the threshold of important ideas in social theory. Marx himself, after all (descended as he was from Rousseau and the ideal of Natural Man), but sought, through hyper-sophisticated mechanisms, to return mankind to the socially untrammelled state from whence it came. And so on. But in the more sober intellectual climate of today we are unable to accept any of these archaically romantic resolutions of our central puzzlement: the relation between person and society. Progressive Education is clearly a practice posited on the primacy of the person, a primacy that gives its meaning to a separate structure of educational practice. There have been times when this practice could continue undisturbed despite an absence of clear definition as to its character. But the times are now hard, and likely to remain so, for this practice, and its continuance may well depend on a clarification of its purposes. Such a clarification, if it were to succeed in its aim of rallying sympathizers to new endeavours, would not have to be blind to the at present debilitating inconsistencies of Progressive Education.

Now it would surely be unimaginably depressing if the philosophy of our own times did not have something to tell us about this state of affairs. The rejection by this philosophy, then, not only of idealist thought but of an ideal language—together with the character of logic (as being intrinsically situational) that flows from this rejection—means that in matters themselves involving language, human affairs, our only mode of investigation is that of conceptual elucidation. Hence, their analysis becomes morphological, and forms are what must be its concern. To accept this is as much as to be freed from the attempt—so long pursued by the social sciences—to construct models of human activities such as might in themselves, with the consistency we look for in the external reality of Nature, represent social reality. It is this unattainable consistency that has yet required of us complex theoretical social models, such as incorporate within themselves both society and the person as indubitable elements of our human experience. Now that we understand that consistency of this kind is a chimera—and that the consistency our minds crave is of a different order—we can allow ourselves to explore such forms as may impose themselves upon us. (As a matter of illustration and of interest, it is in China today—one refers to the 'cultural revolution' of the Red Guards—that we are witnessing the latest, and probably last, attempt to make a social model that embodies a relationship of its members, as persons, to itself. Naturally, it is the children who provide the agents of this attempt.)

The forms that force themselves upon us do not, in sum, constitute a society that has any consistency other than the language in which it is spoken of. We are therefore not obliged to reconcile a form of education we call 'Progressive Education' with the 'orthodox' form of education, by means of any common set of principles (such as, perchance, the protagonists of one or the other form might have misconceived); nor are we obliged to propose that, in some interpretation or other of Truth, one form excludes the other. 'Person' and 'society'—that dichotomy from which our different educational forms derive—are words used to discuss situations that are not comparable. In philosophic terms, they concern different language-games: games played in situations so different that the constructs built upon them scarcely interfere one with another. Thus, it is by the elucidation of discourse that we pursue social reality.

If this view can be accepted it means that Progressive Education—deriving as it does from the notion of the person, and in effect being a language-game conducted around that notion —has an unchallengeable integrity. (Naturally, so also does orthodox education.) Whether this is of more than a candidate status, however, depends upon who is attracted to the discourse in question. These present words are written in the estimation that current conceptual confusions conceal a perennial and powerful consensus, a deep yearning to treat children in a way more religious than that which orthodox education permits: in a way that the very idea of 'children' calls forth. Of course, this is not to say that our ears must be blocked to today's yet louder discourse about society and about how men, among themselves, arrange their affairs. Perhaps it is to say no more (at present) than that the recourse to social respectability, such as recently some progressive schools (in the inevitable course of institutional change, and given our difficult times) have embarked upon, is surely beset with pitfalls and disappointments. As Neill has done, we must keep our courage.

You are not asked to subscribe to the foregoing principles, as such. You may have better ones of your own, to explain the extraordinary, and highly emotional, cleavage between educationalists. Such judgement can be deferred pending a fuller discussion of the subject in the light of these principles. Indeed, they may appear something of a sledge-hammer with which to crack a nut. For it is possible to entertain the rudimentary thesis—and it was put forward at the Dartington Colloquy— that Progressive Education could dispense with progressive schools: that, were these schools for reasons of State abolished, progressive ideas would none the less continue to circulate and be developed.

With admitted intent to be provocative, Elmslie Philip said:

> I dare to query the contention that has been made: namely, that without the progressive schools, what has happened in State schools could not have happened. I don't think this is true. I don't think the fact of progressive schools being in operation is necessarily what has brought about a remarkable change of development in State schools. It is progressive ideas that matter, not progressive schools.
>
> These progressive ideas are bound to be fostered by any intelligent, devoted educationalist, and gradually come to realization. Let us not kid ourselves that the progressive schools have persuaded the mass of English people now to come forward, in a wave, in favour of comprehensive schools. The great British public doesn't give a damn about the ideas we have been talking about. But educationalists do.

It might, of course, well be asked, why they do. Edward Blishen's perception, noted earlier, of the progressive schools as places where everybody involved therein is stimulated by a common outlook, might well suggest itself as the answer. Progressive education is a matter of an intense, concentrated practical discourse: a serious and continuing language-game, whose quality must be obvious to the outsider, even if its meanings are not understood. In any case, however, Elmslie Philip's point—perhaps 'Aunt Sally' would be the better term— was commonly refuted at the Dartington Colloquy. Both Professor Rée and Mr. Schiller, for instance, contended that A. S. Neill's preaching without his practice would have been disregarded. Harry Rée put it as follows:

As a pragmatical nation, we wouldn't have adopted a great many of the ideas in State schools if we hadn't known they had been put into practice. I, personally, remember reading Neill, and as a result of that I introduced a school committee into my school. It was a simple thing and it made all the difference to the school. This was a progressive idea that came from seeing how it actually worked as it was described in the book. I wouldn't have done it if it had come just as an idea. Neill himself, sadly enough, doesn't seem to realize what an enormous debt huge numbers of us owe to him—and to others like him—because he has put things into practice.

Yet there is an element of truth in Elmslie Philip's contention. Progressive ideas in the State schools might well be advanced without their having any reference to the progressive schools. Orthodox education knows its own progressives. Within that body of practice, there is indeed a ferment that creates progress in its own terms. It would, for instance, be impossible to claim that the move towards comprehensive schooling in the State system has in any way derived from the movement for Progressive Education. It has taken place, rather, in the context of the language-game about society.

Marjorie Hourd expressed the matter thus: 'Surely, our ideas in education have changed for a large number of reasons. One is the progressive school; another, changes in psychological ideas and philosophical understanding. There has been a big shift in ideas, taking place from very many sources, of which the progressive school is but one.'

And, indeed, the unspoken presumption that (because of the name) Progressive Education is the source from which progress in education must come, goes a long way towards accounting for the resentment towards that form of education undoubtedly felt by a large body of educationalists. Yet even if this feeling is warranted, it must not be allowed to lead to the grave conclusion that the pervasiveness of ideas as such renders the practice of Progressive Education unnecessary and dispensable. Society is not the monolith that this philosophy of ideas would have us suppose. To think that it is, is to succumb to the confusion of dissociating practice from discourse, and words from ideas; it is, also, to surrender to the tyranny of the ideal. In brief, the continued practice of Progressive Education in progressive schools is certainly essential to its survival. That extraordinary change of climate, for instance, which anyone would experience on passing from a conventional to a progressive school—and which is what Progressive Education is all about—could result only from some commonly held outlook; and it is this, alone, which gives us something meaningful to discuss when we speak about Progressive Education.

These considerations bear upon another and more serious (because more subtle) threat to the practice of Progressive Education. For while most people at the Dartington Colloquy were anxious for the progressive schools to continue (and certainly did not want to accept responsibility for their demise), there were several who voiced the opinion that a place should be found for these schools, within the State educational system, as 'experimental' schools. For Harry Rée, for instance, this seemed the obvious niche for these schools.

> I see no reason [he said] why there shouldn't be set up a Department of Sociological and Educational Research, which would run experimental schools and finance research of all kinds, sociological and educational. This surely would defend your independence *vis-à-vis* the Local Education Authorities. The parents would opt, from all over the country, to send their children to you. You would therefore have parents who wanted this experimental education—and I think you would find that there would be parents enough.

Likewise, Elmslie Philip looked, somewhat obliquely, for a place of this kind for the progressive schools:

> I would have thought that, on the whole, the term 'experimental' would be better than 'progressive'; but of course if your label is 'experimental' it takes a lot of living up to. The danger is that the halo of empiricism slips and becomes the halter of oddity.
>
> You might say, if you are going to be experimental, that in standing aside from general educational practice either you ought to experiment on normal children or

you might experiment in the treatment of abnormal and maladjusted children. If it is the first, how are you going to select children for experiment? Is it on the parents' wishes? Now, unless the progressive school is wholly taken over by the State, one would say that the normal children to be experimented upon would join other children who are not normal, simply in that they have, many of them, been sent by rather odd parents. Or is, in fact, the experiment to consist in the mixing of normal and odd children? If you are somehow going to cater for special groups I am quite sure that progressive schools don't want to become dumps for the impossible children. In a way, in many people's eyes, however, this would be a justification for spending public money—because you would be doing an extra-special job.

You are in a bit of a dilemma.

The idea of the progressive schools as experimental schools presumably arises all too easily from the association of 'progress' with 'experiment', and is uniform with the philosophy of an ideal world and an ideal language in which to describe it; and this is, after all, the way of thinking which, with an ever-increasing momentum, we have prided ourselves on adopting since, say, the Renaissance. Significantly, however, this role for the progressive schools was many times, and often strenuously, renounced by participants to the Dartington Colloquy. Mr. Pidgeon, for instance, said: 'Attitudes have been shown in this gathering to be very important. But an attitude will only stem from a firm belief that what is being done is right; and you don't get this if you are asking someone to do something by way of experiment.'

Michael Young said:

All the suggestions I might make about curricula experiments, and so on, don't quite get to the heart of what progressive schools might contribute, supposing there were something like a marriage, even though a very informal marriage—better call it a liaison!—between them and the State system. The progressive schools aren't particularly cut out for curricula experiments—not specially cut out, say, for letting people do fruit-farming

E

mixed up with mathematics and history. They are, rather, specially cut out for trying to build a special kind of environment, where a certain kind of easy, formal, friendly, considerate relationship between adults and children is at the heart of the school. To ask them to give this up, to sacrifice any of this for the sake of some experiment in individual learning, would obviously be quite wrong. The schools must keep their character.

The question is, though, whether they can be a little more systematic than they have been in examination of their character, so that more is known of what their particular régime does for children.

It was, however, King Harris who most passionately repudiated this 'experimental' role for the progressive schools.

We are told to be more deliberate about ends and means and not to run a school just by intuition. Can children be made, consciously, the subject of experiment? I am not a sociologist, but I have very grave doubts about making children consciously the subjects of experiment. We may do experimental work—but we do it when we're absolutely convinced that it's the right thing to do. Other people perhaps call it 'experimental'; we don't call it experimental. We call it the right thing.

It is surely important that those who really are doing what some people would call 'an experiment' must believe in it? To them, it isn't really an experiment. Take, for instance, the teaching method of I.T.A. Those schools that have gone in for this have really been such as were already convinced that this was going to be a big improvement in the teaching of children to read. To them, this isn't really an experiment. They believe in it. Anything in the nature of a social experiment proper must have control groups—and this, with live, genuine children, seems to me a dubious proposition.

There is a real justification for this refusal of the progressive schools to take on any role as 'experimental' schools for the State system. It is not just the case that State schools must, and certainly will, carry out their own experiments in the practice of orthodox education. But this serious fallacy about the character of progressive schools could have arisen only from an analytic failure: from failure to appreciate that such understanding of education as we can attain is morphological in kind, is concerned with the forms of education and how they are articulated. The progressive schools are concerned with a form of education, called Progressive Education, which is distinct from orthodox education and not at variance from it merely in the minor degree which is permissible to experiment, before experiment disqualifies itself by establishing too many variables. Experiment with a form itself is, of course, a possibility. A progressive co-educational boarding-school is perhaps in itself an experiment. But it can only be undertaken given a shared conviction of its participants in the validity of the form, in its meaningful potential—not if they treat it as a variation of some other form, wherein their convictions still vest. These considerations may perhaps help explain what, sadly, appears to have happened to certain essays in progressive schools undertaken by well-meaning Local Education Authorities.

Hitherto, of course, it has proved notoriously difficult to reach agreement as to what systematic observations might be made of progressive schools, with a view to clarifying their concepts and establishing their typology. How, indeed, does one measure achievement in a process in which, to paraphrase Rousseau, 'life is the business that one would have children learn'? Indeed, the essentially religious attitude that permeates the movement for Progressive Education—the respect for children, and so for life—is undeniable and is virtually unmeasurable in any conventional sense. Dr. Henderson, for instance, was at one point of the Dartington Colloquy moved to say:

> Surely, what all our educational institutions (since the virtual demise of the traditional philosophy of our Western civilization at the end of the nineteenth century) have been lacking is an understanding of the role of evil and of the nature of death, as presented to children when growing up. Therefore, when Kenneth Barnes used the word 'tragic' it struck a chord in me. What do we have in our educational systems that enables us and our children to

cope with these problems? This seems to me an absolutely
vital point in the whole discussion—and unless progressive schools face up to it they might as well shut up
shop.

This underlying attitude has always led to resistance to the
facile measurement of the 'results' of Progressive Education.
Such measurement, in so far as it is sure to be related to social
criteria, is suspect among the progressive schools. The 'success'
of ex-pupils?—how? in income levels? citations in the Honours
Lists? divorce rates? suicides? All too easily, such tests lend
themselves to the sophistry that Progressive Education is but a
device for achieving the same ends as orthodox education but
by more subtle means. But in any case such tests are scarcely
relevant to an educational practice which among other things
believes, as Kenneth Barnes pointed out, in recognizing the
importance of failure. He said:

> One of the points I would emphasize is concern for the
> general preparation of our children for difficulty, for
> failure, because so much of educational preparation has
> hitherto been preparation for success—especially, in the
> past, in matters of sex. We have too easily made the
> assumption that if we imbue children strongly enough with
> ideals and right standards they will make the right kinds of
> relationships in life—and so proceed smoothly to a Darby
> and Joan end. We've got to realize that life just isn't like
> that: that life is full of errors, mistakes and failures. What
> we have to achieve is an attitude of resilience, an attitude
> which makes redemption continuously possible.

A practice of education, then, centred upon the idea of the
person is evidently not one that can be tested and elucidated
by any of the conventional criteria of social observation—except,
of course, in a way that is likely to demonstrate its social in-
adequacies, from the gaining of 'A' levels onwards! However,
recent ideas under consideration in the U.S.A., and spreading
now to this country, allow of a cautious hope that techniques
are being developed such as could throw new light on the
practices of progressive schools. This refers to techniques designed to show the component of 'creativity' in children's

characters. The caution with which this concept should be approached stems, not least, from what appear to be the historical origins of this enquiry: namely, a dissatisfaction, in America, with the originality and inventiveness of those scientists produced by the conventional academic system and set to work on applied scientific tasks. The conformist, or 'convergent', thinking of this kind of educational product has seemed to set a premium on the original, or 'divergent', thinker.

This premium could conceivably, of course, prove too high a one. As Dr. Susanna Isaacs said:

> I think the word 'awkward' is a good one, but I think it is important to note that being awkward is not necessarily being constructively awkward. One is tempted to think that every time one is awkward one is being an innovator.
>
> Still, I think it's tremendously important that those who are awkward in practice and whose awkwardness turns out to be constructive should have someone to back them.

The concept of 'creativity', in fact, has overtones which should warn us against taking too *simpliste* a view of any necessary connection between a tendency of children to show divergent characteristics in their thinking and the outcome of that tendency. This entire approach, in fact, was evidently new and strange to many present at the Dartington Colloquy, and a certain amount of scepticism was shown towards it. Kenneth Barnes, for instance, likened its impact to that of the Kinsey Report: 'Here are alarming conclusions that may be profoundly modified as one moves into deeper levels and becomes aware of greater subtleties at work in the situation.' Lois Child, however, drew a common-sense conclusion.

> If individualism and non-conformity [she said] are the real source of creative thinking, then it seems to be plain that the progressive school deserves a great deal of consideration. A non-conformist child has always found his place in it. It is, in essence, a non-conformist community. Indeed, if you live in a progressive school a constant factor in your life as teacher is the keeping of the non-conformer

within the bounds necessary to the well-being of the rest of the pupils. You don't have to think of his pleasure—he thinks of it himself! I think there is no evidence at all that the security of his situation blunts the edge of his non-conformity. What I think a school like this does is to stop him from developing his non-conformity into a defensive system. It makes him free to use it as a dynamic. This is because he is genuinely accepted; and if he is not beloved of all the staff he certainly never fails to find protectors among them—and even partisans.

The whole question of 'creativity' is evidently open to debate. As Kenneth Barnes pointed out, evidence that scientists as a whole tend to be 'convergent' thinkers (some merely less so than others) makes one want to look again at the assumptions being made about the concept of creativity. Such a look, however, far from discouraging employment of the term, may lead us, not perhaps to any refinement in measurement of this property in children, but rather to a deeper insight into the idea of creativity itself, and so into the reasons why it seems meaningful (as it does) for us to employ it. This is how an analysis by conceptual elucidation advances—as much by alteration of its terms, or their greater characterization, as by illuminating that to which these terms refer. It at least seems probable that 'creativity', in contradistinction to 'intelligence', is a characteristic that can be usefully applied to the children in progressive schools. This is not to claim that those children are somehow made more creative by their schools; it is, rather, merely to illuminate a syndrome. If investigation seems to show this to be true, then the idea of creativity itself will have achieved a certain recognition—and the people (teachers, children, parents) who between themselves conduct the dialogue of Progressive Education will have achieved more understanding of the form with which they are concerned. It is in this light, and not as a conventional 'scientific' research exercise, that Isabel Cabot's contribution to this book should be viewed.

Yet when all has been said—and much more could be said—about Progressive Education as an autonomous educational form posited on the idea of the person no acknowledgement has been made of that other reality, society, for which, even if orthodox education does make it its sole concern, it would presumably be irresponsible not in some degree to prepare children. The disciplines inseparable from society are a reality which, it might be thought, only at some risk can an education ignore. In a sense, Progressive Education does indeed accept something of that risk—though it does so upon the implicit understanding that it is the mark of a more advanced civilization (perhaps, even, a condition of its perpetuation through continual renewal) that such a risk should be taken. (As Dr. Henderson put it, 'The fostering of children's timely growth is a luxury in any society, which has to be paid for at luxury prices.') The risk here being taken is not only that of handicapping a child socially but also that of society being turned topsy-turvey as a result of the fresh view of it taken by the young when not by their schools committed to its drills. Yet, in fact, society will surely impose its rigours upon the products of orthodox and progressive schools alike. It would be a disservice to the latter children to leave them quite unaware of the temper of society. At some point they will learn with less or more of a shock that they and the boss will not be on Christian-name terms: that social conformities will be required of them, not only in the very earning of their livings but also to fulfil their ambitions for achievement.

Historically, Progressive Education has relied upon extra-educational experience to teach children about society and its ways—just as, conversely, orthodox education has relied upon the home to supply the upbringing of the child as a person. Society, after all, is not an ogre to be kept hidden from the child. He will see enough of it (the theory has gone) for education not to have to make it its business to teach him about it; the world is, anyway, too much with us. This principle has continuing validity (it would seem), and the progressive school remains, very much, a place that continues the beneficent work of the home at a stage when the home no longer has the capacity to continue it; but the world itself is a changing thing, and Progressive Education must beware of clinging to a shadow, not the substance.

Perhaps this problem is, crudely speaking, a matter of age levels. How late dare we leave it, with the world ever-more importuning the growing child, before education orientates itself upon society and its exigencies? It may prove helpful at this juncture in the discussion to introduce the concept of the 'college'; for, traditionally, the college has been concerned with just this transitional role, with the situation of young people learning to fend for themselves in the world. Do not our progressive schools need, at some stage of the age-bracket, to transform themselves into colleges? Arguably, by this means it might continue to prove possible for people to have their adolescence when they are adolescent—and not, disastrously, some twenty-five years later.

To conclude this account of how at the Dartington Colloquy the progressive schools laid the foundations of a recovery of their self-esteem, there is a note of optimism to be struck. Numerically, Progressive Education is a minority movement. But it is custodian of a body of ideas concerning a central contradiction (no less, perhaps, than that involved in rendering unto Caesar that which is Caesar's) in our kind of civilization: ideas ranging from Rousseau's concept of Nature (which was far more pregnant than, today, we seem to recognize), through Victorian Romanticism, to Freud and the exploration of the psyche. To suggest in what way (if any) the next wave of these ideas might develop would be to risk a synthetic confection. However, it can be said that the evidence is accumulating around us that once again our inner natures are, in contrast to our social passions, becoming our dominating concern. Superimposed on this tendency, or perhaps part of it, the novel phenomenon of teen-age culture is breaking down our received customs and casting self-doubt upon the orthodox education that purveys these. It should therefore once again not be ignored that, for the times we live in, Progressive Education arguably is becoming the most appropriate of educational forms.

The student unrest now erupting throughout the world is entirely relevant to this theme. Subsumed in this revolt—in its rejection of institutions themselves, in its condemnation of all bureaucratic machinery, its cultivation of nothing but what is in process, its dread of alienation—is a rejection even of that education which has produced the genus 'student' itself. This is the cultural revolution—profoundly so—and is, in much, to be welcomed. Youth alone, one now recognizes, because perennially it is uncompromised, can push back a little the frontiers of a rat-race culture and so redress the distortions of our value-orientated civilization. Alas! however, that these revolutionaries have nowhere to go but to the opposite extreme from education as a socializing exercise: to anarchy, and a pathetic dependence on man's natural goodness. (Alas! also, that this must be wrapped up in the Marxist package of degenerate idealism.) Progressive Education, however, because it has been through the fires of self-doubt, may now be well placed to lead us out of the labyrinth of contradictions in which we are otherwise trapped, making use of the constructs of contemporary thought to avoid the sterile clashes of contrary idealisms.

3

The Anti-School

We are becoming more familiar nowadays with the notion that
it is never in achievement that the essential lies, but in action—
and that achievement, which but recognizes itself, is the dust of
action. Not surprisingly, this notion seems reflected in the period
of exceptional social flux through which we are passing, in
which as never before whatsoever is established is questioned
purely because it is established. The notion itself, however, also
touches deeper levels; for one thing, it is sounding the knell of
idealistic social thought. The implication lies within it that
idealism's monumentalities are a chimera, and that the flux of
discourse provides our true and passionate concern.

Currently, out of this attitude, has developed that class of
things whose reality is anti their accepted selves. 'Anti-art' is
perhaps the best known example of this: a concept which infers
that 'art' is that which, in becoming accepted as such, acquires
other characteristics—say, the picture for hanging in the smart
living-room, or for confirming the Art Establishment itself—
and so loses the force it had. Only the creative process is anti-
art; art itself is moribund. Analogously, then, it may in passing
be helpful to think of the progressive school, because of the
place it holds in education, as the anti-school. For such a
school exists in testimony against the self-perpetuating academic system. This system, for sure, is one that readily insulates
itself from the opinion, the dislike—even the contempt—which
now growing numbers of adolescents and, customarily, the
adult population at large can be said to have taken against
'school'. On the other hand, for those who believe in Progres-

sive Education 'school' has nothing to do with the all-important ferment that arises out of the personality of the child. For them, therefore, only the anti-school is valid.

If we are concerned with the personality of the child, and simultaneously understand that the ideal school does not exist which would develop this to its full capacity, we must hope that the progressive school can somehow achieve its own perpetual revolution. Clearly, this revolution is one that must use the ever-unpredictable resources of children's personality as its dynamic. Somehow, then, the progressive school if it is to be a continuing entity—is not to blow up—must survive the effects, wayward as they may be, of this dynamic. Hence, in providing the environment that fosters the development of numerous young personalities together, the progressive school will have to accept that as a social organization it itself may have to own to many inconsistencies. Such inconsistencies may seem unintelligible, meaningless, to the adult world, that world which chiefly formulates our rules of discourse—although to the children involved, could their inventiveness of language but rise to it, these inconsistencies might seem perhaps quite plain. The hierarchies and observances in orthodox schools, the rational administrations to which they submit in the interests of the school as an institution of a certain kind, obey (although sometimes grotesquely) general institutional principles. Conversely, however, the progressive school consists of an environment which makes small pretence to mirror, or apply to, the conduct of worldly affairs.

The progressive school is, after all, a children's world, having that kind of logic. The freedom its children enjoy would, if transferred to the work-a-day world, make the running of many an institution difficult or impossible. More particularly, such freedoms pose problems for the staffing of any school, problems of which the orthodox school gratefully makes certain, by its regulations, that it is spared. The disciplines the latter school imposes provide an environment, for the staff at least, that ensures adult institutional sense: an environment that has recognizable and generalized form, and in which the roles of teacher and pupil can be played without undue overt difficulty, tension, embarrassment or, perhaps where applicable, even fear. The progressive school, on the other hand, must face up to the difficulties inherent in cultivating an environment conducive to the development of personality, but not necessarily logically consistent as an institution.

In large measure, the resolution of this problem for the progressive school consists in its constitution as—to use established but technical sociological terms—a community, rather than as a corporate social structure. Without going too deeply into the description of this fundamental distinction, perhaps by itself it sufficiently conveys the difference between a loose, informal order and a rigid and formalized one. The point is, that the former is in certain circumstances a quite viable kind of social form. In the case of a progressive school, it is not the functional relationships—as, say between teacher and pupil, or between pupils of one status and another—that give character to it, but the relationships that indirectly flow from the functional ones. These informal relations—involving such things as Christian-name terms between children and staff, non-hierarchical relations between different age-groups, uninhibited relations between girls and boys, etc.—are of so great an importance compared with the formal enclosure that school as a disciplinary institution must provide that they can in a progressive school be said to have burst institutional bounds and joined the larger community of the normal world outside. Thus, the progressive school escapes from the suffocating atmosphere of 'school'.

Despite the absence of institutionalized hierarchies in progressive schools, however, there should be no illusion but that conformism is present among the children of such schools. Michael Young expressed the situation as follows:

> There is obviously more freedom for children in relation to adults in the progressive school than there is in another sort of school. But there is also the question of the relationship of children to each other. How much freedom do they have in relation to each other? Coming myself to Dartington School first from a very orthodox preparatory school, I remember being enormously relieved by the sudden relaxation of adult authority and of the great array of rules that there were in the preparatory school. But I was conscious—as I think all children of all schools are conscious—of the unwritten code of behaviour which the

children had and which was enforced, not by punishments nor ordinary sanctions, but by the power of local public opinion inside a tiny society and the sense of some sort of collective.

The morale that grew out of this collective was, I think, very strong, and obviously in all schools children do have these unwritten codes. In progressive schools and all boarding-schools these codes are particularly strong and do press on certain individual children and may make them really uncomfortable. I think it possible that, certainly with some children, the less the weight of adult authority, the more in a sense they need a bevy of unwritten rules about behaviour, which they build up on their own—perhaps as a way of giving some sort of security to themselves which they otherwise wouldn't have.

What I think we don't know in a systematic way is how this works in progressive schools as compared with other schools. We don't know how far the attitudes of the responsible people—the adults in progressive schools—do communicate themselves to the children, and so lead to what they would think of as the right kind of behaviour: how sometimes a mutation of the adult's ideas occurs and perhaps creates too clinging a children's small society—that is, for children's individuality at least. I wonder what children in progressive schools feel they need to conform to in order to be members of their own little society?

There were conflicting views among others at the Dartington Colloquy as to whether in progressive schools there were significant pressures for conformity to a children's ethos—though there was, perhaps, a general acceptance that these pressures had increased of recent years. Eleanor Urban, for instance, said:

I have noticed, in the last few years, pressure groups among the children—a thing we hadn't noticed before at Monkton Wyld—and it started when there was an Aldermaston March. There were certain children who went on the Aldermaston March (and some of them were not really very peaceful children!), and we found they were exerting tremendous pressure on some children who were just not mature enough, and perhaps knew they were not mature enough, to understand these things. That was the first of that sort of thing. I would say, now, it's not a school pressure—it's nationwide. The whole Beatlemania, Rolling Stones and what-have-you. There is quite a strong pressure among, say, fourteen- and fifteen-year-olds, of that sort.

One advantage in a progressive school, however, is that you can talk about these things without the children necessarily thinking that you are going to put something across them to make them change their minds. You can have a more intimate relationship because it is a smaller school, I suppose, and because it is a boarding-school.

Freedom, of course, is what we must associate, not with an absence of all impediments, but with a variety and choice of contacts, each incidentally often involving tensions at levels higher than those in any state of captivity. It is certain, as Michael Young said, that more might be learnt about this in relation to Progressive Education, and it is obviously important that it should be learnt. It is equally possible that what Miss Gardner has called the 'half-baked' approach to Progressive Education could lead, say, to bullying among the children— and, prima facie, there are benevolently paternalistic forms of education that are more worried than progressive schools seem to have been about this sort of thing. However, what remains important about the loose social structure typical of the progressive school is that it is a society of peers: that the conformities, inescapable in this as in any society, are those intelligible to children themselves.

This directly raises the question of those organs of 'self-government' that have usually provided a facet—though often a chequered one—of many progressive schools. At the Dartington Colloquy experiences of these were, in fact, scarcely mentioned—perhaps significantly so. For it may be that there is some disillusionment with these 'democratic' devices, coupled with a consciousness that, since the self-government they can assure is often more apparent than real, more harm than good can ensue from a naïve dependence upon them. Yet the conclusion, surely, is precisely not to be jumped to, that the ultimate impracticability of school self-government—barring, of course, those dire occasions when adult participation, overt or heavily cloaked, dominates the proceedings—finally eliminates that children's world upon which the progressive school's justification depends. Probably in all such schools the moment arrives, from time to time, when the 'Moot' (or whatever it's called) has to be closed down. This but faithfully reflects the ebb and flow of life in progressive schools: the understanding that the school does not stand or fall by some fixed and imposed pattern of order. In a sense, therefore, these organs of self-government in progressive schools illustrate the case. They are part of a children's, not an adult, society. What matters about them is that they should come and go and yet come again: not that they should be faithful replicas of institutions in the adult world. So long as they are in being, they are part of the communications among the peers of the community that is the school. When they are discontinued they are a promise—and so also remain part of those communications. They are not so much important in themselves as they are reflections of an attitude which, if sometimes it does not express itself through them, must find other means of expression and which is a continuing thing, being centred on the personalities of the children.

Questions of the institutional organization of schools lead directly to questions as to their size. There was a perhaps significant difference as between the old and the new progressives at Dartington simply in this matter of size. For the former, a small school was an assumption to be made almost without question—and this is not surprising, because, prima facie, the organizational problems of any institution will tend to increase out of proportion to the capacity of each of its members to determine its activities. For the 'State progressives', however, large size held its merits, and (seemingly) precisely so as a means to the ends sought by the others. Evidence was given of the impressive array of classes available to the children of comprehensive schools. It was emphasized that these served not only the scholar but all children in finding their 'place in life'. (It perhaps takes some conviction about the nature of 'life' to contend that this may not be the purpose of education.) Nevertheless, it remains true that these claims for the large school carry a certain conviction. They do so not so much because of the better world that the resultant skills will help bring about as because the specialisms they encourage, being a function of so great an opportunity of choices, represent the sort of freedom in which we like to think maturation of the personality best occurs.

Now, imperceptibly perhaps, this discussion is narrowing on to the adolescent and his secondary schooling. The recognition is widespread, after all, that in primary education the battle for Progressive Education, if far from won, is at best fully engaged. In secondary education, on the other hand, and with a traumatic suddenness, the facts of life as orthodox education has always understood them still rule nearly supreme. (Nor is this gainsaid by any contention that secondary education is nowadays full of technical innovations.) And, in simple terms, this situation is readily understandable in the light of the relative proximity of children, young and old, to the claims made by society upon them. Yet Progressive Education itself has never easily recognized the distinction between 'primary' and 'secondary' education. Its kind of education has been all one, and progressive schools have tended to want children to pass through the experience they offer even from nursery school to school leaving. The reason for this is, surely, to be found in the irrelevance to society of education—and, conversely, the relevance of personal development—as conceived by the progressive schools. (This, let it be remembered, is not to suggest that society, *per se*, is irrelevant: only that the role of educators towards it is somewhat more humble than they suppose.) It follows that if Progressive Education persists in asserting its relevance to secondary education it is seeking no less than to push back the frontiers of society's intrusion upon the person. For this reason, the secondary schools of today are one of civilization's battlegrounds.

All this being said, intransigence and educational ideology are the enemy of us all. In any case, Progressive Education cannot be confused, in its concern for the personality of the child, with that form of British classical education sometimes said to have been posited on 'the whole personality'. This education, as is well understood, was concerned to impart proconsular skills and, thus, was to a high degree socially motivated.

(Of course, those were other times, other people!) Rather, Progressive Education has generally accepted that the deep pursuit by a child of perhaps some one particular interest is often the key to an unlocking of personality development. To this extent, when one comes to the adolescent stage especially, it can seriously be argued that large schools with their opportunities of specialization truly have an element of the progressive about them.

It was indeed notable at Dartington that remarks hinged around the advantages of large schools in curricula matters centred upon older children. Such children, all over the country and including those in progressive schools, are in fact making increasing use of Technical Colleges as a means, while escaping from school, of continuing their education. This but reinforces the contention, surely, that if schools wish to keep children in an environment in which they can continue to grow as persons—deferring their immature but desperate entanglement with the artifices of the world—they need at some stage to become more collegiate in character.

Clearly, then, as far as size is concerned and the opportunities it proffers, progressive schools might be wise to take this matter more seriously. Comprehensive schools, it has earlier been suggested, handicap themselves in terms of Progressive Education by reason of their size. Obviously, however, balances here must be sought and struck; what matters is that in neither case should they be sought for ideological reasons. For their part, progressive schools should perhaps weigh Dr. Winnicott's words in the balance: 'I don't have to remind you how absolutely different a fourteen-year-old is from a sixteen-year-old, and a sixteen from an eighteen. I mean, the extreme changes they go through, just getting from one little bit to the next.' What may matter is not that a school should be progressive all through but that there should be more progressive schools for all ages.

At some stage even the very impersonality of today's Technical College may provide something of the shelter from unwelcome personal intrusion—from those best-meaning of attentions that nevertheless are not quite to the point—that a young person desires. Such a stage would, presumably, be one in which a child had begun to set off down its own path in life

F

and at which, therefore, not even the most comprehending and sensitive of adults could, in some personal relationship, any longer touch it at many, let alone all, points of its personality. Yet it is becoming all too plain that young people might often benefit from developing in the environment of a school, rather than in society at large. It could follow, then, that there is a point for the progressive school of the future at which the informalities of its structure as a community should pass into something more formal: something that can offer, because of its greater variety and complexity, actually greater freedom to the more mature child. The judgement of when this point is reached, as also of how the various parts of such a school should relate to one another, is something to be left both to individual discretion (relating to particular circumstances) and to further enquiry.

Immediately, these considerations raise in our minds the thought of boarding-schools. This could, of course, be treated as a subject in itself; also, because of Dr. Lambert's absence through illness from the Dartington Colloquy (for which he had written the background paper on this subject), there is perhaps insufficient material here to report and comment upon. What can, of course, be noted is the prejudice which exists nationally on both sides of the question of the educational significance of boarding-schools. First, these schools are predominantly associated with the independent sector of our educational system—and so they are hard to disentangle in the arguments for and against that sector. Secondly, the day-school having become predominantly associated with the State system, there remains in certain quarters a feeling that any child sent to a boarding-school is being 'put away'. Edward Blishen, having confessed his personal ignorance of boarding-schools, described this matter thus:

> The little virtue there may be in my otherwise disabling innocence of mind may lie in the evidence I can give as to the unfavourable view of boarding education that was held in the circle in which I grew up and which, I think, is still held by a large number of people in England. When we heard that someone was being sent to a boarding-school we didn't think how very grand and fortunate a

fellow he was. I remember we felt, very distinctly, a sort of shadow falling over his home. He was being sent away, and this could only mean there was, behind the event, some sinister secret story—his parents had come to detest him, or he had proved unmanageable in some way. I think this went side-by-side with a perfectly practical understanding that this was how things were done at certain levels—the boy concerned was merely following in the footsteps of Harry Wharton and Bob Cherry—but a sense of something untoward, something cold and un-natural, was usually felt.

The concomitant of this latter prejudice, furthermore, is an idealization of the home, as a place for children of all ages (i.e. until marriage)—an idealization as dubious as that idealization of the child as repository of all virtues which has been laid at the door of Progressive Education. Kenneth Barnes touched on this point when he said:

I think we ought to go a little more deeply into the significance of the home. You see, we tend to talk about the home as an absolute—something unchanging—and I at once think of the Catholic presentation of the home: almost sentimentalized, as though this were an unques-tionable unit that never changes and always has the same significance. In point of fact, the home is changing and has changed profoundly. The home of today is a unit of perhaps four people, frequently moving from one place to another, not rooted in any kind of community. This is going to increase as labour becomes more and more mobile.

The family of the past wasn't just two parents and two children; it was two parents and quite a number of children, who lived in a place where there were also uncles, aunts and cousins and, in a sense, they were all members of the family. The adult–child relationship was then not within a tight little compact group; it was a child–adult relationship spread over quite a large number of adults. (If you take youngsters as I have seen them in Africa, and the Africans I have had in my school, when they talk about brothers, for instance, they include a lot

of people we would call cousins. I am even completely
confused as to who is the father of my Nigerian boy at the
moment—two or three people have turned up whom he
had called 'father'. I wonder how the Oedipus situation
resolves itself in a unit as large as that?) So what do we
mean when we talk about 'the family'? I wonder whether,
in our present situation where families have become so
small, there isn't a real necessity for putting children in
boarding-school? In such a school a child doesn't feel
he's got to make a close and urgent adjustment as to
mother and father, but may have a sense of detachment
and freedom in his relationships with adults, in which he
can choose the adults with which he makes an adjustment.

Perhaps this argument could be taken a stage further by
saying, in all seriousness, that 'middle-class' people—and
perhaps we are all becoming more middle-class—are so complicated in themselves and in their lives that it is often better
for their children at some not too late a stage to leave their
homes. The analysis of the educational significance of the
boarding-school is, however, now in hand—not least on the
part of Dr. Lambert—and is not to be anticipated here. The
Dartington Colloquy did, however, have the benefit of some
balanced comments by Edward Blishen that are worthy of
report. He said:

> I believe there is an enormous need for boarding-
> school education. I am thinking of the problem-children I
> know in the 'Newsom' area of London. I remember the
> very specific harm and damage that was done to children
> where there was not even the minimum of security and
> stability simply as to where they were located. I believe
> that it would be an enormous advantage if it were possible
> for such children, without paying fees and without feeling
> they were entering this as a sort of glass cage, to be able to
> go to a boarding-school, not necessarily for the whole of
> their secondary schooling but perhaps for a part of it. I
> think of children whose need for stability and pleasant
> considerate relationship made day-school quite inadequate
> for them. I think of the children I taught who in fact
> turned the day-school into a boarding-school, in the sense

that they stayed after hours, as long as they possibly could, because the school did offer a communal stability, a sense of security, a sense of purposeful activity, which they were not going to find once they walked out through a not very attractive school gate and went home.

If, indeed, the choice of boarding-schooling were a parents' a great problem would be to get people to identify themselves as being parents of children who need this kind of security. I think there would be a whole world of enquiry needed there to find out how this should be done.

I must say, however, that personally I think there is a serious limit to the usefulness of boarding-school education. We have heard the saying, 'The adolescent is not at home at home', but many of us know that this is part of the very agreeable comedy of having one's children educated in day-school. The 'not-at-homeness' of the adolescent is not always a tragedy; it's often, I think, a very pleasant comedy for both sides. I am a little worried by the argument that the boarding-school provides a necessary form of stability in a society which, indeed, does subject children to a very exhausting and bewildering cross-fire of values. (Some of you may have read this argument in a book written by John Wilson, Second Master at Kings, Canterbury, in which he argues very strongly that one purpose of education in the future might simply be to provide children, in a society which is increasingly confused, with an experience of unconfusion.) This seems to me to touch on the area which our proceedings here have frequently approached: the degree to which children should be protected.

Agreed, there is frequently an attempt in our society to make profit out of men's weaknesses, and it is perfectly true that today's children live in an environment which makes it very difficult for them to become whole and unconfused persons. However, this in a sense is the human struggle, and I merely say this in order to suggest that, in the isolation of the boarding-school education, there's always bound to be an element of detachment and abstraction from society. One of the important things that benign boarding-schools must do is to attempt to limit, as much as possible, this element of isolation which takes children out of what for most people is the natural environment. It seems to me very important to work out exactly how the element of what is 'unnatural' should be limited.

At least, then, it is perhaps more widely recognized than it was that boarding may have some educational function, as opposed to the various social purposes it has been said to serve; the bounds of this function await more precise description. Can it be said, however, that Progressive Education itself expands or contracts those bounds? Historically, there have been very few progressive day-schools, but this might quite simply be ascribed not to anything inherent in Progressive Education but to the limited demand by parents for this form of education, which, just like the traditional foundations of the Public Schools, has imposed a concentration of resources necessitating the pupils being brought to the school, rather than the reverse. As a practical matter, this state of affairs is likely to continue, and even if it comes to be accepted that boarding-school education is desirable only for restricted categories of children, Progressive Education may have to continue paying this price for the sake of its very continuation. Were this so, it would surely need to be shown that the price was a very high one before those dedicated to the idea of Progressive Education would be convinced that it was not worth the paying.

Touching on the factor of the boarding-school's isolation—which is, presumably, the unresolved central conundrum about its educational virtue—Michael Young had some proposals to make that were perhaps specially relevant to the progressive school.

I think [he said] one of the great strengths of Dartington School—and this is something that Leonard and Dorothy Elmhirst saw at the very beginning—was that it was set in a community where, to some extent, other skills and achievements could be drawn on for the benefit of the school. I often wish it could be done more than it is. But all schools, it seems to me, could benefit in the same kind of way if only they could to some degree break down the wall which separates them from the rest of society and bring in teachers who are in some sphere or other outstanding, whether it is in bricklaying, ballet or science.

To take a leaf out of the Russian book—and not just the Russian's, but something that was also done for older children at Antioch College in America—I think there is something to be said for trying to link school and work during the years of adolescence more closely than is usually done in boarding-schools. One of the great merits of Dartington School for me was that I was able to study fruit-farming ('study' isn't quite the right word: I practised it in a very elementary way) while also learning a modicum of arithmetic, etc. Later on, when I found out I wasn't cut out to be a fruit farmer, I was even able to go into an architect's office (about a hundred yards from where we're sitting) and pretend to be a minor junior architect. This experience of mixing some kind of work and the ordinary sort of academic schooling was, to me, certainly tremendously valuable.

Obviously, because it cannot help but break down the atmosphere of 'school', this latter aspect of Michael Young's suggestions is important for Progressive Education. Indeed, it has antecedents in that spontaneous nineteenth-century movement of schools for workers' children centred upon craft disciplines, schools which sadly and ironically were stifled by the advent of compulsory public education (i.e. academic teaching). The difficulties of implementing these ideas are practical and well known. It may be, however, that the time has come for progressive schools to make renewed efforts in this direction. The retention of many children in school, where surely they ought to remain in order just to grow a little more, may depend on the development of this kind of practice. The informality of a progressive school should, from the school's point of view, allow it to happen. It could indeed be a further way of partaking in a wider community, such as seems an essential way of preventing the school itself from becoming an adult-ordered institution.

On the merits of the boarding-school issue itself as it affects Progressive Education, there are two opposing considerations to be put. On the one hand, that children's world which it is the purpose of a progressive school to foster can, prima facie, best be sustained in a boarding-school and there given a much enhanced significance. Moreover, this 'world', since it is a loosely structured community, need not involve the isolation from the local community that is typical of the conventional boarding-school. Progressive school-children have, in general, been much freer to mingle with their local communities than have been their orthodox counterparts. The unorthodoxy of manners typical of the progressive school-child is, by and large, quite easily assimilated in the wider community around the school—while the school, itself, remains none the less essential for generating the ethos that this unorthodoxy expresses, and which indeed would be untenable in a more closely structured school. The apartness (of a kind) typical of Progressive Education was, after all, typified in the régime of 'Emile', the original progressive student of them all!

On the other hand, it is possible that the freedoms of a progressive school are, at some times, going to be damaging to some of the children boarding in the school. Kenneth Barnes, for instance, has already been cited as expressing concern about girls' sexual frigidities, which may have been produced by these schools in the past. Should this be so, a progressive day-school could be said to have an in-built safety-valve for such children. Indeed, this consideration only leads, once again, to the common-sense thought that generalizations about Progressive Education that ignore the important distinctions between age-ranges are not very helpful. Hu Child, for instance, was careful to make the point at Dartington that in his experience pre-adolescent boarding should be the exception for a progressive school, rather than the rule. And, once again, not only discretion but further enquiry is obviously needed here. Meantime, a practical conclusion might be that there should in the future be scope both for boarding and for day progressive schools, because in all probability there is no inherent educational superiority in either of these types of school. Social and other extra-educational considerations are generally likely to determine which of them, at any point or moment, is to be engaged upon.

Yet it must be recognized that one category of problems is

today far more acute for the progressive boarding-school than for the orthodox boarding-school. This arises from that very mingling of its pupils with the world-at-large which ensues from its own informal character. For the world-at-large has itself become much freer in its ways (has, in fact, itself become more of a child's world), so that the problem is less whether the local community can occasionally assimilate the unorthodox behaviour of the children from the progressive school in its midst as whether, reciprocally, the school can withstand the importation of behaviour—particularly such as stems from the autonomous youth-culture new to our times—which, because it is not moderated by the continuing responsibility for the school of those who belong to it, puts an undeniable strain on the informal structure of the school. (The problem, for instance, of relations with the local Youth Club is often a real one nowadays for the progressive school, whereas for the conventional boarding-school the problem as such is overtly not allowed to exist.) Furthermore, it is certain that contemporary attitudes to sex and drugs are posing new problems for the progressive boarding-school. June Ottaway expressed the position as follows:

> Our children may turn to adults for guidance, but they have only to take a straight look at the adult world to see irresponsible, illegal sex rampant. Films, plays, novels all thrust it at them. If they go to John Osborne's *Inadmissible Evidence* they find the hero bedding-down on the office floor with his secretary, and although Osborne isn't advocating this, he may well seem to be holding the mirror up to Nature. Children may get the set-up and miss the moral (if there is one)—and what view of the sex life of adults does this lead them to take? I remember being very uncomfortable once, when I had a play-reading of *Waltz of the Toreadors* with a group of sixteen-year-olds, so vivid is the depiction of the seamy sexuality of the middle-aged General.
>
> Now, of course, one doesn't want to censor their reading or restrict their play-going. They'll read *The Group* and see *Who's Afraid of Virginia Woolf*, and they will want to talk about them. But it does seem they are beset on all

sides by this discouraging presentation of sex which, none the less, simultaneously encourages its promiscuous practice. (If everybody does it, why shouldn't they join in!) They may well become impatient of the hypocritical society which says 'No!' but shouts 'Yes!' from every hoarding.

In these circumstances it presumably needs to be asked of a progressive boarding-school whether the informality of its structure, its child's idea of order, will not indeed verge upon the chaotic and, if so, whether it is, perhaps, only in the day-school (where the strains will somehow be taken elsewhere) that Progressive Education can henceforth be carried on. The question is hypothetical because of the generalities in terms of which it is phrased, but evokes the perhaps worthwhile answer that the position is indeed probably tenable so long as it is not 'half-baked' Progressive Education that is being practised: so long, that is, as there are teachers such as Mrs. Ottaway involved in it, who are capable not merely of leaving the children to themselves but of offering them (to be accepted or rejected) experiences that could be of significance to them. And this, further, leads to the tentative conclusion, that some progressive schools may need seriously to think about becoming larger than they are, in order to generate from inside themselves that variety of interest and experience which they will need, in order to withstand an ever more importunate world-at-large.

Of course, for a progressive school at least, this does not imply a closing out of life beyond the school. This danger was touched on by Mr. Snape, whose comprehensive school includes a boarding element:

> There are some parents [he said] who want to contract out of all the aspects of modern society they find upsetting —long hair, jeans, leather jackets—and we have tremendous pressure from these parents to bring up the boys in our boarding-house completely divorced from contemporary adolescent culture. Now, I think this is a cowardice on the part of a parent, because if you reject modern adolescent culture I don't think you should withdraw from it; I think you should get to grips with it. If you

don't like it you must change it. You can't withdraw from it and then despise it, or despise adolescents who adopt it and parents who accept it.

At the same time, it cannot be claimed that in principle this problem of the assimilation of two cultures has yet been mastered. One proposal for mastering it, canvassed at the Dartington Colloquy, is for the establishment of neighbourhood boarding-schools, where weekly boarding would be practised, with the children returning to their homes and to the general community at week-ends. Royston Lambert broached this possibility in his paper, and Mr. Schiller indicated some of its possibilities when he said:

> I would mention one aspect of the idea of the local boarding-school which concerns the bringing of parents into closer association with the school. I think the experience of school dinners throws some light on this. When they were introduced the effect of school dinners was quite remarkable. Their socializing effect on the children was quite remarkable; not only that, but—what was a little puzzling—there was the effect on the relationships of the parents with the school. It dawned on me, then, that nearly everything that happens in a school is quite remote from life for a parent. You see, most of them can't do the things that are done in most schools; they're quite remote and different. But they do all eat their dinner; and the mothers are extremely interested in the sort of dinner and how it's cooked. That very simple thing, without any doubt, did bring the parents into appreciably closer relationship. When I think of a local boarding-school I am thinking of a place where most of the parents live within half an hour's walk. I would expect to find them in closer relationship with the school because they would be able to share and understand more of the ordinary life of those boys and girls.

Hu Child, among others, pointed out some of the practical, including geographical, limitations of the efficacy of this idea of a neighbourhood boarding-school; he further made the point that it was precisely at the week-ends that the boarding-school proper had its greatest educational opportunities—even though it then as often missed them. There was, however, no objection in principle made at the Colloquy to any attempt to establish neighbourhood boarding-schools, provided these constituted only part of a pattern of boarding-schools. But the point perhaps needs here to be made that this very idea stems from a concern to modify the isolation of the orthodox boarding-school and to amend its effects by the application of certain counter-balancing forces. As such, it is an idea somewhat irrelevant to the character of the progressive boarding-school, which seeks to operate as a community, not isolated from its locality, but whose isolation and quality consists solely in the structure which a children's way of life imposes on it. To reinforce this point, it is also perhaps here relevant to point out that in progressive boarding-schools generally it has always been customary both for parents to have *carte blanche* of entry and for such children as wished and were able to do so to return to their homes at week-ends.

In all practicality, however, it has to be recognized that until the central question of sexual conduct is faced up to, a progressive boarding-school will be unable to resolve—in a way that recognizes rather than avoids the problem—the difficulties posed by the relationship of itself to the changing world around it. Co-education is, of course, integral with nearly all our progressive boarding-schools; yet it is not only the questions this nowadays raises of the relations as between the children of a school but also the questions that are raised about the relations of the children with their contemporaries not in the school that have to be answered. Co-education itself is something without which the movement for Progressive Education could hardly survive; its importance in providing the climate in which personal maturity can take place is (assuming this is the chief aim of education) by and large probably undeniable. By way of illustration of this point, some comments of Kenneth Barnes may be quoted:

> We have a great opportunity in co-education [he said] to make girls more natural, to make girls more normal and wholesome than they are when they get segregated

from boys. I get a terrific shock whenever I leave the world of co-education and am, for some moment, in the world of the girls' school, realizing how typed a girl can be when she is in a single-sex school. I know also what terrific changes girls go through when they come from a single-sex school and come into the co-educational school. When we have boys and girls together, of course, we are forced to get rid of our romantic notions and accept the fact that both boys and girls are equally crude. It doesn't make them any less likeable. (I have discovered how incredibly crude an eleven-year-old girl can be—but I am delighted with her at the same time.) And what encourages me about co-education, where girls are concerned, is the way they can grow up accepting their sexual nature in its relative primitiveness and crudity, and yet making it part of their integrity. In most instances that I have kept in touch with there is nothing phoney, nothing artificial about it; it is real, it is part of a woman's nature.

June Ottaway added to this theme:

Our society hasn't adjusted itself to sex; merely, it seems to have become obsessed with it. The young do marvellously to cope as well as they do. The very freedom of the progressive school, however, gives them a chance to work out their relationships. What we think does emerge from our relaxed situations is that, where relationships do spring up, they are, if in miniature, valid ones. The promiscuity of the outside world seems not to attract these children—and that is something achieved! Mystery, glamour, contrivances are all absent. We seem to turn out womenly, rather than feminine, people.

It was Dr. Hardy Gaussen, perhaps, who gave most complete, albeit partly oblique, expression to the beliefs that traditionally have underlain co-educational practice. In speaking generally to the Paper Kenneth Barnes had contributed, Hardy Gaussen said:

My first reaction to Mr. Barnes' Paper was that he'd said it all; the advantages of co-education can't be questioned. Then, I felt there was something missing in it—and I wondered what sort of man was this that had written so. I turned it over in my mind. I slept on it—and I looked again and thought, 'Well, nobody can say it all, in five thousand words or so. I must meet Mr. Barnes.'

It all sounded too rational, too clear (almost too down to earth), when I read it. After a bit, I thought that, possibly, his premises are incomplete. For at the opening of his Paper, Mr. Barnes says, 'When we put boys and girls together, we are producing a sexual situation.' Surely I thought, even when we are born we enter into a sexual situation; we are all bi-sexual from the word go! We all love and have to meet the opposite sex—both without us and within us. That is a fact of life, and we remain in a sexual situation—all our lives.

Boarding-school is but a minor incident, and for a few people. It is those who attempt to deny this, for example by single-sexed schools, who are mistaken. It is people who try to get away from, or to control, sex, to repress it, who block the road to development in the individual child, who produce the one-sided, crippled and specialized pseudo-adults we see around us.

So I went on thinking about it, and it seemed to me there was a word missing—and here, of course, Mr. Barnes has given us an explanation, and he's used the word this morning.

When discussing sex and sexual education he has explained he hesitated to use the word 'love' because it is too ambiguous, too commercialized. (It occurred once in his Paper, when he said that when boys and girls fell in love it was in some quarters regarded as 'silly'.) He called falling in love 'warming-up relationships'—and I thought to myself, 'Well! shades of Romeo and Juliet.' He has seemed to regard education as a means of controlling sex—whereas I would regard love as the driving and moderating force in human relationships, and sex as the manifestation of love.

Where is love without the body, and where is the body without love? It is this wonder and mystery of love that is felt by so many boys and girls before physical desire appears: romance, idylls, springtime, that prepare the way for the summer heat. Sometimes, alas!, the physical and the psychic are widely separated. Physical passion may, of course, not be integrated with tenderness; or the embodiment of love may be feared and fled from. It is this process of bringing together, and its completion, that we hope for—and when we see boys and girls awakening to what lies before them the possibility of 'the other' (the other sex, the other person, a new creation), it is all there, in that crude beginning.

My work is mostly with children in their own families and in day-schools. There is a trend for more schools to be 'mixed', and I think this is a very good thing. The single-sex schools have some advantages at certain ages; there are ages when boys prefer boys and girls prefer girls and when nothing will get the two sexes together. You recognize that puberty comes two years earlier in girls—and communication at that stage is quite impossible between the sexes. Even allowing for this, boys and girls need each other as much as do men and women.

Taking the whole community—head, heart and hands must all develop together. Sometimes one aspect takes the lead, sometimes another, but it is often what the poets call 'the heart', the whole life of feeling, that is neglected. (That, I think, goes for all schools, and for our community at large.) Acquiring facts, or passing exams, have left us no 'time'; competition, getting on, acquiring skills have won approval. This life of feeling—life based on the very ties that bind humanity—gets lost. It may then appear as a sexual drive. I think the one can turn into the other, and this life of 'the heart' may find a substitute expression in 'sex'. I think if there are marriages where this has happened terrible failures sometimes occur as a result.

The insecurity, the deprivation, the loneliness that masquerades as 'sex'—yet which can never be met by sex—is known to everyone who works with people. For instance, the unwanted girl, at odds with her mother, spurned by her father, wanders the streets and haunts the cafés. She finds she can get a passing warmth, she can get attention, she can get a kind of security by using her sex-attraction. (She is not her feminine self at all—she is far too immature for that—but she can use allure; she can create an illusion of being wanted by somebody.) No wonder her need overwhelms her—and no wonder she often has a baby!

No wonder the baby often grows up to repeat the pattern!

You will see in this, that my experience has been of the deprived and of the unloved, and of those who have not really joined the human family; they have remained outside the pack. Often, they get pushed away to boarding-school—and the parents or Local Education Authority will pay for it. Those unwanted ones make a nuisance of themselves; they have what we call 'symptoms'; they misbehave, they are delinquent. Indeed, how can they love if they have not been loved? and what more natural than to turn to 'sex' for solace? They do not know what they want (but think they want sex) because the primal link, the link which makes common humanity, has not been forged.

As I mused on Mr. Barnes' Paper, I saw the missing word was there—this was after quite a time; that when he gives sex-instruction he is showing his feeling, he is evaluating his pupils as people, as people that he wants to help to grow. With his enlightened and liberal attitude, Mr. Barnes is, as it were, himself a good parent, who has been through it, who is on their side; and when I came to the end of the Paper and read that 'education is re-demptive', then I know that what he means by 'education' is what others call 'love'.

It's love that redeems and transforms and, as it is the 'love' of the physician that heals the patient, so it is the love for and by the teacher that can make whole the child.

There are, to be sure, other aspects to the totality of conviction about co-education. Perhaps chief of these is the insight it gives into the quality of discipline that teachers exercise in schools of one kind or the other. Life in a school in which adolescent boys and girls are mixed together becomes, presumably, several times more complicated than one in which they

are segregated. For the teacher of authoritarian mind, therefore, co-education is an impediment to discipline. Co-education
is, rather, a plan innately conducive to that children's world
which the progressive school is concerned to achieve.

Granted, however, this basic principle about co-education,
the progressive movement still must struggle to instil reality
into the practice. At one extreme, as Ruth Foster pointed out,
the concept of co-education is prostituted into what, more
truthfully, is sometimes called 'mixed' education. She said:

> There has been a good deal of talk about the justifica-
> tion, or otherwise, of the independent progressive school. I
> think there are several justifications for it, but I think
> co-education is one of the great ones. It has been said
> here that a number of schools are becoming 'mixed'. This
> indeed is the word for it: not 'co-educational'. There are
> very, very few co-educational secondary schools within the
> State system. Where they exist they are, with one excep-
> tion in my experience, run by women; I have encountered
> only one run by a man.
>
> Very little thought is given, within the State system,
> as to how boys and girls can really live and work together
> and complement each other. It's something that's assumed
> simply as an administrative convenience or, at best, as a
> 'good thing'. A good thing it is, but most people in the
> State system don't find it a thing worth consideration—
> and, in fact, don't achieve it. In school after school you
> can go into Assembly and find the girls on one side and
> the boys on the other. One kind of address is likely to
> make the girls impatient, and one kind of address is
> likely to make the boys impatient. There is quite a lot of
> antagonism between boys and girls between the ages of
> twelve and fifteen—maybe this is true in a progressive
> school too?—and it sticks out a mile in school after
> school in the State system.
>
> You will often ask teachers how, for example, they
> manage subjects like History and English with a class of
> boys and girls. Often they will reply, 'Well, of course, we
> have to think about what the boys will take.' Over and
> over again this happens. In most State secondary schools

G

it seems to me, with a few very honourable exceptions, we haven't found out how to help boys and girls, young men and women, to live and work together. In independent progressive schools, though, certain achievements have been made, which have helped those schools to establish true co-education.

The reasons, however, for the introduction of co-education in progressive schools do not lie solely in the authoritarian cast of orthodox education (though this must contribute to the position) but in factors with which the progressive schools must also contend, and the baffling reality of which is shown by the considerable difference in reactions among themselves that these schools make to them. June Ottaway stated matters quite simply in saying:

I sometimes wonder whether by, as it were, providing facilities for them to sleep together, and then telling them not to, we aren't being a little unfair. Would the children appreciate having it made more difficult; or would this simply act as a stimulus and challenge? The sleeping arrangements for boys and girls differ from school to school. At Bedales they have their own separate houses; at Wennington separate floors; at Dartington only separate rooms. Have we, with our freedom, put children in an impossible position? Or is it good for them that they are trusted in this way?

Hu Child added to this, when he said:

It isn't necessary for a boarding-school to cut itself off—as they nearly all do, by persecuting modern styles of dress, hair and expression—from pop-culture. In most progressive schools children are not thus cut off. Our children can go to cafés and cinemas as much as they please in their free time, provided they've got the money. Maybe, however, the school that deliberately cuts itself off has an argument. It can say this is not the kind of culture for which it wishes to educate children: that it wants to educate for something better. (Whether it does so or not may be an open question.) In our case this is a worry, because we get a number of children who spend every minute of their spare time in cafés in Totnes—and we try to do something about it, though we don't forbid it.

Undeniably, the facts of our times are that—unlike the desirable congruence movingly described by Hardy Gaussen— love and sex are not any more, in one way or another, integral with each other in contemporary discourse. 'Sex' is, seemingly, an invention of our days—presumably it was an inescapable one, when once the puritan shroud had been drawn over mankind in Victorian times. The point was put, with purposeful crudity, by Peter Sutcliffe:

> Mr. Barnes and Dr. Gaussen [he said] are associating sexuality with high ideals. I would like to hear discussed this problem of crude sex. It has always seemed to me a terrible shame that, whereas we supposedly are sexually most able—more or less like ping-pong players—before we are twenty-one, yet we neglect those wonderful opportunities.
>
> In a boys' school masturbation goes on all the time. There isn't any way of having a satisfactory sexual relationship, one that is freely condoned by society, until people get married at twenty-five or so. This is something we've got to cope with, particularly in a situation, as now, where people are going to go on continuing their education for a longer period.

Needless to say (one hopes), this is not how the situation is seen to exist from within a progressive boarding-school. But it is as it is known to exist outside it and, since such a school depends very much on its not being isolated from the general community as such, conflicts of a serious kind are hereby generated. (It would make a fascinating speculation for another occasion, as to whether the generally 'wholesome' relations between the sexes within progressive schools are a left-over from a previous era—made still possible by the degree of protection in which relations between the sexes there can develop—or a precursor of a new balance of masculine– feminine relationship.) What the Dartington discussion there-fore fumbled towards was consideration of the possibility of developing what might be called a stable code of casual sex relationships. Peter Snape expressed this position in the following way:

> Isn't Kenneth Barnes seeking to replace the 'Christian' taboo on casual sex with a new kind of restriction upon casual sex? I think he is probably right in this, yet no one here yet has explained why casual sex really is to be avoided.
>
> I think society is moving towards a new view of sex. Certainly, I think some of our young people have sexual relations which don't seem to make them particularly unhappy. Some young people don't feel uneasy about it; some do. The fact that for some children casual sex relations are a miserable experience may well, in fact, rather be a reflection on other things—an unhappy home, for instance. I think nobody really knows—although this is within our dealings with young people—whether casual sex relationships are important or unimportant, or whether they matter at all to some people.

It was perhaps natural that at this point eyes should have been turned towards the experiences of the progressive boarding-schools in these matters. Professor Harry Rée, while taking it upon himself to act Devil's advocate to a solution at the opposite pole to the progressive school, posed the relevant question:

> I wonder if we can hear from the 'experimental' schools what the victims—i.e. the children—really feel about this? I was at a Public School where sex relationships were continuous and casual without any dangers at all, because no babies were produced. It was a very pleasant way of going through one's teens. One wasn't in any way repressed. It was accepted by the whole community, and the masters didn't take any notice of it. I suppose this is terrible, but, looked at in one way, we felt this was the Greek way of doing it—and other people who have been at Public School will recognize this. I honestly don't think it did many of us much harm. (Arguably, I know of course, it is harmful, as happens with most upper-class English-

men, for their initiation in sex to be with the same sex.
But much of what is harmful about it can be adjusted
later.) But nowadays, with the danger removed of babies
being born—and shall we assume that this probably is
so?—have we to move into a completely new attitude on
the part of adults to the young's casual sex relationships?
Has this already started in 'experimental' schools? I shall
be interested to know.

Hu Child gave an honest answer to an honest question:

I think it is very difficult to enlighten Professor Rée on
what happens in co-educational progressive schools,
partly because I don't think any one school is like another
in this or in any other respect, and partly because I
would not pretend to know just what does go on in my
school. All one can describe is what one thinks goes on
and what one observes.

Dartington, in which the mixing of the sexes is perhaps
more thorough than in most schools, might be taken as
one example of the situation. There we have these mixed
boarding-houses, which have single rooms. Each boarding-
house has a roughly equal number of boys and girls in it,
all mixed up together, and they are perfectly free to
associate with each other in their rooms—except they are
firmly told that we cannot allow them to go to bed with
each other.

Now it is very difficult in these modern times—as
people will realize—to give one's reasons for this. All we
can say is that of course there is the danger of pregnancy.
Ourselves, we don't believe that people should engage in
full sexual relations until they are emotionally secure
enough to take the full emotional consequences. Of course,
you can say this to an adolescent until you are blue in the
face. He will say he agrees—but that doesn't mean he
feels exactly the same way about it at the bottom of his
heart.

All we can say is that we have tried to work out an
ethos in the school community, such that sexual relations
are recognized as something you have to wait for until
you are mature enough to take all the risks involved,

emotional and physical. To what extent this is accepted by the children it is very difficult to say. There are, as we all know, always the odd rebels who will not take any notice of what you say. The children are, it must at least be said, uninhibited in the expression of their feelings for each other, and a couple will go about hand-in-hand and, without undue embarrassment, will embrace in the presence of adults. So, where one has a couple who are getting very thick in this way one obviously takes the opportunity to discuss their problems with them and find out if one can help them. (Actually, the number of couples one gets are conspicuous by their small numbers.) They do in our school, I think, live a very unselfconscious life about sex—except, of course, the child who doesn't get the affection he should have in his home. This is exhibited in their dress. The girls, for instance, wear the ordinary uniform of the adolescent—dark sweaters and jeans—but make-up and fancy hair-do's are fairly conspicuous by their absence.

When Professor Rée suggests that modern contraceptive techniques have altered the whole situation I would agree that in a way they have—and yet it doesn't seem that the number of pregnancies out of wedlock is declining. It seems they are very rapidly on the increase, and this is rather a peculiar phenomenon. I have a fancy that Nature has a way of circumventing our methods.

Kenneth Barnes likewise adopted a pragmatic attitude to suggestions that some new ideal situation in co-education was but waiting to be brought into being. He said:

It may be we are moving to a world of free sexual relationships. I am not one who says a particular moral pattern is essential for the survival of humanity. I just don't know what the world of ten years hence will be. I think in this we have to exercise 'negative capability': to develop the capacity to live in a state of transition and uncertainty—and I don't see why the children shouldn't know that I'm in a state of negative capability, living in uncertainty.

I feel perfectly prepared to say to my children, if they

question me, 'This is the state of uncertainty that I'm in. I'm not the kind of person who leaps from one place to another without any evidence for what I'm saying. For the moment, although I realize the world is changing, I think you must restrain your sexual impulses because I ask you to be restrained.' This is not the same thing as exercising a taboo. A taboo can be a dangerous thing, because it pushes things down into the unconscious, where they churn around, producing effects that you don't know of. A conscious restriction is not necessarily an imputation of evil in the thing you are restricting.

I know that many of my children will enjoy pre-marital intercourse—and I use the word 'enjoy' quite definitely. They will enjoy it and they will be enriched by it. What I've got to do is to give my children a preparation for anything that might happen—so that whatever happens to them, even if it is quite different from what is expected to happen, they may be open to redemption and it may be something enriching. That is as far as I can reasonably go, I think, in the world as it is. People thirty or forty years hence may ask, 'Why didn't he go further?' The answer is that I'm not living thirty or forty years hence. I am living here, now.

The tentative character of some of these points of view expressed at Dartington cannot, surely, in itself be objected to. The discussion there only reflects the confusion of the situation itself. A comment of Dr. Winnicott's indicated something of the extent of this confusion.

When a boy [he said] lately came to talk to me about sex and when I asked him something like, you know, 'How is it?', he replied, 'Well, I'm not perverted'—as much as to say that it hadn't occurred to him there was such a thing as impotence! Now, this seems an awfully interesting reflection on the present day; impotence seems to have gone out of the window, while perversion as it used to be has almost turned into loose affairs without any intention of marriage—simply because that is now the most wonderful defence against homosexuality.

I remember a discussion we had in the 'thirties with the

Heads of Progressive Schools, when we went over the whole ground—of masturbation and the value of masturbation, the value of homosexuality and the flight from homosexuality that can be found in a school that is always fostering heterosexuality. (We can say, for instance, that a deprived girl, who psychiatrically is wanting and needing a regression—a few months of being spoilt by mother, as to speak, in a very intimate way—has to have homosexual relationship. That's the explanation of half of the homosexual problems that come my way.) At that Conference we went into all that and there was included, then, a rich description of the fantasy life that belongs to sex. But I think it's a very confusing discussion we're now having. We are talking about adolescents and what they are like everywhere in a society that is changing, and changing not only here but in the whole world of the adolescent at the moment.

For the progressive boarding-school, indeed, it cannot be pretended that this discussion in itself resolved its problems of internal–external compatibility: of a resolution, that is, in some way ensuring the continuance of its children's freedoms. Yet enough that was hopeful was said, and enough to establish to what considerable lengths it would be worth going in order to preserve the potentially great benefits for the development of personality that a progressive co-educational boarding-school confers. If it must be recognized that children may sleep together, then surely it is vital for the school to ensure that they are instructed in contraception? If promiscuity is to continue to be meaningful and therefore to be discouraged—because of the offence it causes to the community in which it is practised—then surely an organization on collegiate lines for the elder children is called for, an organization in which those children bear responsibilities (and have privileges, e.g. driving motor vehicles) such as become increasingly realistic in adult terms? And if it is becoming increasingly difficult to refrain from shutting out the inhibiting intrusions of the world-at-large, then, again, surely the progressive school must think about increasing its own inherent attractions, not least by an increase in its size?

Perhaps it is the easier to make this latter proposal because of the, at present, very small size of most progressive schools. First, however, it has to be recognized that this smallness of size is often a function of poverty. Secondly, a suspicion could be entertained that a virtue has here been made of necessity. The stress laid by progressive schools on personal relations is, given any constant staff–pupil ratio, surely not so much a matter of size as of the character of organization. Relations as of person to person are indeed important for these schools, if only because, being concerned with personality, it is for them not the roles played by children in the institution that matter, so much as that children should be children in their own right. Nevertheless, as with growing maturity the personality becomes more definitely structured, personal relationships become an ever more difficult basis upon which to sustain a community. It is, in fact, more than arguable that our concern for personality must consist, all along the line, in allowing it such freedom as from stage to stage it needs for its growth—a freedom which even includes release from personal relationships that can be too oppressive. This freedom, as has already been argued, is very much a question of providing the right ranges of choice at the right times. (This principle is surely foreshadowed by those large classes of many of our primary schools nowadays, in which teachers have mastered the art of allowing children, individually or in small groups, to busy themselves with their separate activities.) Of course, however, a larger progressive school would have to be one capable of resisting the forces of adult administrative convenience. There are many patterns that could be followed to ensure this, which it would not here be appropriate to go into. The over-riding requirement, however, would always need to be that type of Head whom Marjorie Hourd cited as quite typical of progressive schools: 'A dominant person who is always examining his dominance—for that, partly, is why he is what he is and is doing what he is doing.'

If the progressive school indeed is the perpetual 'anti-school' there might in the foregoing suggestions be found some of the material needed for its continuous renewal. As some of these suggestions should imply, to break out of the conventions of 'school'—always closing in on us, as they are—one essential may be the practice from time to time of that neglected art of scandalizing the bourgeois, itself ever being renewed. However, to complement this pastime, we would be wise also to have more positive stratagems in hand. This is the subject of the next chapter.

4

Some Common Ground?

The general ideas of the last chapter lead, fairly directly, to a range of particular questions. These concern the topical problems of learning, of how children do learn, problems of acquiring skills and of submitting to their disciplines; matters in relation to which it is important to know the standing of Progressive Education. Does Progressive Education stand aside from these? Or might the ideas now in ferment here prove important for its own development?

The attitude of Progressive Education to these matters has hitherto been distinctive; it might simply be described as one of resistance to pressurization of the child. Such pressurization, of course, includes that of learning, and hence has induced an indifference to novel techniques of teaching as being educationally irrelevant. Combined with this there has gone an innate confidence in the child's own capacity to select and acquire such knowledge as he will need, not to achieve status in the academic microcosm (unless the child is a scholar) but in that world of adult life at which he will in due course arrive. Yet (if this be a fair description of the attitude in question) for this still to withstand the pressures put upon it itself by an importunate world is, surely, becoming ever more difficult. To arrive at the adult world without some mastery of the skills this world requires is increasingly for the child to find himself at a disadvantage, the tolerable limits of which must now be being reached. Very possibly, this is a fate which orthodox education itself holds in store for an increasing percentage of its own products—those who fall by the wayside during the process of

secondary education. This is the characteristic of our merito-
cratic civilization. And orthodox education faces its own
problems in beneficently providing for the quiescence of this
new race of helots. But progressive schools cannot simply turn
their backs on this situation, trusting in their children to rough
it in the adult world for a while and confident of their capacity,
in the end, to reach an accommodation with it. Progressive
Education cannot do this, because the world intrudes increasingly into the school and, realistically speaking, cannot be
kept out. Arguably, the failure to impart skills—as the world
demands these—is itself to stunt personality development: is to
place a young person in an inhibiting situation. For better or
for worse, the distinction between 'school' and 'life' is becoming
less tenable. Orthodox education, in these circumstances,
appears to react by trying to make life like school. Perhaps it is
reserved for Progressive Education to make school like life.

A helpful introduction to these questions is provided by the
distinction which, at the Dartington Colloquy, Dr. Pidgeon
sought to draw between the essential characteristics of 'primary'
and 'secondary' education.

> I want to point the distinction [he said] between
> primary and secondary education. I have myself always
> been uncertain as to what the difference here is. I don't
> mean in terms of physical appearances; that's easy enough.
> (In primary schools it's usual to have a teacher who
> teaches all subjects, whereas the secondary school intro-
> duces specialist teachers.) But what, essentially, is the
> difference between primary and secondary education?
>
> Well, I want to suggest that secondary education is that
> stage at which an individual learns because there seems
> so much to be learnt; he is habituated to learning as such.
> I would like to illustrate this from my personal experience
> —which I wouldn't do if it hadn't been confirmed for me
> by that of others. I can remember, then, in my school days,
> that I was very loath to learn; I learned simply because I
> had to. I had to learn certain things which were, in a sense,
> remote. I was forced to do that and nothing else until
> one day, when I was about thirteen, I was in the school
> library (playing about as usual) and something hap-

pened. Other people went out. I was alone; I was sitting in a chair looking at a row of books, such as I would never have dreamt of taking out, when suddenly I saw a title. (I can't remember now what it was.) I took the book down and started reading; I thought, 'My golly, this is interesting!' Then I looked up at all the other books and I thought, 'Heavens above! Isn't there a fantastic amount? I haven't got time! What have I been doing all my life? I'm now going to sit down and start learning.' And from then on, learning took on a completely different aspect.

Perhaps this is a silly anecdote, though maybe other people here have had a similar experience. However, I do think there is a stage of learning that can be induced, and I myself think of the primary stage as that of bringing about the need of learning for its own sake; the secondary stage can then take it on from there.

One of the first things in the primary stage is learning how to learn; learning that learning is, in fact, something which only the self can take part in. Being a member of the class with a teacher at the head, listening to something or occasionally glancing out of the window if it gets boring: acting on the assumption that this is what education is, is just not good enough for the child.

Perhaps there lie here the seeds of some sort of reconciliation between the two groups of progressives represented at the Dartington Colloquy. If learning is 'something which only the self can take part in' it presupposes that 'self' and its maturation. It was instructive to note how so much of current pedagogical attention, as mentioned by Dr. Pidgeon and others, leans in this way towards solutions sympathetic to the attitudes of Progressive Education. Yet it does so without, on the one hand, emphasizing the primacy of personal relationships or, on the other, viewing the child as social material. It does it, rather, by reason of its emphasis on the developmental processes of the child as a person. Some more words of Dr. Pidgeon will serve to illustrate the point:

My idea [he said] is to challenge some of the basic assumptions on which classroom-teaching is founded. First, all children are different and, in particular, they understand in different ways. They think differently. A teacher, therefore, cannot stand at the head of a class and expect a complete overlap with all children in a class. Some of them will understand him, some will not. Thelen, in America, has taken this point further and has experimented on what he calls 'teachability grouping', whereby pupils are grouped together in classes where they are compatible with the teacher. This is done in a variety of ways, but the idea is to get a group of pupils, under a teacher, who are in sympathy with his mode of approach and his personality, so that the pupil–teacher relationship is as clear as it can be.

Another point, in this class–teacher situation, is learning. The teacher in a class has a set of ideas about what he thinks his pupils are capable of learning. (I am primarily thinking here about a subject teacher.) What determines this set? Of course, a large number of factors: the whole background of the pupils, the teacher's background, the circumstances of the school and so on. All these factors determine what the teacher expects of the pupils. And, of course, there's the reverse: the pupils' expectations about themselves. Let me give you an instance of how these factors can affect what is learnt.

I did a short study in schools which had three classes in a year-group and which separated these classes by age. The classes were not divided by ability but by age, so that one class was of the top four months of the age-group, the middle class the middle four months and the third the bottom four months. We gave some reading tests to the children, and it was perfectly easy, from the calculation of the performance of the whole year-group, to calculate the expected performance of the three different classes. You would expect that the older children would do thus much better than the middle group and so on. However, what happened was that the oldest group achieved a level much higher than expected, the middle group achieved just about the level expected and the bottom group achieved a level much lower than expected. We found this in each of three schools studied separately, all of which streamed by age.

How does one explain this? I may be wrong, but my interpretation is that, simply because the oldest class is older, the teachers (probably quite sub-consciously) know that they've got a slightly better class and so expect more of them. (Whether the pupils do the same, I don't know.) And the reverse happens in the bottom class.

The crux of this approach is the concentration of attention, not upon teaching, but upon learning, and because this is concerned with the child rather than the adult, it surely reflects, in the traditional sense, a 'progressive' attitude. Together with this concern for learning there goes a belief in children's potential, such as conventional teaching practices have been prone to suppress. As Dr. Pidgeon said:

I think there are two lines of approach in educational research that are now coming together. On the one hand, you have those who are making a deep study of a subject and are beginning to get down to the ways in which this subject should be presented for learning, so that there is a continuum in it and the early learner starts at the bottom and gradually climbs up this continuum. On the other hand, you have the work of psychologists, post-Piaget, who are getting more understanding of how children do learn concepts. These two approaches can now be put together.

We have to work out how individual learning can be brought about in schools which have pupil–teacher ratios of perhaps 20 or 25 to 1. I know it can be done. I have seen many classes that have done it, both in primary and secondary schools. What I think is needed, however, is curriculum reform. We must look with far greater care at what it is we are expecting children to learn in any subject. We have to give a great deal more thought to the sequential order in which topics are presented. I don't say there is always a unique order; the only thing I say about the order is that at no one time should a child be presented with a concept which, as it were, subsumes an earlier concept which he may not have fully learnt. Dienes has done a great deal of work in this country showing the order in which mathematical concepts should be presented. I don't know how history, say, should be presented, but I am quite sure there are a number of people who do know how this should be done.

It is perfectly easy, in mathematics say, provided children are given concrete experiences of the world of number, to develop a programme of learning—not the kind of rigid programme used in a teaching machine— such that the pressures of the environment are towards the gaining of early concepts. The proof of whether a concept has been understood is always that a child can recognize it in different contexts. You cannot develop any concept if it is not experienced. Children must be put in situations in which they can experience a concept before they are able to have any idea of what it means to be able to use it. My suggestion simply is that from the early stages children must be introduced to the notion of how to learn and of what learning is; they must be introduced to situations in which they can carry out their learning, and then, as they progress, the stage will come when they are ready for secondary education, in which they are able to continue the seeking out of information for them-selves.

In summary, we have to think in terms of bringing some of the practices from the primary school up into the secondary school. I would also think we must bring some of the sixth-form practice downwards.

Alan Brimer continued this line of thought, putting special stress on the question of children's capacities to learn.

The notion is still widespread [he said] that Intelligence Tests measure some form of inborn capacity, and that this inborn capacity somehow or other places limitations on what can be learnt. We still hear the kind of statement which suggests that the child can't do it because he hasn't got it 'up there'. The general attitude towards the per-formance which actually children give, as an indication of what they are capable of doing, still comes from this general expectation that some fundamental limit is present. In practice, we have no basis for assuming that such a limit exists, except theoretically. We have every reason to suppose that learning can improve for every child beyond what it now is—and there is no contrary evidence.

While many people now accept this notion, there is still a good deal (particularly in their teaching) which suggests they have the old ideas in mind. The organization of classes into streamed groups is based on the assumption not merely that it is easier to teach groups that are relatively alike but also that there is some intrinsic character in each of these groups suggesting that one group will never improve to the extent of a higher one. I think that this notion of the individual difference between children constituting an innate characteristic is one of the greatest stumbling blocks in producing a more progressive kind of education. We cease, as a result of it, to experiment. We adapt our circumstances to the point at which we think we have diagnosed what a child 'is'.

Unfortunately, this notion of a natural limit to what children can learn has appeared to gain some force from the work of Piaget himself. From this, it has seemed that certain orders of conceptual development are possible only at given ages. But the fact that certain children, in a particular part of the world, attain certain conceptual levels at a given point of life, is no indication at all that we couldn't make matters otherwise. Indeed, in Bristol we have been engaged in showing that concepts can be accelerated. Whereas Piaget quotes certain ages at which children begin to conceive of number, we have been able to show that it is possible to accelerate the formation of such concepts to a very great extent. There is a necessity, therefore, for us as teachers to continue to try to improve beyond what we achieve at the moment.

One of the things we have learnt from Piaget is that we have no basis, as adults, for regarding the child's way of thinking as in any sense inferior to ours; that there is a necessary respect for the way in which children think at any point in life; that their ways of reconstructing the world and producing reality-adjustment are as important for them and merit as much attention as the way we think we ourselves ought to look at matters.

H

Alan Brimer dissociated himself from notions of promoting sequential and linear programming of instruction, holding that these could encourage 'the notion of some external rate-forcing process, rather than an intrinsic rate-forcing process'. But he went on to suggest that our increasing understanding of learning processes contained implications for the character of our schools. He said:

I would suggest there is another way of looking at how learning takes place, one which makes more use of the motivations which children are able to display to us. If we accept that learning is the process by which children go through continuous reality-adjustment, and that the business of education is to make this reality-adjustment more effective by whatever means this is achieved, then it ceases to be necessary to enclose this reality-adjustment in rigidly organized subjects. I also think it has implications for the organization of schools. I agree that more individualizing is necessary, but this individualizing can't go on in the kinds of buildings that we now have, or with the kinds of attitudes teachers now have to learning.

Schools now are organized for group instruction, rather than for individual learning. I would think that the school of the future ought to aim at, say, 70 per cent of the child's time devoted to individual learning, something like 25 per cent to very small group processes (perhaps no more than eight children in a group, with a tutor) and 5 per cent in very large groups—much larger than we usually use at the moment.

The reorganization of the school to make this possible would be considerable. It also implies a reorientation of teacher attitudes. It suggests a more humble approach on the part of teachers, a greater respect for what the child is searching for. It would mean, I think, a breakdown of the subject specialism we have at the moment. I would think that teachers could themselves be much more versatile in their guidance of children—so long as there was the specialist help available, as necessary. I can even see the whole curriculum being reorganized in quite different systems from the one we now have. There could be the notion of language as a fundamental aspect of human activity. Within a notion of language, mathematics could be studied, as a part of language; literature, the means by which people communicate mechanically; the process of symbolism, and so on. There is a whole realm of study possible, within this, which is relevant to reality-adjustment in an individual child and which does not have to fit into a particular subject-period as we know it today.

There was at Dartington, however, a suspicious resistance to much of this body of thought, as presented by the educational researchers. It came in large measure, indeed, from those who stood by the current practices of the progressive schools. Hu Child expressed these suspicions when, in talking generally about curricular matters in progressive schools, he said:

All kinds of school these days offer practically the same curriculum. This was not true when the progressive schools started. They started by changing the curriculum to a considerable extent, particularly by altering the emphasis on the classics. But nowadays, at any rate in the secondary stage, all schools offer the same curriculum, not because they want to, but because they more or less have to. Their curriculum is, very largely, dictated by the national examination system; even progressive schools have to play in with this to a considerable extent—although it is perhaps true that they don't impose the same curriculum on all children to the extent that orthodox schools do. (One of the distinguishing features of the progressive schools, when they started at the beginning of the century, was their emphasis on arts, crafts and music—and, in most cases, this continues.) As to method, I think all schools are able to experiment with teaching now, and all kinds of school are doing so. Here, though, I would want to say that the progressive schools are perhaps a little antipathetic to the fashionable methods of the moment; that is, those of programmed learning and the use of machines. This is because one of the main beliefs of these schools is the feeling that the really important incentive to learning is the relationship of the person to the adult who is teaching.

It was Ted Fitch, however, as a practising teacher in a progressive school, who launched the most sceptical case against the suggestion for more individualized learning such as forms the backbone of the claims of these new ideas themselves to be progressive.

I am not [he said] an eagle in this soaring gathering; I am very much a worm, and I think a worm's eye view may help to bring us down to earth. The two things about a worm, I believe, are that he can't see far ahead, and he is remarkably timid. I will, then, restrict myself to a few comments, based on my experiences at Dartington. These embody old-fashioned, conservative doubts, probably very heretical now, but they may do you a service by showing you what you are up against.

Dr. Pidgeon makes an assumption that a pupil's will to learn can be increased and his frustrations overcome if he is given an individual programme, one logically structured and adapted to his capacity. But does every child clamour wholeheartedly for individual attention? The more unique his programme, the more he is isolated—yet many children wish to be involved with others. Even under ideal conditions, individual work can be boring. Some people love it; I have known others who have hated it. I have found that many a voluntary assignment is dropped just for this reason—the child is working on his own.

We once experimented at Dartington with a modified Dalton plan (all Dalton plans seem to be modified ones!) to suit individuals. The end we had in mind was to ease their anxieties by letting them work at their own pace, in their own time; and it was dropped because it had the opposite effect. I'm not saying this is bound to happen, but it's what did happen here. What we found was that, without the frequent supervision of a teacher to act as a brake, there was an anxious rush of the conscientious to complete their work, while the lazy suffered from a sense of guilt or of despair. Moreover, pupils would insist on comparing assignments and so could not be prevented from deducing a general level of expectancy, which they then anxiously compared with what they were achieving.

Next, I would like to deal with this question of abolishing groups. All schools, from time to time, have bad spells and, when this happens, pupils usually concentrate their frustrations on two main things—food and classwork. Now, eating is a group activity and a dining-room riot can well clear the air. But if work were individually planned, children would be deprived of this focus for an outburst, and a creeping paralysis might take over. I think the assumption that group work is at best a necessary evil, should not pass unchallenged. At Dartington we allow children to choose their own tutors; this is a recognition that perfect communication cannot be achieved between any teacher and every pupil. But to expose a child to the direct influence of an incompatible teacher may do more harm than good—and if you are doing individual work only a very large school could afford the multiplicity of specialist teachers you would need to avoid this. I find that group teaching can cushion the clash of personalities, and very often antipathies wear down in time.

Another point I would question is the contention that learning takes place during activity. To stimulate the imagination, must one be active? Every teacher has met the child who opts out of all participation, yet remains interested, and carries over what he absorbs into his private life. And the more you attempt to involve him, the less he will respond. I believe that, to a certain extent, all adolescents at some time desire non-involvement; they want, and probably need, to be left alone—but not to be neglected. Does not group teaching achieve this compromise? Moreover, I have found that it is only in a group that standards can be persistently upheld; I mean, a kind of craftsmanship, without any descent to personal nagging. You can, if you like, address a group week after week; but week after week addressing individual people, that is a very different matter!

Finally, is there to be no place for the teacher who is a born lecturer? Wouldn't he be wasted without an audience? and wouldn't his usefulness evaporate with individual

repetition? Such teachers can achieve a momentum of
enthusiasm in a group—whereas individual pupils might
well be unresponsive to him. Group inertia, we all
know, is deadly; but a good group is more than the sum
of its members. I feel that the ability to rouse the sense
of corporate excitement over a common task is no bad
thing.

This is the authentic voice of Progressive Education, and
yet, within that matrix, as Ted Fitch himself in fact allowed,
also a duly conservative, practical voice. After all, however, it
can fairly be noted that whereas the classic régime of Progressive Education—that prescribed by Rousseau for 'Emile'—
was indeed one involving a personal, one-to-one, relationship
between pupil and teacher, yet, in another sense a régime of
individual work by the child might be conceived as but the
next and logical stage beyond that old régime: the abolition of
all teachers, so that the child alone, as a person in control of
his situation and according to his capacities, becomes the
concern of education. (Sometimes, indeed, one wonders what
would be left of any child's personality after it had experienced
an individual tutelage by Rousseau!) At all events, the impression must not be left that at the Dartington Colloquy the
progressive schools were uniformly antipathetic to develop-
ments in the techniques of individual learning. Eleanor
Urban, for instance, claimed quite simply that at her school
these principles had been put into practice over many years past.

> We have been doing this kind of thing [she said] minus
> the programme imposed externally on the child and with
> some fixed sequence, for twenty-five years—and we haven't
> found the snags apparently experienced at Dartington. I
> think this was probably because we thought it was a good
> idea, we believed in it and we all wanted to do it; we
> modified things gradually. We do break out into all kinds
> of group-activities, for all kinds of purposes, when there's
> a meaning in the group; but we avoid the passive role of
> the child.
>
> It's great fun for a teacher to give a good lesson. I think
> that's one of the troubles—that teachers don't like to sacri-
> fice their satisfaction in giving a good lesson. It can, too,

on occasions have a good effect. To some extent, we allow for this by having a weekly work-meeting. Children, then, can give lessons, and teachers take part.

So it isn't rigid! There are plenty of active experiences, expeditions, discussions and that sort of thing. However, the basic background is the subject-room and the learning situation. The teacher is in the humble role, as has been suggested—just catering for what each child needs. It is rather like a big jig-saw puzzle; even if you put in a bit of blue sky there, and you put in another piece at the bottom, you get the whole thing finished without following some necessary sequence.

There is very little machinery. There are subject-rooms and subject-teachers, subject-books and equipment, and the children just go into whatever room they feel like going into at 9.30. If they've been to the school before, they know what they're going to do and they start doing it. If they are new children, then of course there have to be consultations. We are waiting, then, all the time to see a gleam in the eye of the unmotivated pupil, because we do get children coming to us who have been years elsewhere, working, say, for 'O' levels in an automatic way, and who are pretty unmotivated towards learning.

We are so pleased with the way all this works that, rather than argue about it, I'd simply say, 'Come and see it!'

Roy Potter took a mid-way position on Dr. Pidgeon's thesis, when he said:

I feel that the insistence on learning rather than teaching is an excellent one, because I think there is still far too large a body of teachers who feel it is the effort they put into teaching that determines whether or not they are being successful, not the amount of learning that goes on. But the notion of even a third of a child's time being spent as an individual is, to my mind, in complete opposition to the idea of learning as an active operation. I think not only the pleasure but the value of learning as a social group-activity has here been underestimated. One is influenced in this by one's own subject-teaching experience.

I myself would find it difficult actively to teach a language given this degree of private study, even with modern machines and tapes.

It was left to Christian Schiller, however, to express a certain emotional dismay at these ideas of individual learning.
He said:

Ever since Parliament granted tax-payers' money for education, there has been no doubt at all as to what is the purpose of school: school is a place where children go to learn—there's no possible doubt about that. For a large number of years Parliament specified exactly what children should learn. For some years now that responsibility has been handed over to the L.E.A.s, who themselves have handed it over perfectly squarely to the Heads of schools. Now, as to class-teaching, in the schools which I visit class-teaching has been dealt with long ago. This picture of boys and girls sitting there in rows is a kind of funny story one tells to students. (There are still primary schools like that, because there are always schools that faithfully reproduce practices that were common twenty years ago. That is why you can always give a lesson in educational history on the spot—you can show it happenning.) Well, in effect, it's all gone.

It has been mentioned that you can bring forward the age of conceptualization of number, quite appreciably. Indeed you can! There is a piece of 'research' going on in America, teaching children to read by putting them in a glass box at the age of two. Why do you want to teach them to read at two? I thought the whole idea was that children should be children—and to most of us the idea that a child should read before he can properly talk, or that he should conceptualize number before he really knows much about counting, is just horrifying. Of course it can be done! The alarming thing is that you can do almost anything with young children. But why?

We have been realizing here how difficult it is to carry on an effective exchange between those whose experience has been in the progressive schools and those in the State schools. (It does seem to me important to try to get much more in common between us.) But, however little common experience there is there, there is much less common experience between what happens in the classroom and what goes on under the name of 'psychology and research'. You see, there are things one takes for granted: one knows them from one's experience! I don't think it helps to put them into long words.

The grounds for this kind of suspicion are understandable. Pressurization of the child to learn is contrary to the tenets of Progressive Education, presumably however interpreted. Yet there is a distinction between pressurization of the child by the teacher and pressurization (if that is the word) of the child by the subject. The former holds all the connotations of an authoritarian social structure; the latter presumes a relationship of a child's innate capacities with the world as it is known. For progressive schools, the approach to learning here under consideration appears hopeful because it holds promise of filling a gap in their argument—a gap to which they at increasing peril turn a blind eye, and which they have hitherto sought to fill merely by dragging themselves into line with conventional curriculum practice. That a concern for a child's capacity to learn should not degenerate into an exploitation of that capacity must be dependent on a continuing recognition of the child as a child—and the environment of any school may, or may not, reflect this concern. But there need be no incompatibility of this attitude with a positive fostering of a child's talents and interests. Perhaps the current clouding of this issue would be clarified by a greater use of the idea of expectancy in this context: of the significance, for learning, of what is expected of the child.

For Dr. Pidgeon, the idea of expectancy was central to his notions about learning.

In a sense [he said] one aim in learning (I'm trying to avoid the use of the word 'teaching') might be to set an expectancy: a standard for pupils which is just far enough ahead of them to reach up and try and get. If it is too far ahead, of course, there are difficulties; they may become discouraged and react to that. On the other hand, expectancy can be too low. Somehow, I think, children react to these different situations rather like chickens faced with a pile of grain: they'll anyway eat just so much of what is in front of them. In a similar way, children will learn so much, very rarely achieving 100 per cent of what they are expected to learn, but a proportion of what is in front of them—and the less of what there is, the smaller the amount learnt. This, coupled with the fact that children are individuals—they all do develop and progress at different rates—makes it wrong, I think, that we should go on with the assumption that the classroom is the correct approach.

Marjorie Hourd explored this idea of expectancy more profoundly.

We have here [she said] an idea of expectancy linked in a very useful way with the problem of motivation to learn. The idea, as I understand it, is that there is a direct relation between a child's achievement and what is expected of him—as that, if children are taught as a large class, then the teacher will be bound to impose an unwarrantable degree of standardization on its members, so that the notion of expectancy operates according to the situation in which children are taught. Thus, if we expect a high level of performance we're likely to get it; if we expect a low level we're probably going to get that too. Expectancy is also influenced by classroom background, by what we think about the intelligence quotient.

I would suggest we could add infinitely to this. We could say that expectancy is influenced by the physique of the child; it is influenced by his speech—and in very many ways. In fact, this is an extremely complex and important idea. The attitudes on the part of both pupils and teachers to what learning is and of what learning is possible, to no small extent influence what in fact is learnt. I am left wondering how far we yet realize that a teacher's attitude can change learning. For many years now I've set for post-graduate students a question which reads something like this: 'You cannot regard or judge a child's behaviour and learning without taking into account the attitude taken to them.' Usually, only about five students out of one hundred and forty choose this question. Even they find it extremely difficult—and I may also say that some of my colleagues did not understand it. So it's evident we have a long way to go in grasping this idea, though we may pay lip-service to it. It follows, further, that children are capable of a far higher level of performance than is normally expected of them. This, again, is something we haven't fully grasped. It has been quite a relevation to discover in children's writing and their art work what a really high level they can and often do reach.

Following on from the notion of expectancy, however, we are asked to believe that it's easier to reach a child's true level through individual teaching than by group work. Now, in this connection, I deplore all the wasted effort that goes into too much seeking to please, but I doubt if one could complete any task of significance without trying to win someone's approbation. We shall probably never be able, each one of us, to eradicate a certain amount of attention-seeking in what we do.

Here, however, I think we have to recognize the value of negative purpose, as well as of positive purpose. I think the concept of expectancy is greatly enriched by taking this into account. A teacher also needs what, in my own mind, I have called 'multiple expectancy', which I would take to be an aspect of creative learning: that is, being able to allow the child his whole experience.

I don't see how in English literature, or the arts, or in any subject where what we've called 'divergent thinking' is important, one could possibly have a planned continuum of stages of learning. I don't think we shall discover how to teach a subject from within the subject itself (nor how to find the incentive to learning from within the task itself) unless, as teachers, we do cultivate the quality of negative capability. Children are very much interested in a teacher's way of teaching; they watch it, they imbibe it and they care about it. It fascinates them. They are perhaps as deeply involved in this as they are in their own ways of thinking. We are, whether we like it or not, in the grip of a revolutionary idea: that learning is not the result of an omnipotent force from without, nor of a benign submissive attitude, but of a complex and curious relationship as between a child who has plenty of maturing and growth in him, and a grown-up who has plenty of the child.

I think the teacher needs very great understanding here. He does have to go out on a rather courageous mission and there risk the unfulfilled parts of his nature—in a way, incidentally, that no other profession is asked to do. If we are not going to be able to say that teaching is a highly risky procedure—though very gratifying when it comes off—we might, instead, be finding it said that teachers aren't really necessary. (It might turn out like this in the end, but we must come to this conclusion only for a good reason.)

The combination here submitted, therefore, is of an exploration of children's individual potential to learn, together with the cultivation by teachers of their own 'negative capability', of their capacity to expect the unexpected. (Such a capacity, indeed, arguably could inhere only in those with the classical attitude of Progressive Education to the child.) This combination perhaps suggests the recipe for which the progressive schools must seek if they are to remain compatible with the world around them. If so, it could have many practical consequences, from the break-up of the classroom to the creation of new architectural spaces, and to various techniques for the programming of learning, etc. Yet there would seem to be more than that to the story. How, for instance, might this recipe be brought to bear upon the difficult question not just of children's motivation to learn but of actual adolescent boredom? This, in a progressive school where it is not hidden by imposed occupations, can be manifested in ways which defy easy remedy and which, however rationalized, remain disturbing. Of course, it is arguable that here the educational confrontation reaches its climax: that orthodox education is the refuge precisely of those who cannot endure this ultimate (seeming) waste of life-energy: who at this point find too high the price demanded, of letting children be children. Granted the truth that lies in this test of mentalities, however, a legitimate grain of doubt remains as to the immutability of adolescent boredom itself.

Hu Child bravely faced up to this situation as he knew it.

Public boarding-school week-ends [he said] are, apparently, and for large numbers of children, tracts of unbearable boredom, relieved by bouts of indiscipline, punctuated by compulsory rituals and, for the younger boys at least, filled with admittedly time-killing activities. I would like to make a comparison between that kind of week-end and the kind we have at Dartington. Our weekends are potentially quite as boring, in that the children are completely free from lunch-time on Saturday until Monday morning, and have nothing that they must do. Therefore, they are liable to be bored. But this is a deliberate policy because, while boredom is a real problem for them to face, we do provide for them a lot of things they could do, if they wanted to. The idea is that, perhaps through being a little bit bored, they will find creative activities to occupy their time in that long week-end.

Dr. Winnicott, however, made a more positive claim for boredom as an inalienable concomitant of adolescence and as something, therefore, only to be repressed at risk.

It seems to me [he said] that there's a place, for such as can bear it, to meet the essential doldrums of adolescence. Adolescents, you see, have to endure just being unable to move. They can't suddenly go back, yet they can't go forward. They decide there must be no false solutions, that they must just wait; and they don't know what they're doing. (Sometimes, it's quite a help to let them know something of what they are doing: waiting for growth to carry them forward.) And they gang up with people exactly the same age, who are in exactly the same position; so if there are certain groups of other people who are able to tolerate this and all its consequences it seems to me there is a very great value in it—because these adolescent people do come through. Those of them who come through, helped by such tolerance, probably do so to a more stable kind of adult development. Still this does put a very great strain on the adults around—and you won't find many groups that can go with this.

The alternative (which may then be much the best one) is to fill up their time in the ordinary way with 'schooling'

—soccer, cricket, Cadet Corps and that type of thing. In other words, if you don't have your adolescence at the time you wait until you are forty-five and have it then. It would, perhaps, be unrealistic to expect there would be a large number of groups, everywhere, able to hold children in the doldrums and see the value of it. But doing so could provide a meaning of the word 'progressive'. If an orthodox school has failures it isn't the school which is said to fail; it's simply thought that the children are naughty, or something. But if somebody really working with adolescents has failures—and there have got to be failures— then he will rather say, 'We all failed.' This seems to me a more mature attitude.

Adolescent boredom, then, is a phenomenon not lightly to be put out of mind, nor brushed out of sight. Yet what does not follow is that the only alternative to doing just this is to abandon adolescents to themselves and to it. 'They decide,' said Dr. Winnicott, 'there must be no false solutions, that they must just wait.' Yet could it not be the case that this adolescent decision not to decide is endemic only to our culture and is a sceptical reaction to nothing other than education's own rarefied distillation of that culture? Might not the alternative, therefore, be for schools to involve the adolescent in life?

If it is the week-end, then, that is the moment of boredom in a boarding-school, progressive or otherwise, conceivably this could become precisely when a new Progressive Education should take place. (But 'week-end' here signifies only an accident of time that education has had to admit as a gap in its defences. It is an accident that must be seized on.) Progressive Education, as it is here coming to be thought of, is almost whatsoever is not 'school'. 'School', for one thing, embraces a curious collection of 'subjects', whose *raison d'être* is to be found largely in the misty realms of the history of Academia, and including the generic group of 'games'. To escape from 'school', however, it may not suffice—though it may help—to invent new subjects. Such new subjects, just as they have done, for example, in American universities (grudgingly as this will be admitted), indeed cannot help but freshen up the airless rooms of education. But the case goes deeper than the creation of a new Academia; it allows of the penetration of Academia by life itself.

What patterns of educational activity does this call to mind? For some adolescents, of course, it only means continuing academic study, though in a more collegiate environment: for others (still their colleagues), apprenticeships of an experimental kind; or temporary employment (daily, weekly, monthly, quarterly) mixed with academic work. For some of all these there would be boarding in the school; for others, living at home; for others, neither living at home nor at school, but in neighbouring digs. It means, also, conceiving of the school not as something monumental and static, symbolized by its buildings, but as a process. Thus, a school might exist simultaneously in several places: country and town, home and abroad, North and South. Its children, circulating between these, could taste of the differences of life they offered, yet without, in so doing, being cast out from both home and school as today they must be. All the till now separate ingredients of, for instance, technical college, youth club, hostel, college, holiday camp, etc., might go into the making of this new community of a progressive school.

Such ideas but seek to draw together, and to formalize in a new concept of school, many of the things that are nowadays happening anyhow in education. Needless to say, of such a programme the very first victim would be the week-end itself. To participate in life in this way, a progressive school would need to take its 'week-end', if at all, in mid-week. But this would nowadays be a relatively trivial departure from our remaining academic mediaeval constraints.

(Arising from these thoughts, but something hardly brought up at the Dartington Colloquy, is the curious question of school holidays. This teacher-dominated and anachronistic convention is surely ripe for assault by a revivified Progressive Education. Hu Child, alone, touched on the subject, and that negatively, when he said:

One of our headaches is the kind of life our children lead in a place like London in the holidays. From a cultural point of view such places are, to my mind, getting steadily lower—even though some of our children may come from the well-to-do intelligentsia. The temptations of London life are pretty devastating for the children of all classes, and if a school is not going to fight this in some way or other, then it is not doing what, to my mind, all schools ought to do—try to educate children's values, which is so much more important than educating the intellect.

Better still, it might be suggested, and perhaps less controversial, would be an annihilation of 'the holidays'—with all their tedium—by somehow making an end of the divorce between home and 'school'.)

It is to be hoped that this digression into the 'cure' of adolescent boredom will seem justified. One says 'cure' because this is not firm ground. Progressive Education, however, is of its nature an adventure; it adventures in the personalities of the young. It is hard to believe (though it may still be found to be true) that the world, in all its marvellous complexity, is of so little consequence to the young that only by breaking their spirit (in effect) can they be brought to participate in it. It seems a task apposite to Progressive Education, therefore, that it should seek to renew itself by finding the way whereby the young might on their own terms enter and animate society. Should this succeed, Progressive Education would have pioneered some common ground with orthodox schooling—and new meanings would have been brought into our speech.

5

Progressive Politics

The very name of Progressive Education leads everyone to suppose that it must stand on the frontiers of educational discourse: that it must for ever march in the vanguard of progress, of whatever is new. Only partly—even inadvertently—is this belief true. The impact made on society and on society's educational organs by Progressive Education is unpredictable in terms of the logic of social institutions themselves. The child whose creativity is nurtured (as well as its intelligence) is, for better or for worse, prone indeed to scandalize the bourgeois. Progressive Education's field of discourse, after all, is that of human personality, not society. In the sense, therefore, that Progressive Education is continually, if fortuitously, inciting orthodox education to question its own premises, it is indeed to be found on the educational frontiers. Further, with all its unpredictabilities, Progressive Education is a constant threat to those influential social idealists—ever with us—who see education as their only instrument for producing the society they desire and upon which their minds are fixed. In this sense, and perhaps in this sense alone (that it can never be assimilated to the social establishment, no matter how this be constituted), Progressive Education is perpetually on the frontiers.

Progressive Education, nevertheless, has its own body of discourse. Within this body, some of its schools, some practices, are more peripheral, more adventurous, than others. Conversely, of course, orthodox education, too, has its adventurers, its own progressives—schools and people concerned with the adaptation of education to a changing society, rather than with conformity to a vanishing one. It is useful, therefore, to bear a

rough-and-ready typology of schools in mind: within the
categories of Progressive and Orthodox there are also the sub-
categories of orthodox Progressive and progressive Orthodox.

Clearly, then, Progressive Education, while it can hardly
avoid finding itself in the educational vanguard, is not tolerant
of every meretricious new thing; it is not the refuge of no
matter what the latest educational theorem may be. As a result,
the educational debate of recent years has passed the progressive
movement by, and the disappointment felt on this account by
many well-meaning people can be ascribed to the very ambi-
guity of a name. There remains, none the less, this emphatic
difference of kind between the two forms of education, guarding
an integrity for Progressive Education that resists the debilita-
tions of mere novelty. To say that this difference has to do with
the human spirit may arouse resentment, even incredulity, but
how otherwise—given the tiny minority that creates it—is the
persisting fascination, the spell, of this problem of difference to be
explained? Unquestionably, after all, a progressive stands aside
from that orthodoxy in education—of academies in their hopeless,
narcissistic quest for certainty—upon which Shakespeare placed
his lasting sentence: 'Light seeking light doth light of light deny.'

Nevertheless, in remaining outside the current ferment of the
educational language-game as a whole, the movement for
Progressive Education has run a grave risk: the risk of stag-
nating within its very own bounds, and so of losing even the
respect of an uncomprehending opposition. Because of this, the
dialogue with the State has become the most difficult that
Progressive Education has to undertake. It was this, certainly,
that at the Dartington Colloquy most obviously brought hidden
resentments to the surface, disclosing an irreconcilability, not
just of two groups of educationalists but, it began to seem, of
two ways of living, such as came close to wrecking the discussion. To the practising progressive educators there, the threat of
the Leviathan of the State was an ever-present reality.

It was, for instance, out of personal experience that Hu Child
was talking when he said:

When I was in a large urban area I was asked by the
Education Committee to make a survey of educational
backwardness there. I was delighted to do this and thought

the study would make a very interesting document. Knowing this, I asked my most senior colleagues if they would support the publication of the document when it was complete, and they agreed.

About a year later, I pitched in a preliminary report of my findings—and the result was not a meeting of the Education Committee itself but of the Chairmen of all the Education sub-Committees: a formidable body—but not gathered to discuss education. They were very complimentary about my document, but they said, 'Mr. Child, you can understand, can't you, that this can never be published?'

I turned to my senior colleagues, hoping they would say something—but they said nothing at all. You see, I had discovered there were certain areas where the backwardness was quite appalling. Before the war, when similar enquiries had been made, this had not been so—and they couldn't face this being published. So that document never saw the light of day.

For me, this was a very shaking experience and is one of the main reasons why I'm here, at Dartington School, because in this case and in many other ways I found myself hampered by politics: and I mean, politics. Everything one did was scrutinized, first, from the political angle, and only then from the educational angle. I think that not only progressive schools but all independent schools will one day have to face this.

Indeed, there need be no pretence that this political threat—of incorporation, or 'integration', of independent schools into a State educational system—does not exist. It is something held desirable—incorporation, that is, not merely influence—by a respectable school of thought. Peter Snape expressed it directly at Dartington—'I feel that the integration of the independent schools is essential'—and Dr. Cook justified it on the grounds that, as he thought, parental choice of school was as much a myth for the independent sector as for the public sector, not so much because it did not exist, as because:

You are in fact giving parents their choice, as regards the independent schools, to select utterly unsuitable schools for

their children. An enormous amount of damage is done by
the exercise of parental choice. I would suggest that we
could be much more positive by saying that you (the progressive schools) should come right into the State system,
because you will be surprised by the variety and freedom
you can have within the system.

The illuminating thing about this threat, in so far as it is
exercised against the independent progressive schools by those
who also think of themselves as progressive, is its resolution into
the proposition that, until such incorporation has taken place,
the State system itself must be less than perfect. The perfection
of the State system is thought to require all progressive parents
(significantly, it is not so much the children as the parents
whose participation is required) to be within it.

This well-known point of view was expressed at Dartington
too by Peter Snape:

> What we in the public sector miss above all [he said] is
> the sense of involvement of people with progressive ideas
> with the State system. Here is Hu Child, objecting to a
> situation elsewhere and coming down to Devon to escape
> it. Now, if something was wrong with my school in Totnes,
> how effective it would only be if we had a few parents—
> articulate, powerful, forward-looking parents—who would
> say, 'We won't stand for this!' How helpful it is to the State
> schools if the best, most articulate and powerful parents
> are involved in the welfare of ordinary schools!

Elmslie Philip took the argument a stage further when he
mused, as follows, about the future:

> So, what about your [the progressive schools'] relation-
> ships with the State? I don't see, in practice, any Commis-
> sion itself appointing Governors directly. In effect, the
> L.E.A. is bound to be the agent for any Commission. If,
> then, the progressive schools enter our fold, could you re-
> tain your character? Are we compatible, you and us?
> This needs discussion. Let's just say, the fold would be a
> little less respectable in future. I sincerely hope there
> will be scope for more choice. (This is a thing that worries

us in the public system; there is not enough choice among schools, both for individuals and for minorities.) There should be a territorial relationship, but not too parochial. There would have to be links: a few Governors brought in from the L.E.A., for one thing, and for another, professional access of the L.E.A. to the school on the level of administration and teaching.

So this is feasible, I think, given two things, one on either side: a newer and more liberal attitude from the authorities, both nationally and locally; and secondly, that the progressive schools should (no offence to anyone in this please!) shed some of the arrogance of voluntaryism, without losing the vitality of the pioneer.

It is tempting to contend that we are here entered upon an exercise in naïvety, one that can end only if and when the incorporation of all activities under the State's proprietary control has somehow brought about the transformation of human nature. (One day it may be learnt that people who favour the conduct of social affairs through political action are of a certain type; political democracy itself may come to be recognized as the dominion of the extroverts. This is just a harmless fantasy, of course.) Meanwhile, however, we have to consider what is involved for progressive schools in such suggestions as having 'a few Governors brought in from the L.E.A.'.

Setting aside whether there is anything innate in politics to give reasonable grounds for anticipating, ever, a 'newer and more liberal attitude from the authorities, both nationally and locally', it would be as well to remember that a progressive school (if earlier analysis has any validity) is a discourse, a language game, between those who are concerned with that form of education. Of what service to such education would be the admission to that discourse of others not in tune with it? Of course, if the State were able to introduce to these schools persons who had somehow been debarred from them but who secretly desired to foster them, such communication could not but benefit the schools. This, of course, is not the purpose of State intervention. Perhaps here it needs to be underscored that the progressive schools of Britain are of the order of personal affirmations by those, few as they are, who accept responsibility for them. To destroy the character of these affirmations would be to imperil the education that stems from them. And there would be no surer way of doing this than by forcing such schools to accept Governors from the L.E.A., for no other reason than that such Governors 'represented' the L.E.A.

Elmslie Philip, as he was honourably bound to do, made it clear that if representatives from the L.E.A. became Governors of a progressive school they would do so for reasons of 'public accountability'. He was saying that the State was not something static and dead, but itself progressive 'at a modest pace', and that it was flexible within limits.

> What are these limits? [he went on]. Baldly stated, the limits are those of what you might call public and communal accountability. That phrase 'public account-ability' is usually used with a financial connotation, and that obviously is the first one. But the second form of public accountability is the necessity to think in terms of mass organization and mass thinking. We have to take into account the general tempo of thought throughout the country.

These sentiments seem impeccable. There is just, however, the question of language. If it be so, that Progressive Education is a matter of communication, a discourse, among those involved in it, and if the progressive school itself provides the only situation in which that communication can take place (if Progressive Education confined within the covers of books would wither and die), then certain difficulties of communication, of 'accountability', would arise for such educators relative, say, to Councillor This or the Mayor of That. (Perhaps it would help here to remember the adage that it is their common language which prevents the British and the Americans from understanding one another!) The parameter of social respectability is, indeed, unavoidable in the administration of public affairs. As Elmslie Philip was himself to confirm, there could be no place in the public sector of education for those 'madmen' cited, and seriously so, as the lifestream of the progressive movement.

Of course, there are tolerant and liberal people in authority in our State educational machine, and under their wings daring innovators have, to the general good, been able to practise their beliefs. Remembering his schoolboy Greek, however, Elmslie Philip himself confirmed that it is by stealth that such administrators often have to act: 'He escapeth his own good doing some.' And the intermittency, fortuity and precariousness characteristic of any such discourse within the State system is what seems significant about it. Hu Child, in speaking of this, illustrated the point as follows:

> To give you my first example, I asked the Senior Inspector in charge of our own School's recent full inspection what the feeling of the Inspectorate would be towards a school such as ours, which had no daily Assembly for worship, or no religious instruction of any kind. He said, 'Well, since you are an independent school, that doesn't matter at all. If you were not an independent school, however, it would be a very different matter indeed.'
>
> My next instance covers a school I was very interested in when I was working for one of our larger L.E.A.s. This was a very enterprising adventure in Progressive Education, in one of the most difficult areas you could imagine, and the headmaster was an astonishingly courageous man and, I think, a very successful man. (The question of parental support just didn't come into it, because the kind of parent you get in that area is someone indifferent to anything you might call 'education'.) But he was attacked by the local magistrate—a very well-known person—who took every opportunity he could, if a child from this school appeared in Court, to say something about how awful the school was. All this duly appeared in the Press.
>
> Now, when that headmaster died of heart-failure (and I am not surprised that he did so) it was very carefully seen to that a similarly progressive-minded headmaster was not appointed in his place, simply because of all the resultant difficulties for the Council.

General reinforcement of this theme came from Roy Potter, himself an educational administrator, when he said:

The idea has been mooted that the new progressive school will not be the progressive school we see today, but a neighbourhood school—where one consults with customers. My experience leads me to believe that this would inevitably result in the most conservative approach to education in the broad sense that one could possibly have. In fact, I see a tremendous advantage in the future of the progressive school, precisely in that it would not be dependent on having to try to convert sections of local opinion. Rather, it could take bold, imaginative steps without having to face up to such reactionary opinion as would, quite inevitably, centre around a school serving some neighbourhood and which was foolhardy enough to try the same sort of thing.

It is all, in fact, a question of language: of the dialogue in terms of which a school is conducted. Those who believe in that form of education known as 'progressive' are, at present at least, spread somewhat thinly on the ground. To conduct an effective dialogue, they need to take rational measures to concentrate together at a relatively few places. What would render their dialogue ineffective, even in those few places, would be if they were forced continuously to interrupt it in an attempt to explain themselves to others who did not comprehend their language yet who were in a position to demand a continuous interpretation. (It is, perhaps, as if the researchers of some large industrial concern were continuously being pestered by the Directors to justify their investigations in terms intelligible to the shop floor.) If our language games become too intermittent, they break down and cannot be played at all.

This must not be read pessimistically. There must be communication between different worlds of discourse. There are people to be found who speak two different languages and can interpret one world to another. It is important, only, not to delude ourselves into supposing that all can be solved by one world embracing the other. Hence, if for its own sufficient reasons, or because in practice it has generated a Gadarene momentum that it cannot stop, the State were to determine that its educational system must incorporate the independent progressive schools, and if (as seems to be the case) the State would then have a conscience about preserving and protecting something whose nature it does not fully understand, it ought to make quite certain that the status of those schools generally, within its system, is one of autonomy: that the discourse conducted within, and between, such schools continues un-impeded, and that such nominees as the Government may feel impelled to place on their boards should be people (their selection justified in some curious way, by reason of their being externally appointed) who nevertheless enjoy a mutual respect with those who conduct the schools.

The feasibility of this actually happening depends very much upon the public debate about Progressive Education being kept alive. If the climate of thought is such that the Govern-ment of the day cannot ignore the existence of a living body of Progressive Education, such as would be tampered with at some peril, the future could be reasonably secure. This, in its turn, depends upon the schools remaining in existence to practise what they preach. But there should be no illusions about the difficult character of that foundling, so to speak, which some well-meaning Government might be thinking of taking under its protection. (A hornet's nest might be a better metaphor.) For instance, the things that any progressive school will be thinking about today must include collegiate treatment for its elder children, involving realistic attitudes towards drink, motor-cars, contraceptives and drugs. Are these things that a Government wants, or is able, to become involved with? Again, any progressive school today must be concerned as to whether it should not opt out, either altogether or by drastic deferment, of that very examination system which the Government finds an increasingly essential yardstick for its own 'rational' expenditures of educational resources. And so on, and so on. And in twenty years time all may be different or reversed, so that the substance of today's progressiveness may be tomorrow's shadow, with the Government of the day left clutching at educational straws. For how long would it work?

There were many people at the Dartington Colloquy expressing from either side goodwill towards the other. It would be true to say that the very depth of their educational experience and conviction allowed those from progressive schools to express their concern for the social problems of our times, while yet not conceding for a moment that a watering-down of their educational principles would be relevant to the solution of these social problems. Eleanor Urban, however, went as far as anybody dared in expressing the wish of the progressive schools to meet the seeming requirements of a putatively progressive State educational system. She said:

> I wonder if it might be possible to get social justice without taking away our autonomy: whether there mightn't be ways in which children at large could qualify for our kind of school? But L.E.A.s do vary considerably, and though there are some with which it would be very nice to play ball, I think that with something like a central Inspectorate there would be more chance of our finding enlightened attitudes. (Some L.E.A.s know a good Head when they see one, and allow her to do the right thing. However, I have heard with my own ears of one L.E.A., for instance, which with a wagging finger told people that even at primary level, crafts could be cut out and nature study could be cut out.) I myself would rather be under a central Inspectorate than at the mercy of an L.E.A. To the existing Inspectorate, I would willingly hold out my hand. However, I am not so keen on some new research body acting as a supervisory organization, because things like that are subject to fashions, and one of the points about being independent is that you can do what you sincerely believe in. The existing Inspectorate, I think, allows you to do that.

Certainly, however, other progressive educators would fear that Eleanor Urban's goodwill had there got the better of her judgement. A lot more proof is needed, surely, than at present exists, that the progressive schools' problem could be solved by their throwing themselves upon the mercy of the existing In-spectorate. Were those schools able to sit in judgement on the Inspectorate, rather than the boot being on the other foot, there is at least some prima facie evidence that the correlation between them in terms of a common educational language would be found to be surprisingly small. If the Inspectorate could mobilize within itself a 'Progressive Schools' Section' the situation might be transformed. An outsider, however, must be left wondering whether the Inspectorate could be brought even to pose this question to itself at all.

The counterpart to Eleanor Urban's goodwill was that also expressed by Professor Harry Rée. Significantly, he had himself seen the acceptable grounds for the inclusion he desired of progressive schools within the State system, as in their role of 'experimental' schools. (He even, logically, insisted upon this nomenclature.) Equally significantly, as has been seen above, it was just these grounds and this kind of supervision that Eleanor Urban, among others, found unacceptable. It is important, then, to be very clear about this dangerous word 'experimental'. At the Dartington Colloquy people were using the word to mean two quite different things—and became bruised when they discovered what difficult confrontations with one another this led them to. There is, on the one hand, experiment that occurs to satisfy curiosity. Such experiment treats children, perfectly harmlessly, as 'guinea pigs', and is concerned, say, with varying the hour of bed-times, or with programmes, or teaching methods, etc. The other experiment occurs out of conviction, and is 'experiment' in the sense that it is concerned with actions that somehow are a-normal. In this case it is necessarily morphological in kind, appertaining to the form of action. This is the sense in which progressive education is experimental; it is a different form of education from the normal. Hence, to think of it as experimental in the empiric sense, simply as varying in some one particular (or at most a few) from the practice that makes up the normal, is to miss the point that it is different in kind. Harry Rée's goodwill fell upon this stony ground.

> Isn't the point this [he had said] that if somebody wagged a finger at, say, Kenneth Barnes, what would happen? What we need, in the State system, are Heads with some personality who will stand up to these jacks-in-office. I would like to issue my word of warning. I think that if you do show yourself so withdrawn—as some of you have done—so fearful of association with the State, you may go down, and this I'm sure would be a pity. But if you came forward and said, 'We are prepared to

come in, on condition that we retain our independence'—
this is of course important—people would I'm sure agree
with this.

Quietly, from his detachment, Dr. Winnicott's comment
returned the issue to its starting-point:

> I feel I now want to say one word, because when
> Professor Rée was speaking he seemed to be saying
> something which is common sense and absolutely logical;
> and I felt I was back in the thirteenth or fourteenth
> centuries, and someone was saying to the Lollards, 'Why
> don't you come into the Roman Catholic Church? Then
> we won't burn you!'

Is there, then, no alternative (assuming that the *status quo*
is, for some reason, intolerable to certain powerful political
forces) to an, at best, precarious condition of protection by
the State of the progressive schools? At the Dartington Colloquy
the alternative uppermost in a majority of minds was that of
partnership or 'marriage': that is, of co-operation as between
equals. Some remarks of Mr. Zoeftig might help set the stage
for a consideration of what this could mean:

> The inception and growth of progressive schools is
> dependent upon the freedom of individuals to go out
> and carry out their ideas in practice [said Zoeftig]. Can
> this freedom for individuals (and groups) be continued in
> a less free situation: that is, supposing all schools are
> permitted to function only within a certain laid-down
> framework?
> What are to be the qualifications of a person who wants
> to start a school? If permission is refused, what does the
> determined person do? Should we then see another
> group of Pilgrim Fathers, with mothers, children and
> teachers leaving these shores to find freedom elsewhere?
> (What new Continent would they find?) What would a
> future innovator like A. S. Neill do? Or have we reached
> the end of originative thought and practice in education,
> such as stems from really complete freedom of action?
> To an independent observer, it would appear that the
> position of progressive schools is basically similar to that

of the other independent schools. They do not wish to surrender their autonomy, and they wish to practise what they preach. The independent schools, whether progressive or otherwise, are the aristocracy of our educational system. The majority looks upon such privileged groups, as always, with a compound of admiration and envy. Yet it remains understandable—and desirable—that parents should demand the best possible education for their children. Because it is sad that all cannot be satisfied, should this be denied to the few? If not, how are the few to be chosen?

From some such base as this it is possible calmly to assess the alternatives to putting gratuitously at risk something of intrinsic value: something which, moreover, if it can find no new Continent, may manifest itself more destructively nearer home. From this base, also, one can look with a detached eye on the currently fashionable nostrum, that it is education which determines society. (Rather, one has even to resist the more cynical dictum—too unpalatable for educationalists easily to entertain—that a society gets the education it deserves.) Likewise, from here, one can understand a point made by Dr. Winnicott, that it is as much the failures as the successes of the independent progressive schools that have justified their existence. ('Some of them have done terrible things and some of them have got into trouble, and from my point of view these are all part of the success.') All in all, in fact, these considerations prepare one to seek a more genuine base of 'marriage' as between the State and the progressive schools.

Dr. Pidgeon was one who was looking for this base.

It has become clear [he said] that the State system itself has need for liaison with the kind of experience that the progressive schools can offer, at least for putting certain children into environments which State schools simply cannot provide. I would feel that, instead of the progressive movement offering itself to be absorbed by the State—and hence adding to that monopoly, with all its resultant problems—the idea of a partnership is an extremely good one. It would leave the progressive movement independent. (This is always a kind of safety valve, isn't it, for any home,

any parents, anybody, in fact, who wants the possibility
of opting out of something?) An offer to assist—whether
it is done on a national scale or, as I think more advisedly,
on a school-to-school basis—this is a positive way of
looking forward.

Yet, at the end of the day, it appears that if this desirable
partnership between such seeming unequals is indeed to be
brought about it is not so much for the schools as for the
State to put its house in order. It is upon the question of the
availability of choice that, at the last, attention must settle.
It is the (admitted) absence of choice for parents and children
in the State system that now makes unreal the idea of a partnership between it and the progressive schools. And this absence of
choice within the State system has even become a virtue made
out of necessity; it has nourished the belief that in education
there is only one right way of doing things, and that way the
State's.

Michael Young devoted a large part of his comments at the
Colloquy to this question of the availability of educational
choice and to the function of the progressive schools in helping
to provide it. He attacked the question on several different
fronts. First, from the point of view of educational minorities:

> It is surely right that a very proper function of pro-
> gressive schools, or other private schools, is to serve minor-
> ities. The parents in Islington, as a matter of historical
> fact, didn't like Mr. Duane's progressive school there. But
> there are still some parents—a minority, maybe—who
> apparently very much did like that school. In the future,
> however, that minority—perhaps only 10 per cent or
> 5 per cent, we don't know—are not going to be able to have
> the sort of education they want, because another man is
> coming in who will run the school in a way more accept-
> able to the generality of parents. Obviously, there are
> small minorities in every district whose needs can't be met
> by the State system. So far, the only way we have found of
> meeting the needs of these people, provided they have
> the money to pay, is to establish private schools for them.
> I should have thought the fundamental question for us

here was as to whether we do see any way of liberalizing the State system, of making it possible for parental preferences to be met rather more readily than they often are by comprehensive schools or any other sort of school, so that the small minorities (which add up, one on top of another, to something quite substantial) can be more fully satisfied than they are at present. If this cannot be done within the State system, then certainly there is a very great case for private schools, especially progressive schools, of one kind and another.

And even if it can be done in the State system, there will still always be a limit of toleration to what the State, representing as it does the majority of taxpayers, is prepared to stand for. The heart of the matter, indeed, lies deeper yet. For we should not only be concerned to meet minority interests, however crazy-odd these may be. We should also be prepared to facilitate those minority interests which, in ten or twenty years time, may turn out to be majority interests. Somehow, we ought to be trying to pick out crucial minorities, important ideas, which now only can be shared by a small number of people. A relatively small number of parents, with ideas, always can—if these are given a trial, and discussed and put into practice—influence for the good the majority of schools, in the long run

Next, Michael Young attacked the income-barrier to choice.

I think [he said] that the progressive school would benefit (as I think other schools would) if the income barrier, which prevents so many children from going there at all, were removed or at least reduced. I don't yet feel, in my own mind, that I have been able to answer the question as to what particular form the progressive school must take in the future. All I do know, is that I desperately want progressive schools not to stand completely aside should it be decided to get on with what will be another chapter of experiment in the whole story of experimenting in British education.

The great danger of the Labour Party's proposed reforms is that they will do nothing but bolster up the

Public Schools (which, unfortunately, are not with us to speak for themselves at this gathering). But if the only kind of 'marriage' into respectability is to be one between Public Schools—still, to my mind, the acme of formality—and the State, then a great deal of the point of the whole programme will have gone. Indeed, further, the real danger would exist of the progressive schools being swept, by default, into the conformist net and so facing extinction. It is only, rather, if there can be an injection into the State system of the different mode of thought represented by the progressive schools, that this experiment in breaking down the income barrier might educationally turn out to be a fruitful one.

It is as part of this prospective marriage that we feel a need for a much greater variety of choice for parents. We need a greater variety of kinds of school for children, such as will correspond to the extraordinary variety of types of children themselves. Unless we get this as part of our prospective reforms (if you call them reforms) I think we shall, rather, be losing a great deal. And if only two or three progressive schools would agree to give it a trial, then I think there might be a chance of something very worthwhile coming out of it. It would also depend, however, not just on Curzon Street but on the view taken of these prospects and ideas by Local Authorities—a view, if our discussions here are anything to go by, that is unfortunately taciturn.

Michael Young also endorsed the suggestion of direct exchange arrangements between different kinds of school, as part of a practical programme of widening the range of children's opportunities. In this connection he said:

I am very attracted to the idea about treaties between progressive boarding-schools and particular schools within the State system. I can see these treaties as being of all degrees of formality and informality. One might, for instance, be able to arrange for children in a progressive school even to go and see Boarding School No. 56 in Moscow, while children from Mrs. Chetwynd's school, or from the marvellous school that Mr. Zoeftig used to run in the south of London, would come into a school in the country. That sort of thing can be done almost without any L.E.A. intervention.

Out of research findings, Michael Young supported an extension of State-aided boarding-schools, largely on the grounds that this would widen the at present narrow range of choice in this respect. He also wanted to go further than has been gone, say, in Russia, and to seek means of giving expression to children's own preference for boarding-schools. He saw a potentially large scope for this in the period of late adolescence. He also saw scope for establishment by the State, as part of a programme of widening the choice of educational opportunities, of specialist progressive schools, schools specially catering for interests such as music, the arts or languages. For him, the question was not as to whether progressive schools should be for the many or the few. Rather, the issue was one of choice: 'Money and income shouldn't enter into it. There should be a much greater freedom of choice than there is.'

Logically, Michael Young should have added that residential constraints also 'shouldn't enter into it'. At present, it is this as much as anything else that limits a parent's choice: that, and a restriction of opportunity by Local Authority boundaries that are often archaic. Restriction of choice on these counts must bear a good deal of the responsibility for the haphazard rise and fall, already remarked on, of the occasional progressive school under Local Authority aegis. Such a school cannot build up a supporting body of parents to ensure its continuity. (In an ultimate sense, it must be autocratic if it is to exist at all.) Clearly the importance of boarding as an instrument of choice is as important as it has ever been—really, in fact, has nowadays become still more important. For Progressive Education itself, the importance of these considerations lies in the breakdown of the State's educational monolith, such as is implicit in the provision of a real range of choice. Should this happen, the chances would improve of that practical educational discourse continuing, within the situation of each and every progressive school, which elucidates the actual conduct of Progressive Education for those partaking of it and which alone assures its continuance in practice.

K

This need for the educational autonomy of a progressive school, if it is to survive at all, was finally hammered home by King Harris. He said:

> Let us accept in good faith the need for the abolition of fee-paying privilege, and where do we arrive? (But is even 'privilege' the right word? Perhaps 'tradition' is better, because there is a fee-paying tradition among a group of people in our culture. 'Privilege' means, one supposes, something that everybody wants—and, in this case, they do not.) Where do we get, then, if we accept this position?
>
> There have been suggestions of treating our boarding-schools as aids to industrial mobility, or as facilities for full-time female employment, etc. This seems to me a very materialist conception, one that puts children second and social organization first. As such, it is only marginally different from another suggestion to which we have been treated: that of using progressive schools for maladjusted children. This latter at least does seem to put the children first—but I must make the point that this approach, too, is educationally superficial. I believe that State-school educators are so very liable to misunderstand what we can do for these so-called 'maladjusted' children (a word I shouldn't be using, because I don't think it has any meaning at all unless its use is carefully defined). There is the real rub: the fee-paying, 'normal' children are absolutely vital to our achievement with the handicapped, special children!
>
> Our achievement with the special children is, of course, acceptable to the most extreme egalitarian view. This, therefore, raises the crucial question, as to how this sort of educational practice can be forwarded if not with the support of those who, believing in it, are prepared to pay for their beliefs? How can the progressive schools be forwarded without this essential ingredient, in face of the fact that the majority don't want this privilege (if it is a privilege)?
>
> Various suggestions have been made about our possible relations with the State. That we might have direct

relations with a Commission is one of them. This, it seems, would involve selection of 'suitable' children, but not by the parents. (One wonders what say the schools themselves would have in such selection? This is vital.) Where is this levelling of privilege, then, to come from? One's fear is that if 'suitable' children are to selected, then these will be the children who 'need' this kind of school. But what, then, about the sort of children, the 'normal' children, that the school itself needs?

King Harris went on to reject, out of some first-hand experience, selection of children arising either from incorporation of a school into a Local Authority or out of an (anyway) unacceptable role for the progressive school as a test-bench for 'experimental' research. He drew the only possible conclusion: that if the progressive schools have in all justice a right to survive they must be allowed to do so in terms of parental choice.

> I am sure [he said] that the progressive schools would be willing and ready—I hope this does not sound negative, it's not meant to be—to play their part with the State. If parental choice could be extended, within the State system, to the progressive schools, giving them a voluntary-aided status, in so many ways this would provide a wonderful opportunity. (Perhaps the parents would have to find the boarding fees, while the public authority would pay the tuition fees.) This could be something essentially exciting—so exciting that maybe it's bound to develop.

For the progressive schools, this question of parental (and child's) choice is vital. It is all of a piece with that affirmation about human personality and its autonomy, relative to society (not its supremacy, that question does not arise), such as makes of Progressive Education a distinct educational form.

This form is one that is speaking ever more clearly to the times we live in: one to which youth itself is increasingly responsive. If the State, well-meaning but clumsy, destroys this form civilization will be the loser.

Epilogue

Education is the unending dialogue between youth and age. It is the greatest of all our language games, in which age speaks from its established authority and youth speaks—we hardly know from where, nor from what springs; but speak for itself it does. There are times when this comedy loses its savour, when the misunderstandings in the dialogue seem absolute. This happens when age forgets that in bringing youth to take its meanings, youth is causing age itself to change: that age and its social paraphernalia are not something immutable, to which youth simply adapts: that it (age), too, is involved in a game. And this, in turn, happens never so surely as when age speaks to youth, not from life but from the static refuge of 'school'. Then, indeed, education ceases to be a game and becomes a thing of gloom.

The Dartington Colloquy passed fleetingly across the scene. As do scudding clouds, it left the landscape only fitfully illuminated. But it was a necessary event if in Britain Progressive Education (or whatever this comes to be known as) is to participate in the future. If this record of what transpired has not faithfully reproduced the discussion it will none the less be excused if perhaps, out of what was said, it has fairly elucidated the function that Progressive Education is now surely required to fulfil: that of restoring balance to the education game—so that indeed it becomes a game again. Marjorie Hourd, it will be remembered, put the matter more poignantly: 'We are, whether we like it or not, in the grip of a revolutionary idea: that learning is not the result of an omnipotent force from without, nor of a benign submissive attitude, but of a complex and curious relationship as between a child who has plenty of maturing and growth in him and a grown-up who has plenty of the child.'

Leonard Elmhirst closed the Dartington Colloquy by giving the following quotation from Whitehead:

> Ideas won't keep; something must be done about them. The idea must continually be seen in some new aspect; some element of novelty must be brought into it freshly from time to time—and when that stops, it does. The meaning of life is adventure.

Part Two

EXTRACTS FROM PAPERS

A Retrospective View of
Progressive Education

BY H. A. T. CHILD & L. A. CHILD

In this first paper we are asked to give some picture of the background of the Independent Progressive Schools, to examine something of their history and present circumstances, and from this at least it will be clear that without a doubt they arose in protest against contemporary practices in education and that half a century later they are still autonomous and still protesting.

It is not our intention here to enumerate the schools and describe their various foundations, but in the relationship of the first two, Abbotsholme and Bedales, two factors existed which have remained characteristic of the movement. Cecil Reddie at Abbotsholme had no truck with co-education, but John Badley, who left his staff to found Bedales, soon admitted girls, first the sisters of some of his boys and later equal and unrelated members of both sexes. There has always been some diversity even in major matters between all the progressive schools, and this divergence according to the personal views of heads and of governing bodies has remained a consistent pattern, a safeguard and a growing point. Thus, though in the main co-education became and remains a common factor, freedom from religious observance begun by the King Alfred School in Hampstead and continued later at Summerhill, Dartington and Monkton Wyld has never been accepted by the schools as a whole. But as there has been divergence, so there have been close personal links and associations. It was at Abbotsholme that Badley first saw the practicability of new ideas, and it was from Bedales that a rationalist group of parents in London found the first headmaster for the King Alfred School.

At Abbotsholme and at the early Bedales the first major change was in the academic curriculum offered. At Fettes and at Rugby, from which Reddie and Badley had come, as at the similar boys' schools of the day, the classics had been the centre of studies. Reddie and Badley after him relegated Greek and Latin to a minor place and instituted a programme in which English, History, Modern Languages and Science were given an equal share. It is difficult to think of this step now as a pioneering one, so quickly did the change in this direction come in both State and private schools. But to Badley, who was a distinguished Cambridge classical scholar, it represented a revolution in school life. In the field of curriculum perhaps the situation now has once more come full circle, and when all schools for academic children, whether private or public, conventional or progressive, are linked to the requirements of the General Certificate of Education new pioneering in curriculum will arise, and the signs of this are already apparent.

But there was another side to the change of classroom curriculum linked with the emphasis which was now being put in the new schools on the relevance of learning to living. This was the belief that motivation in the classroom should come from pleasure in the work in hand, and that competitive marks and form orders, and all the apparatus connected therewith, were outmoded.

Life outside the classroom was no less different. The country estates in which the first new schools stood became an integral part of a new learning situation. Outdoor work through every form of maintenance was taught, and craft shops where all sorts of skills could be developed were considered an essential part of their equipment. Help with the domestic chores by boys and girls was a part of daily life, and part of the whole resolve to educate children in the belief that manual labour and skill in craft added to the stature and dignity of man and was of comparable importance with intellectual pursuits.

Aesthetic education also claimed a major place. Music of all kinds and art of all kinds were part of daily life in schools where philistinism had no admirers. Simplicity of living was the rule, but it was a simplicity designed to promote good health, and comfortable and unconventional dress and planned diet perhaps ameliorated the stress on early bed, cold baths and morning runs.

From the first the notion of savage punishment came under fire, and there was a slow growth in the belief that the most important thing about punishment was that it should fit the crime. The last boy was beaten at Bedales in our early days there—and this was a unique occurrence asked for almost as a dare by the offenders. The total abandonment of corporal punishment by all the schools is now a matter of history. Yet for all that, the originators of the movement had no belief that choice of what a child wanted to do or not to do was part of the programme of his education, and the degrees to which a pupil's choice enters into his work and play remained, and remains, a matter of variety between the schools.

Jingoism was totally absent from the first. The welfare of mankind regardless of creed or colour was taken to be the natural concern of all young people. No pre-military training was ever contemplated or has ever arisen, yet there was no pacifist indoctrination. Political indoctrination indeed was always frowned on, and freedom of thought for members of the staff of the schools was part of a pattern of freedom of thought for those they taught. But the duty of service to the community was a factor in education which was stressed from the first and has been consistently taught by all the schools in their various ways. Where monitorial systems still existed, which was in most of them, Dr. Arnold's privileged prefect with punitive power and a claim to the slave labour of the younger boy gave place to the senior, whose duty was to befriend his juniors and maintain order as helper rather than disciplinarian.

More important, perhaps, was the steady growth of a conviction that to train children for life in a democracy meant at least a measure of democratic life in school. School parliaments, representative councils and elected committees with various degrees of power and responsibility became a feature of all the schools, and as was inevitable, this cultivation of a democratic way of life tempered the autocratic tendencies of all the adults concerned. Irrational prohibitions or rules for the sake of rules in turn steadily diminished and, as a corollary, no environment was provided in which the often more irrational strictures on each other's behaviour, which have always been such a source of anxiety to younger members in orthodox private schools, could arise.

All the schools were small schools, and this fact, together with their total way of life, emphasized from the first the part played by all the children as individuals, which in turn became an emphasis on the importance of individual well-being. There was never much overt class consciousness, since both teachers and taught had, as it were, broken away from the mores of the schools which the class-conscious parent normally used. And this perhaps today still accounts for what must seem an almost naïve attitude to problems of class adopted in these progressive schools. Their concern with education was always their first and foremost one, and this can make them seem the despair of the sociologist.

Finally, the dislike and fear of indoctrination, along with the vivid sense of the worth of all men which was cultivated, was reflected in the way in which the religious life of the schools was organized. It would be difficult to describe the different forms of worship adopted, but the emphasis was, and always has been, on the ethics of Christianity rather than on its dogma. King Alfred School, of the early schools, was openly a rationalist school, though there are now schools in the group which, like King Alfred, give no denominational instruction and have no form of communal worship. For all that, where religion is not part of the life of the schools a distinction must be drawn between those who leave it out on rationalist or humanist grounds and those who see childhood and adolescence as ages when freedom from dogma is a necessary foundation for adult spiritual life.

With the exception of the King Alfred School, which was and has continued to be a day-school, the progressive schools remained within the boarding-school world in which they began, though most of them now include a greater or lesser number of day pupils. Total membership of a community rather than the partial participation in community life of the day pupil was and is thought of as a vital part of the educative process. And since the sort of education in which they believed rapidly divorced them from the preparatory boarding-schools from which contemporary private schools recruited their children of secondary school age, nearly all of them developed junior boarding departments. The many liberal State primary schools which have since come into being have affected these junior departments, but they can still be seen to flourish.

But the co-educational experiment initiated by Badley was the greatest change in the boarding-school world and the one which became for most parents the distinguishing feature of the progressive school, and the one which would be acknowledged by nearly all the schools of the movement as an essential part of their programme. To segregate the sexes seemed and seems to them to be no more practicable as a training for adult life than the practice of submission to autocratic rule as a training for life in a democracy. The degrees to which the sexes mixed, their ways of living together, what was thought permissible and what was not, varied as time went on and as the social climate changed, and still varies. But for those who made the break and for those who came after them a return of segregated schools was not an action which they have felt any desire to contemplate.

The study of psychology had made its first major advance as a coherent and established science almost at the same time as the movement we are discussing. Galton introduced the first objective tests of human capacity around 1880, and Freud began his work with neurotics in Vienna in 1886; Abbotsholme was founded in 1889 and Bedales in 1894. As psychological knowledge expanded and began to make an impact among thinking people, the progressive schools were quick to grasp its educational implications. We need to distinguish between two main fields of psychological activity. One is the study of individual differences and of child development as revealed by objective tests. This has indeed caused something like a revolution not only in progressive schools but in the whole State system through its application to methods of selection in education since the 1944 Act. To begin with, there were some extravagances due to incomplete knowledge; the concept of 'learning readiness', for example, led to schools of thought which believed in postponing any formal teaching, particularly that of reading, to a dangerously late age. But while the progressive schools made some errors in this way, they saw in the new techniques something which accorded well with their view of the child as an individual in his own right, whose particular strengths and weaknesses deserved all possible consideration if he was to make the most of himself. It is not surprising that they were among the first to use tests of intelligence and attainment; some of them employed professional psychologists to assess children and report on their potential, and one at least had a psychologist on its staff for a while.

But it is in the second field, that of depth psychology or psychiatry, that these schools found a new branch of knowledge which offered a support to their own ideals. The notion that the unconscious mind is the source and governor of our emotional life, and the foundation on which social and emotional behaviour largely depend, found ready support from teachers in schools where there was already a strong desire to find ways of educating children other than the traditional ones. The new psychology offered explanations of deviant behaviour entirely different from the old ones based on moralistic ideas, and from the new explanations it was hoped that new ways of dealing with juvenile behaviour would be found. The writings of Freud, Adler and Jung were consequently read with avidity, and the work of Susanna Isaacs at the Malting House School was closely studied. In the new schools, where authoritarianism was minimized in so many ways and punishment had ceased to be part of a rigid disciplinary system, the assertion that deviant or anti-social behaviour could be understood differently was at once welcomed and developed.

Inevitably, mistakes were made. Freud and his fellow workers were not always fully understood or were misinterpreted, and the idea that absolutely any form of 'repression' was wholly bad gained currency in some of the schools. There was much argument about the degree of permissiveness allowable in a school, and the more thoroughgoing of the 'free' communities earned for themselves an unenviable reputation, giving rise to an image of progressive education which did some harm to the movement as a whole.

We might say that the problem of deciding what degree of permissiveness is optional and what degree of restraint is necessary in the rearing of children, whether in school or home, is one which neither the educators nor the psychiatrists have satisfactorily settled. But the non-authoritarian tradition of the progressive school world has enabled it to accept and explore this question, which is perhaps the most vital of our time.

But apart from such early errors there grew and remains an attitude in progressive education towards children and their behaviour which, while not exactly psychoanalytic, does at least owe something to the findings of depth psychology. It is an attitude which readily accepts the idea that children's behaviour of all kinds, including their attitude to learning, is only partially governed by reason and is in fact largely governed by irrational impulses rising from the unconscious. Proper education of the emotions therefore, from which all behaviour, good and bad, springs consists in helping a child to come to terms with his own inner life. This, in the view of most progressive teachers, is the prior task of education, and it requires that children be offered a new understanding and affection from whoever educates them; the adult must be, as is often said, 'on the side of the child'. It is possible to trace a thread of thought and opinion of this kind, starting with Homer Lane (who was born in 1875) and running right through to the present day, when A. S. Neill is perhaps its most outstanding exponent. As Dr. Robin Pedley has said in talking about Neill:

> [He] has done much in general to swing teachers' opinion in this country from its old reliance on authority and the cane to hesitant recognition that the child's first need is love, and with love, respect for the free growth of his personality, free that is from the arbitrary compulsion of elders and disciplined instead by social experience . . . today's friendliness between pupil and teacher is probably the greatest difference between the classrooms of 1963 and those of 1923.

Within the classroom of the new school, too, where milder attitudes had been made possible by the abandonment of the more exacting and avid demands of the traditional curriculum, the new knowledge pointed to the fact that the punishment of failure to learn, like the punishment of failure to behave, might well be an inefficient instrument. Just as corporal punishment disappeared in the early schools of the movement, so it never arose in the later ones, being shown up for what it was by the new concepts of sadism and masochism.

Similar support was drawn from the new psychology for the original schools' belief in organizing both work and community life on a co-operative rather than a competitive basis. For if anxiety and a sense of guilt arising from feelings of inadequacy are reinforced by environmental factors the growing personality will be more rather than less inhibited, and its chances of a more mature adaptation to life will be diminished. It was seen to be the duty of the school, therefore, to minimize anything which could lead to excessive anxiety and guilt; the traditional trappings of marks, form orders and so forth, which the progressive schools had already discarded, were seen for what they were, enemies to real educational progress rather than aids to it.

Following the same line of thought, the schools welcomed many new methods of teaching which originated in the first half of this century, both in Europe and America, as well as at home. Dewey's Project Method appealed to many of them largely because of the opportunity it offered for co-operative work, and the Dalton Plan was adopted by some because it encouraged the pupil to pit himself against his own standards rather than those of his fellows. Some of the schools have now returned to more orthodox teaching methods with new insight into what they can do in the classroom, and one or two are still well-known exponents of the Dalton method. But perhaps the most marked stimulus offered by the new psychology was in aesthetic and creative education. Arts and Crafts and Drama, introduced at first as a counterbalance to the traditional narrow academic curriculum, came to be seen as an essential need for the growing personality in school. The work of art teachers like Cisek exerted a wide influence, and the notion of all education as a creative process became a theme which spread and began to gain wider and wider support.

The study of the transitional period between childhood and adulthood showed up adolescence as a time when the governing emotional factor is the desire to be independent, which comes before there is adequate experience or emotional balance to make the period an untroubled one. Boarding-schools had always been in part looked upon as offering a training in independence, since they separated children from their parents, but the rigid framework imposed by the ordinary boarding-school was in fact but another form of dependence. The independent progressive schools, which already presented a freer boarding life, were encouraged by the new view of adolescence to extend their freedoms. The adolescent was seen to have psychological needs for choice and consultation in his work and play, for greater share in rule-making and for freedom in his personal life. Co-educational schools saw in the mixing of the sexes an essential part of this growing-up process, whatever problems these greater freedoms created. Perhaps the best way to summarize their policy would be to describe it as the provision of an environment in which it was safe to make mistakes.

The Independent Progressive Schools, as we have shown, have never agreed among themselves upon a common policy about religious education, but they still between them offer a variety of approaches, Christian, agnostic and rationalist. But what is the parent who is constrained to choose State education to do if it is against his convictions, for whatever reason, that his child should be subjected in school to imposed religious belief and observance? And this is only one of the difficulties he will have to face. For the child brought up in a home where the proper freedoms and the inevitable troubles of childhood have been understood may still be subjected to a totally different set of attitudes when he goes to his neighbourhood school. Corporal punishment, for example, regulated certainly by local restrictions, but still regarded by many authorities not only as permissible but necessary, as it still is in boys' private schools, is unthinkable in such a home. The whole divergence on questions of punishment, of guilt and anxiety and the like associated with the motivations of living and learning between those of the new and old schools of thought, is a gap which seems hardly to have begun to close. The old motives of marks, form orders, house points and the like, all those ways, that is to say, which reinforce competition as motivation, may be passing slowly but surely from the primary world, but are still prevalent at the secondary level, just as honest attempts to involve the adolescent in choice and self-government are rare.

The cynicism of older children towards authority, both in State and private schools, is a disquieting feature of our time.

L

It must still seem to many that as a country we are educating for bureaucracy rather than for democracy, for uniformity rather than for spontaneity. The child in the primary school can find himself free to paint and model, make music and play in a way often still denied to his contemporary in the private preparatory school, but at the secondary stage, especially if he has been labelled 'academic', in how many State schools will his aesthetic education be given an adequate share of his school time because its importance is regarded as vital? And finally, the parent who is looking for co-education as a matter of educational principle may well find it for his younger children in his local primary school, but he is by no means certain to do so when they have passed the primary stage, and if he does, it may have been introduced more by reason of administrative convenience than because it is accepted educational policy.

The impracticability of setting up a State boarding-school system on a large scale inevitably places the well-to-do parent who believes in its value in a privileged position. But we think it is true to say that many of the parents who now send their children to a progressive boarding-school do so not so much from a belief in boarding education as such as from their conviction of the rightness of the kind of education such schools provide. These schools would be among the first to want to offer a similar education to any non-fee-paying parent who wished for it; they view with no enthusiasm the idea of the State absorbing the orthodox private boarding-schools into its own system, for they feel as critical of these as they ever did. But in the general circumstances of the present as we have described them, they would not willingly surrender the autonomy which still allows them to practise what they preach.

The Progressive Ideas
in State Schools
BY L. C. SCHILLER

After a conventional education and some years of soldiering I began teaching in a 'progressive' school, Rendcomb College, which was then dedicated to self-government and greatly under the influence of Homer Lane, whose son was one of the pupils. Then I took a year off in order to study under Percy Nunn, who was much occupied with the Hadow Report. At the end of this time I was appointed an Inspector by the Board of Education. During the intervening forty-odd years I have been entirely involved in the State system of schools.

I give this short biography because every man is a creature of his will and his circumstances. The ideas which interest me now are rather more 'progressive' than were those of forty years ago; and my concern has been, and is, to contribute to their fulfilment in State schools.

I

The oldest part of our existing system of State schools is the Infant School. No one knows exactly why in this country, unlike all others, schooling has always begun at five years old. Nor is it known why in this country, unlike others, the five- and six-year-olds have always been given a separate school of their own instead of being put into an introductory class or classes in a school for older children. But so it has been; and when I arrived in Whitehall as an Inspector I found that the tradition of the separate Infant School was rigorously respected.

It is a fact that in the early part of the last century, when Parliament was still busy arguing whether or not to establish schools from public funds, Robert Owen established schools for the children of the workers at his cotton mills in Lanarkshire. One of these was a separate and special school for the very young children. It was to be a place, he said, where they should play, and sing, and be happy; in other words, where they should live out the life of a young boy or girl. When some years later Parliament finally agreed to a small grant for public schooling Infant Schools formed part of the pattern adopted.

Doubtless there were many influences which persuaded Parliament to adopt this pattern, and among these was expediency. But mere expediency is not likely to have created a tradition which has lived in the Infant School for well over a century, and today thrives with added strength. In this tradition the purpose of the school and the function of each teacher is to help every child grow to the full. It is a tradition in direct line of descent from the Infant Schools founded by Robert Owen.

Of course, children in the State Infant Schools have not led such a simple idyllic life as this tradition, if unhindered, would provide. When Parliament was persuaded to pay for the schooling of the children of the poor it was chiefly concerned that these should be prepared to take the place which God (they used to say in those days) had chosen for them. They must learn to read, to write, to cipher a little and, above all, to behave themselves.

Thus, not for the first time in an English institution there came into being a compromise whereby two conflicting ideas lived uneasily side by side: preparation for a prescribed place and fulfilment of a stage of growth.

In the middle of the century a new influence arrived in England, the Froebel Kindergarten.

A number of German men and women had come to live and work in this country. Some came as a result of the growing commerce between the two countries; others came because they found repressive the autocratic and reactionary measures taken by their government after the uprisings of 1848. They were not refugees in the contemporary sense of this word. They chose to live in a country closely related to their own through its royal family, where they found life more free and more congenial. Nor were they poor; they were usually intelligent and industrious, and soon they found themselves a place among the English middle classes. One common characteristic they shared: they were concerned for the education of their children, and not least their young children. And so it happened that in 1851 in London was opened a school for young children in charge of a follower of Friedrich Froebel. This was the first Kindergarten.

A second Kindergarten opened in Manchester, and soon others followed. The English middle classes, not slow to take advantage of a good thing when it came their way, began to send their young boys and girls to 'the Kindergarten', where for a small fee their children played and sang and were happy, in pleasant surroundings, with nice companions, in classes which were not large. By the turn of the century there were Kindergartens all over the country. For these schools teachers were being specially trained in independent Froebel Colleges, where the principles and practice of Friedrich Froebel were expounded to them.

Froebel was a man of vision. He held a vision of God, man and nature, in which nature and man lived in a harmony which gave man a picture of the ways of God. From his vision Froebel derived a philosophy which asserted the imminent perfection of every child: all would be perfect if all were perfectly treated. From this philosophy Froebel derived an attitude towards children which led him to observe them closely. Thus he saw, what others had failed to see, that one of the most important ways of learning for young children is play. He saw also that children learn best from adults in a relationship which is permissive. 'Play' and 'freedom' were the outstanding characteristics of Froebel's practice in his Kindergarten.

There is, however, little reason to think that the parents, now almost entirely English, who in such large numbers sent their children to 'the Kindergarten' at the turn of the century studied deeply Froebel's philosophy or were much concerned with the principles which gave rise to his practices. Nor were they disturbed that the Froebelian outlook was diametrically opposed to that of the schools to which they sent their boys and girls when older. At the Kindergarten for a small fee young children could learn happily with pleasant companions in small classes. The Kindergarten satisfied a want for a substantial section of the population, and hence it flourished. But it also gave a home to an idea which had already begun to adventure more widely.

When I first knew Teacher Training Colleges in the 1920s few if any girls trained in Froebel Colleges came to teach in State Infant Schools. From a different social background, they viewed almost with horror the very large classes and the very poor premises which Infant teachers still endured. But some of the best of them, having graduated through teaching in the Kindergarten, joined the staff of State-aided Teacher Training Colleges; it was common for the Infant department of such colleges to be in charge of Froebel-trained women.

Here they exerted a valuable Froebelian influence on future teachers. They influenced also Infant Schools, at that nicely calculated distance which has always separated the Training Colleges from the schools.

II

To many active young men and women the 1920s were nothing like *The Boy Friend*. In the State Infant Schools there was in process a veritable renaissance of the century-old ideal of Robert Owen: a place where young children should live out their life as young children. In this renaissance Infant teachers received help from various independent sources; two were of particular importance. Margaret Macmillan drew attention to the need of fulfilling the growth of children not yet five, and demonstrated how this might be attempted. Maria Montessori, from a different point of view, stressed the importance of training the senses, and provided for the purpose a system of play objects. Both of these emphasized the fact, so easily overlooked in face of a large class, that every young boy and girl learns best in his or her own way.

The Montessori apparatus was too meticulous and too expensive to have wide use in State schools; and Madame Montessori's uncompromising authoritarianism was uncongenial to many English teachers. Nevertheless, her influence was great (at the time no doubt greater than that of Miss Macmillan), hers was the inspiration which gave life to 'individual work', the idea that for at least much of the school day a child should have opportunity to work on his own at his own pace. In those days it was still a novel, though increasingly common sight, to see each of a class of over fifty children absorbed in his own individual occupation. To achieve this in a bare room filled with heavy desks and with little equipment or material required hard work, much resourcefulness and abounding teaching skill. It demonstrated the power of many Infant teachers to take an idea from without and realize it within the strait circumstances of the State system.

The influence of Miss Macmillan was less specific. She revived the knowledge that young children are not incomplete adults but complete persons in their own right. By her work among children in the slums of Deptford she gave renewed strength to those who took as the purpose of their school to fulfil the growth of their children. The Montessori apparatus has passed into the museum; the memory of Margaret Macmillan is still an inspiration.

All this happened in the 1920s, and this was not all. In 1926 was published the first of the Hadow Reports. This remarkable document was called *The Education of the Adolescent*; and it will be convenient at this point to describe the situation of those boys and girls whose schooling now takes place in secondary schools. Nothing has been said about these so far because, in the context of 'progressive' ideas, there has been nothing to say.

At this time most boys and girls received all their education in the 'Elementary School'. After two years in the Infant School they went to a school organized in Standards. Standard I to Standard VII to cover the years from 7 to 14 (then the school-leaving age).

The Standard School, though as old as the Infant School, had not received the inspiration of Robert Owen, nor the influence of Froebel, Montessori and Margaret Macmillan. On the contrary, it had suffered the intolerable shock of 'payment by results'. Now, more than half a century later, the teachers were still haunted by the ghost of that dreadful system.

The Secondary, or present Grammar, School had come into being only in 1902, out of a miscellaneous collection of schools long established, some for several centuries, and new schools which L.E.A.s were now authorized to provide. The first task had been to establish a common and tolerable standard among the old schools and the new, to raise the voluntary leaving age to at least 15 and to lay the foundation of a VIth Form. By the 1920s the first of these had been accomplished; the second and third were well advanced, but by no means completed. The major influence on the Secondary School had been, and still was, that of the traditional Public Schools, from which came nearly all those responsible for guiding the work. The progressive movement had no discernible influence.

The Secondary Schools were recruited from a small trickle of highly selected boys and girls from the Elementary Schools, together with a number of fee-paying pupils. Most boys and girls completed their education in the Standard School, often leaving in a low Standard. This had for long been regarded as unsatisfactory, and the Hadow Committee were asked to consider and report on the problem.

Their Report, *The Education of the Adolescent*, was as remarkable in its ideas as in its name. It described adolescence as a stage of growth. It stated a case for providing schools which would give an education to boys and girls at this stage of growth, an education conceived in terms of this stage of growth. In the Standard School we had previously educated boys and girls in terms of subjects up to prescribed standards, usually tested by an examination. The Report suggested that we should think differently, in terms of growth and its fulfilment. It was a suggestion that required a complete change of outlook in the Standard School. But in the 1920s anything seemed possible, even extending the Infants tradition through the whole of the Elementary School.

The Report was published in the year of the General Strike. Soon afterwards we were all gripped in the depression, unemployment increased and teachers holding a job felt themselves fortunate. There was no money for new schools except those made imperative by new housing. However, there was much enthusiasm for the new Hadow plan, notably in Lancashire, where I had the good fortune to work.

When the older children were taken from a Standard School the school was said to be 'decapitated'—official language is nothing if not precise. The Junior School was what was left after this depressing operation, and often that is exactly what it looked like. Often this forlorn company of children and teachers who had been left behind reminded me of the last remaining spinster of a large Victorian family who found herself in the old home, parents dead and brothers and sisters married and away in a new home of their own, uncertain how to leave a life that exists no more or how to enter a new life still quite unknown. Cut off from the Infants by tradition and removed from the Seniors by physical distance, the teachers had only one landmark, the examination for free-places in the Secondary School, for which candidates no longer came from Standard VII, but from the new '4th year Junior School class'.

It was, however, not to the Juniors but to the Seniors that most thought and attention were given. The early Senior Schools were exciting places. The old Standards had gone— though their ghosts lingered in the mind of older teachers. There was no examination ahead, no predetermined destination which must be reached. No longer would boys and girls leave only half-way up, or even at the bottom, of their school, humiliated before younger children. The teachers could now look on the children they taught each as a human individual passing through a stage of growth and being helped to grow. 'Find out what each needs and try and help him to gain it,' said my senior colleague, 'and let them all, dull or bright, flow through the school like a stream.'

Had we realized that education cannot be separated from politics and that politics cannot be contained in neat compartments labelled 'Conservative', 'Liberal' or 'Labour', but are no less than each man's will to realize his attitude to his fellow man, then we might have paused in our enthusiasm and taken more careful stock of the situation.

The Secondary (present Grammar) School was outside the terms of reference of the Hadow Committee, and was quite indifferent to its Report. The Labour Party pursued a policy whose slogan was 'Secondary education for all'. Perhaps the cognoscenti of the party knew what they meant by 'Secondary'; if they did they did not disclose it. To the ordinary man and woman Secondary education meant education in a 'Secondary' School, and a 'Secondary' School was what we now call a Grammar School.

Looking back, it is easy to see that no government could long maintain a system of schools for adolescents of which one part exemplified ideas quite incompatible with the ideas of the other part. And, still looking back, it is clear that in an acquisitive society the part which consisted of those who had won their place by competition would win against the rest, however numerous the rest might be. But peering dimly into the future, we saw nothing. At the end of ten or more years work it really seemed that hopes were being realized and that the new Senior Schools were beginning to help adolescents to fulfil their growth.

Then came the war.

III

No one can pass through a major war unchanged, though some have tried. When the war was over there was a shortage of all material things. On the other hand, there were many children without a school place, and there were certain to be many more when the birth-rate 'bulge' reached 5 years old. Clearly, buildings came first as a priority, and for the younger children first. Fortunately there was at hand ready for this work a young generation of architects. They had been trained differently from their fathers. They did not ask what building regulations must be satisfied; they asked in what manner and for what purpose was each part of their design to be used. The building was to be an expression of the school. This was a good beginning, literally on the ground; on this level the question had to be faced: 'What sort of school?'

The 1944 Act came into force just before VE day; and later the same year came a Labour government with a large majority. The country had moved farther left than ever before. But 'left' is an imprecise term. One could think of several excellent candidates for appointment as Minister of Education. Not one of these was chosen. The Minister was a courageous and well-tried trades unionist who admittedly knew nothing about education but something about politics. It was a critical time; the Hadow plan was now the statutory system of schooling. What sort of Secondary Schools were we going to have? And also, though it was thought of less importance at the time, what sort of Primary Schools?

The political slogan was 'Secondary education for all'—with

the emphasis on *all*. Its political interpretation now seemed to run as follows. Previously Secondary education, like most good things, had been for the few only. Now all were to share in good things, and among good things only the best was good enough for all. What was the best? Clearly, what had been chosen by those who previously had had the privilege of choosing. Those with money to pay fees had sent their children to Grammar Schools; all should be able to send their children to schools like that or to schools as nearly like that as could be managed. In such a simple philosophy there was no sense in the idea that there might be 'for all' a school just as good but different and with a different outlook. At any rate, the idea was presented and dismissed. The Grammarization of the Senior, now called Secondary Modern, schools began. So died the hope that progressive ideas might influence at least one part of the State schooling of adolescents.

With the new 'Primary education', the education of children *before* adolescence, things were different. The Infant School was little disturbed by the new Act. On the other hand, the Junior School, as it made its appearance in the process of reorganization in the post-war years, was a decapitated body vainly looking for its lost head. But there, on the same site, and often under the same roof, was the Infant School, waiting to be friendly. The courtship was protracted; the lady offered a new way of life, though of course on her own terms; and the legal bond had already been concluded by Parliament in 1944. Slowly and cautiously the gentleman decided to accept the circumstances; and having once experienced the advantages of marriage, he has been enthusiastic about the wisdom of his choice. So smoothly has the Infant School tradition developed into a new Junior School tradition that the old rigorous respect for a separate Infant School exists no more, and there is now a substantial body of progressive opinion that favours a single school for children from 5 to 11 years.

From this happy union have followed several consequences. Men and women teachers now work together in an association not previously known. Before the war it was a tricky business for a woman inspector visiting a mixed school to enter a man's classroom. Men teachers are now happy to work under a headmistress in the narrow confines of a small Primary School. This

pleasant relationship has brought to the Primary School something lacking in schools which were entirely masculine or
feminine dominated. It has also revealed to many men teachers
how interesting and rewarding is teaching young children.
With this has come the development in many men of latent
powers to do this work extremely well and with great enjoy-
ment.

A more spectacular consequence is the appearance of creative
work by children right up to the age of 11 years. Children's
painting has a long history; but in the State schools such work
was once very limited beyond the Infant School. Not only is
painting now taken for granted throughout the primary range
but creative work is no longer limited to painting. In using clay,
paper, fabrics, in movement of the body, in using their mother
tongue in speech or writing, young children have now shown
that they possess creative powers whose extent we do not yet
know.

All these have been made possible by the happy union of the
Infant and Junior School. But there has been another factor in
their cause, the adoption of a progressive purpose for the whole
of Primary education. This can be expressed in various phrases,
none of them satisfying, because the only satisfactory way to
express such a purpose is in action. The young architects
enquired for what purpose was a Primary School to be designed.
They were given an answer and they made their design; as the
purpose became clearer the designs improved. In a well-
designed Primary School the building is part of its site: grass
trees, paths, hedges, paved space, hiding-places, mounds,
holes in the ground, buildings, all together form a whole which
is attractive to young children and gives opportunity for observation and activity. The classrooms are large (900–1,000 sq.
ft.), and within this space are smaller detached spaces, 'alcoves',
'corners', etc., available for particular occupations, noisy or
quiet. In the classrooms are things interesting and beautiful to
see and to handle, plenty of suitable books, tables and chairs,
benches—and at least one sink! There is a large Hall designed
chiefly for movement and other large-scale activities when the
weather is poor; it serves also as a place of assembly.

The architects design the body; the teachers give the life.
The life springs from a relationship which gives each boy and

girl a sense of security and at the same time is permissive; which provides for every boy and girl opportunity to choose in all things up to the extreme limit of the capacity of each but not beyond; which relies on influence and not on power.

Of course, not all Primary Schools have buildings of modern design, not all Primary Schools have modern ideas. But many do, and the number of these is increasing at a speed which is remarkable in a system which is itself permissive. The contemporary scene presents a striking contrast to that of thirty years ago. Whence has come the 'progressive' influence?

Except as already noted, there do not seem to be any individuals or institutions which have had a direct influence. Most progressive schools (at least until recently) have so little resembled anything familiar to Primary teachers that when visited they have seemed merely odd, or worse. The books of A. S. Neill, W. B. Curry and others have been widely read, and have undoubtedly influenced indirectly. But the greatest influence has come from the knowledge that progressive schools exist. When setting out on what to many Primary teachers seemed a voyage on an unknown sea it gave great courage to know that the sea had been sailed on before, though in a different kind of ship. The progressive schools have provided a home where ideas still new to many can live and adventure. That has been an influence whose extent it is impossible to assess. Certainly without the progressive schools what has happened in the State Primary Schools could not have happened.

IV

Peering dimly into the future there is not clear vision. Who knows what our Primary or Secondary Schools will be like in another twenty years time? It may be that, sated with rising in their standard of living, people may tire of the intricate selection and competition which now distinguish our Secondary education and put around it a barrier as impenetrable as the Berlin Wall. It may be that the desire to teach young children, and the younger the better, science, mathematics, a foreign language and other specialisms will leave little opportunity for these boys and girls to grow in their creative powers as we now know they can grow. What can the progressive schools do in face of such prospects?

I think they can remember that there are far more people well disposed to progressive ideas than ever contemplate sending their children to progressive schools. I think they can remember that the State schools in their very nature must respect the mores of those they teach, the children of ordinary people; and that ordinary people find differences in custom odd, and therefore repugnant. Oddness, however, is not an important part of progressiveness. I think they can even come to terms with the State schools if they begin by being interested in them.

The present generation of parents had their childhood during the war. In twenty years time those now passing through our Primary Schools will be parents. They will be a different generation, looking differently at the education of their children. They will expect for their young children something akin to the sort of schooling they received themselves, and it may be that they will expect something of similar quality for their children when adolescents. Perhaps the most important contribution of progressive schools is to provide a home where progressive ideas can adventure, ready for this and any other opportunity when it comes.

Do Progressive Schools give too much Freedom to the Child?

BY D. W. WINNICOTT

In this paper it is necessary for me to deal with the subject that has been given me from the theoretical angle, since I have no first-hand experience of progressive schools, either as pupil or teacher.

My speciality being child-psychiatry, with psychoanalysis as a ground-base, I must look at this subject of progressive schools in terms of the work that I have done with innumerable ill children and sometimes ill patients.

Diagnosis

In all kinds of medical care the basis of action is diagnosis. This is certainly true of psychiatry and of child psychiatry. In psychiatry social diagnosis has its place alongside the diagnosis of the individual patient.

My thesis in this contribution to your discussion is that nothing can be said about Progressive Education except on a firm basis of diagnosis.

Education proper can perhaps be discussed in terms of putting across the Rs or introducing the principles of physics or presenting the facts of history, though even in this limited field the teacher must learn to know the pupil. Special education of any kind is, however, a different matter, and progressive schools have an aim that transcends the banality of teaching and enters the wider field of the individual need. It will easily be conceded, therefore, that those who discuss progressive schools

D. W. Winnicott

cannot avoid having a vested interest in the study of the nature of each individual pupil.

What cannot be assumed is that an educationalist will have at hand a theoretical basis for the making of a diagnosis. Perhaps it is here that the child-psychiatrist can help.

In illustration, should illustration be needed, let me take another problem, the problem of corporal punishment. Often one hears or reads a discussion of the good or bad aspects of corporal punishment, and one knows that this discussion is doomed to remain futile because no attempt is being made to sort out the boys according to the state of their emotional growth. To take two extremes: in a school for normal boys from normal homes corporal punishment may be considered along with a number of other moderately important issues, whereas in a school designed to cater for children with behaviour disorders and, in a high proportion of cases, broken homes, then corporal punishment needs to be considered as a vital issue, and indeed as a detail of management that is always harmful.

(Curiously enough it is in the management of the first group that corporal punishment can sometimes be ruled out by an edict, and it is in the management of the second group that corporal punishment may need to be kept as a possibility, something that could be employed if circumstances seem to warrant, i.e. not ruled out by a committee of management.)

This is a relatively simple problem as compared with the wide subject of progressive schools and their place in the community. But perhaps the analogy can be used in the introduction.

It will be necessary to proceed step by step. (I must assume physical health.)

Classification A

Child normal (psychiatrically)
Child abnormal (psychiatrically)
    What is normal?
    Normality or health has been discussed by many (including myself).[1] This state does not carry freedom from symptoms.

---

[1] *The Child and the Family*. D. W. Winnicott, Tavistock Publications, 1957. *The Child, the Family, and the Outside World*. Pelican, 1964.

It implies that in the personality structure of the child the defences are organized satisfactorily, but without rigidity. Rigidity of defences hampers further growth, and disturbs the child's contact with the environment.

The positive sign of health is the continuing growth process, the fact of emotional change in the direction of development,

> development towards integration;
> development from dependence to independence;
> development in terms of instinct and,
> add development in terms of richness in the personality.

Also: steadiness of rate of development is a positive feature. (It is difficult to assess health in terms of behaviour.) Social diagnosis now needs to be brought into play:

> Home intact, functioning.
> Home intact, lame functioning.
> Home broken.
> Home never established.
>
> *also*
>
> Home well integrated into a social grouping $\begin{matrix} \text{narrow.} \\ \text{wide} \end{matrix}$
>
> Home establishing itself in society.
> Home withdrawn from society.
> Home ostracized by society.

It will perhaps be conceded that the majority of children in the community are:

> Healthy, with lives based on the intact family that is integrated into a social grouping (though this grouping may be narrow or even pathological in some aspect).

For these children schools are to be assessed according to their ability to facilitate:

> Personal: enrichment of personality.
> Familial: integration of home with school life.
> Social: initial interweaving with family's social grouping. Possible widening of social grouping of the individual child growing up to become an independent adult.

M

It is necessary to allow for the existence of a proportion of children who can be called normal or healthy in spite of their having broken families or families with awkward social connections. Among the healthy children will be found those who are ill in the sense of

> Psycho-neurosis
> Mood disorder
> Pathological psycho-somatic interaction
> Schizoid personality structure
> Schizophrenia

Most of such children may be counted as normal or healthy if they belong to intact families that are socially integrated, and such children can be treated by management or by psychotherapy within the home–school setting. These are among the ordinary term-by-term troubles of home–school intercommunication, and they can be ranked with spring-term infectious diseases and acute appendicitis and other emergencies, and with the fractured bone that belongs to the playing of games.

Clearly extreme degrees of these illnesses may affect the type of school that is selected.

Diagnosis of Deprivation

There is one kind of classification that is of vital importance to those who think in terms of educational systems, and yet this form of classification is not always given due place. It cuts right across the classification according to type of neurotic or psychotic defence organization, and it even includes (at one extreme) some boys and girls who are potentially normal. This classification is in terms of *deprivation*. The deprived or relatively deprived child has had environmental provision that was good enough so that there was a continuity of personal being, and then became deprived of this: deprived at an age (in emotional development) at which the process could be felt and perceived. The reaction to a deprivation (i.e. not to a privation) is one that holds the child in its grip—henceforth the world must be made to acknowledge and repair the injury. But as the process is largely working in the unconscious, the world does not succeed, or does so by paying heavily.

We call these children maladjusted. They are in the grip of the anti-social tendency. The clinical picture is to be observed in terms of:

(*a*) Stealing (lying, etc.), staking claims.
(*b*) Destruction, attempting to force the environment to reconstitute the framework, the loss of which made the child lose spontaneity, since spontaneity only makes sense in a controlled setting. Content is of no meaning without form.

The diagnosis along these lines is of utmost significance when the place of progressive schools is being discussed.

A group of deprived children can be said

(1) To need a Progressive School;
   and at the same time
(2) To be most likely to break it up.

In other words, the challenge to those who favour progressive schools is of the following nature. These schools will tend to be used by persons trying to place deprived children. Any idea of providing opportunity for creative learning, that is, of giving a better education to normal children, will be vitiated by the fact that a big proportion of the pupils will not be able to get down to learning because they are busy with a more important task, namely the discovery and establishment, each one, of his or her own identity (arising out of loss of sense of identity relative to deprivation).

A good result is often not to be measured in academic terms; it may be that all the school did was to keep a pupil (i.e. not expelling him or her) until the time came for passing him or her on to a wider area of living.

In this way, in some cases the school will have succeeded in curing or almost curing a deprived child of having a compulsion to go on being anti-social. Along with this must be some failures, tantalizing failures causing heartbreaks because the school has had the chance to see the best as well as the worst (or compulsive anti-social) side of the child's nature.

I think it is important that this aspect of the progressive school work should be stated as clearly as possible, otherwise those responsible get disheartened; and if those responsible become disheartened, then there tends to follow a gradual change over in the school towards being an ordinary school which is suitable for educating healthy children from intact families, but which is no longer progressive.

Lieben und Arbeiten—a Case of Cake and Eat It

BY LIAM HUDSON

In this paper I wish to review some recent psychological research into the nature of original thought; and I shall relate this evidence, some of it relatively new, to the aims of the progressive school teacher. With this programme in mind, I shall adopt, for the next three thousand words or so, a tone less sympathetic to progressive education than my feelings warrant. I hope to pose a dilemma for the progressive teacher in its most uncomfortable and inconvenient form, and fear lest my personal biases undermine me.

If I understand them aright the aims of most progressive teachers are twofold. They hope, very properly, that their pupils will be both happy and fulfilled in their private lives. They also hope that they will work productively—that they will help to mould the culture in which they live, rather than existing merely as well-adjusted (and well-heeled) consumers. Such aspirations have deep roots in the development of psychoanalytic thought. Freud is once said to have remarked that the proper end of man was *Lieben und arbeiten*, to love and to work. And to this day this remains the aim of almost every psychotherapist—both for his clients and for himself. The tendency of much recent research, especially that on 'creativity', is to urge that both these aims can be achieved together. My own contention is that this belief is probably unfounded. Indeed, if the evidence points in any direction it is rather in the opposite one. If I am right it follows that the progressive teacher faces a compromise. His twin goals may to some extent be mutually incompatible. Either he must plan to produce children who are contented or he must gear his system of education to the production of brain-workers. He cannot—or so I shall suggest—do both. The teacher who is all things to all children may end by being nothing satisfactory to any of them.

To review an inbred technical literature in the light of open discussion is not an easy matter. If one is honest one has to conclude—as I shall—that the evidence rarely entails useful or practical conclusions. Rather the reverse; that a surface of facts, or objective data, seems to swell on tides of prejudice and belief. One feels only too often that the beliefs support the facts rather than vice versa; and that changes in emphasis derive not from new discoveries but from changes in the methods and assumptions fashionable among those who do the looking.

Educational psychology is no exception. Traditionally, such work is statistical in nature, overridingly concerned with test scores and marks. Human beings as such are visible only fleetingly in a forest of numbers. Times are changing, however; and our preoccupation with statistical analysis is changing with them. Although we retain a deep respect for numbers and the paraphernalia of measurement, we have recently undergone a shift of attitude. Psychologists are showing signs of an interest in people once again; and even the more statistically minded are increasingly concerned with children's personalities as well as their intellects. We owe this change of climate, partially at least, to a resurgence of interest in the nature of originality—or, as psychological cant has it, of 'creativity'. In discussing this literature on 'creativity' I shall of necessity be highly selective, picking those facts and beliefs that seem most pertinent to our present purpose. And I shall do my best, too, to distinguish psychological fact from psychological fancy, the gulf between these being at times a wide one.

The phenomenon of originality is one which has long intrigued psychologists. What is new about the present effort is not so much its subject-matter as its scale. Very large sums of money have recently been spent on the search for intellectual talent, in the physical sciences especially. And an odd feature of this concern with intellectual excellence is that it has slackened, not increased, psychologists' preoccupation with scores and marks. One might have expected new excesses of psychometric zeal; but in practice precisely the reverse seems to have happened—we have witnessed a new burgeoning of American progressivism. (One reads not of ruthless inculcation but of 'nurturing the creative impulse'.) So, although the cult figure of the 'creativity' movement in the United States is the productive physical scientist, we see a special attention paid not to the virtues of academic conformity but to those of the individualist and the non-conformist. This emphasis will be sympathetic, I imagine, to most of us; but unfortunately, it is one which seems to have biased psychologists in the interpretation of their results.

To say that the 'creativity' literature is somewhat progressive in tone is to acknowledge that it is speculative. And this speculation seems to cluster around certain beliefs or maxims—maxims which will not be entirely unfamiliar. The first of these is that originality in all intellectual spheres is related to the same personality type. For the present purpose we may call him the 'diverger'. The diverger is the man who is intellectually flexible, uninhibited and unfettered by convention. He is the one (some would suggest) who—given the necessary training— can establish novel connections between ideas, and see similarities which no man has seen before.

Unquestionably, the diverger is a type which exists. In my own research I have found his qualities quite easy to measure. He is good at tasks which require him to switch rapidly from one line of thought to another; relatively poor at close, logical reasoning. If you ask him to suggest uses for everyday objects he will frequently make suggestions which are unusual, witty or violent; he usually holds liberal and minority opinions and expresses them vehemently; he has 'human' rather than technical interests; he is liable to work in a slapdash fashion on an intelligence test; and so on.[1]

However, the factual connection linking the diverger to originality is not robust. The only convincing evidence is that of MacKinnon.[2] He and his colleagues invited the most original

[1] Hudson. L., 'Intelligence, Divergence and Potential Originality', *Nature*, **196**, 601 (1962).
[2] MacKinnon. D. W., 'Nature and Nurture of Creative Talent', *American Psychologist*, **17**, No. 7, 484 (1962).

thinkers in a variety of fields to submit themselves voluntarily to close psychological examination: famous scientists, architects, novelists, etc. He discovered, among other things, that within any given field the more original men were the more divergent. Original scientists are more divergent than unoriginal ones; creative architects are more divergent than the non-creative; and so on. Sadly, though, the inference that we draw from this discovery cannot be a straightforward one. We know on good evidence that all physical scientists tend, compared with arts specialists, to be the opposite of divergent—that is, convergent. In her famous study of great scientists, Roe found all physical scientists tend to avoid the more personal aspects of life, and avoid imaginative thinking.[1] My own results are consonant with Roe's.[2] At the Sixth Form level, mathematics and physical science attract boys of a markedly impersonal, rather inflexible turn of mind, while the divergers—the boys who are intellectually flexible but weak in close argument—are drawn naturally towards the arts. We can only conclude that all the scientists are convergers; the unoriginal more so, the original less.

We know, then, that different types of persons are attracted to different intellectual fields; and that these differences are measurable. We suspect, too, that originality in all these spheres is intimately tied up with questions of personality. Another of MacKinnon's findings supports this. He discovered that his highly creative men and women were not distinguished from their contemporaries by their scores on intelligence tests, or on tests of any other mental ability. The only tests which did distinguish them were those which reflected in some way or other differences in personality:

> Over the whole range of intelligence and creativity there is, of course, a positive relationship between the two variables. No feeble-minded subjects have shown up in any of our creative groups. It is clear, however, that above a certain required minimum level of intelligence which varies from field to field and in some instances may be surprisingly

[1] Roe. A., 'A Psychological Study of Eminent Psychologists and Anthropologists and a Comparison with Biological and Physical Scientists', *Psychological Monographs*, **67**, No. 2 (1963).

[2] Hudson. L., 'Personality and Scientific Aptitude, *Nature*, **198**, 913 (1963).

low, being more intelligent does not guarantee a corresponding increase in creativeness. It just is not true that the more intelligent person is necessarily the more creative one.

Our data suggest, rather, that if a person has the minimum of intelligence required for mastery of a field of knowledge, whether he performs creatively or banally in that field will be crucially determined by non-intellective factors.[1]

Such cut-off scores occur, as MacKinnon says, surprisingly low on the I.Q. scale. It seems, for example, that a physical scientist stands to little advantage by having an I.Q. much in excess of 120–125. My own results fit neatly with MacKinnon's. I have given tests to groups of clever boys at Public and Grammar Schools, and then traced them through their later school and university careers. I find that there is little difference in I.Q. between a Sixth Former who will go on to win an Open Scholarship at Oxford or Cambridge and gain a First Class degree and a form-mate who does poorly in his A level examinations and leaves school with no distinction at all. When faced with a classful of Sixth Formers, in other words, I cannot tell from their scores which are the exceptionally bright and which the relatively dull.[2]

Since measured intelligence is not closely related to achievement (even in examinations), it seems likely that the vital factors are personal. Such a connection between intellectual productivity and questions of personality is implied by all the relevant research. Psychologists who study eminent men seem invariably to find that their intellectual qualities are intricately interwoven with their personal ones. One reads of uncanny devotion to work; of single-minded pursuit of the right answer; of intuition. Although there seems no one recipe for success, one has the clear impression of men *driven* to think—men who have set some primitive emotional forces to work for their own enormously sophisticated intellectual purposes. But what these forces are and how they can be geared to the task of thinking productively we can, at the moment, only guess.

This leads us to a second fashionable belief and one intimately

---

[1] MacKinnon, D. W., op. cit., pp. 488 and 493.
[2] Hudson, L., 'Future Open Scholars', *Nature*, **202**, 834 (1964).

related to the first. Psychologists seem at the moment to assume not only that the diverger is more intellectually productive than the converger (which, as I have suggested, is misleading) but also that the diverger is psychologically the more healthy of the two. This belief stems from the more basic assumption that we are both healthy and creative inasmuch as we have access to our unconscious impulses. Again, I am sceptical. In my own research I am struck by the extent to which the diverger's openness is deceptive. He seems in many cases to use the display of his feelings, his concern for people and his taste for controversy as a means of avoiding emotions of a profounder and more disturbing nature. As far as I can tell, the difference between the converger and the diverger is not that between the neurotic and the healthy, rather that between one defensive system and another. The converger turns his back quite explicitly upon everything that he finds alarming. The diverger appears to take most emotional matters in his stride, but achieves this at the price of a certain hollowness.

Whether or not my analysis of convergence and divergence is correct, one thing is clear. The very highest achievement in some spheres, science especially, is achieved by intense devotion to work—and consequently a relative disregard for the more personal and private aspects of life. As Roe says:

> It must be pointed out that it is likely that the kind of person who has gone into social science may have had a biasing effect on the theories produced by social scientists, particularly with regard to the desirable or the mature personality. Practically all current psychological theory of development stresses strongly the central importance in any life of the richness of personal relations as a basis for 'adjustment'. But the data of this study demonstrate, and it seems to me quite conclusively, that a more than adequate personal and social adjustment, in the larger sense of an adjustment which permits a socially extremely useful life and one which is personally deeply satisfying, is not only possible but probably quite common, with little of the sort of personal relations which psychologists consider essential. Many of the biological and physical scientists are very little concerned with personal relations, and this is not

only entirely satisfactory to them but it cannot be shown always to be a compensatory mechanism (nor are compensatory mechanisms necessarily undesirable). It can also apparently be satisfactory to others who are closely associated with them. That divorces are so much commoner among the social scientists is of interest in this connection.[1]

Psychologists, in other words, do their best to live fully both intellectually and personally, but the evidence suggests that they pull off this feat only occasionally. It seems likely, therefore, that psychologists have used their own goals in life—*lieben und arbeiten*—as a prescription for Everyman. On this argument, anyone unlike a psychologist is automatically judged limited or neurotic. I would argue that, quite the reverse, although there are many different tactics and priorities which we use in coping with the pressures of our work and private lives, no one tactic is intrinsically worse or better than any other. Each has its own characteristic weaknesses and strengths; and the neurotic is not the man who adopts one particular intellectual and personal style, but the one who having adopted a style suffers its weaknesses without enjoying its strengths.

And this leads me to the third and the most immediately pressing of the research maxims about creativeness. The suggestion is that orthodox schooling in English and American schools stunts children's creative impulses, and therefore ought to be changed. This is backed, or appears to be backed, by a number of interesting facts. MacKinnon found that his creative individuals were frequently undistinguished academically. They were disliked by their teachers; they gained only moderate marks at school and university; they were opinionated and rebellious; and, more often than not, they were unhappy. Getzels and Jackson report similar reactions of teachers to their divergers (or, as they call them, 'high creatives'). Most teachers seem to dislike divergers, even when they are academically successful. They prefer to teach the relatively more docile and conforming converger.

That conventional education is uncongenial to independent spirits seems to me incontestable. Also that much of what

[1] Roe, A., op. cit., p. 50.

passes for education in this country and the United States is a waste of everybody's time, pupils and teachers alike. On the other hand—and it seems vital that we should recognize this—such conclusions do not follow from the evidence in hand. The harsh fact is that MacKinnon's eminent men are eminent; that men like Darwin and Einstein, who were unhappy at school, nevertheless produced theories of evolution and relativity respectively. This datum is open to at least three interpretations. The one drawn by most progressives is that Einstein and Darwin survived through luck or genius; but that thousands of equal, or nearly equal, potentiality are yearly suppressed or extinguished. MacKinnon's eminent men are the lucky ones that got away. The second possibility appeals to people of a more pessimistic temper: namely, that the unhappiness of these great men was a causal factor in making them great. Had they not suffered boredom or frustration at school, they would have led comfortable, mediocre lives like the rest of us. The third possibility is that their unhappiness was concomitant but not causal: that they were unhappy because they were remarkable, but their unhappiness did not affect their creative potentialities one way or another.

The issues at stake here are central ones: yet what we make of them really remains largely a matter of taste. My own bias is towards the second interpretation of the three. I suspect that progressive schools make most children happier than authoritarian ones, but that they withdraw from them the cutting edge that insecurity, competition and resentment supply. I would predict that wherever we adjust children to themselves and each other we remove from them the springs of their intellectual and artistic productivity. Successful brainwork, demonstrably, is the outcome of dedication and single-mindedness, and happy children may not be prepared to make the effort that excellence demands.

To some extent, of course, the validity of such argument about progressive teaching depends on the context in which it is used. If we force children's noses to the academic grindstone, as happens increasingly in English Sixth Forms, the amount of elbow room left for the unusual, non-conforming child is dangerously reduced. Pupils in such schools are less taught than brainwashed. This seems to me a distortion of education, and one which is bound to have dire results, however natively resilient pupils may be. On the other hand, we certainly cannot use the creativity literature as a stick with which to beat academic education of a more leisurely kind, whether along the lines of some English Public School Sixth Forms or those of an American High School. They may be inept, without necessarily 'driving out creativity'. In fact, they may provide precisely the background of mild conformity and incompetence which reinforces the potentially original child's conviction of his own worth. It may be the ideal background against which to rebel.

The gulf, as I have said, between the evidence and the practical decisions facing the progressive teacher remains large. But still, even though we cannot make hard and fast deductions, we can at least look for straws in the wind—and these there are in plenty. The most obvious is the emphasis which all research workers place upon the importance of motive or drive. Successful scientists, successful artists are rarely dilettantes. They work not for pleasure but from emotional necessity. And I find it hard to believe that such dedication does not involve the channelling of powerful impulses—away from the sphere of personal relations and into that of work.

A clue here may lie in the homes from which such thinkers spring. MacKinnon, Roe and other experimenters find that these have two characteristics. Future intellectuals seem to come from homes: (*a*) which provide them with great self-confidence; and (*b*) which, for the scientists especially, are emotionally cold and puritanical. Although his parents have great confidence in his abilities, he finds that in certain crucial respects they are not warm or intimate with him. The implication for the progressive teacher is an awkward one. He does his best to instil self-confidence; but he also seeks (and for the best motives in the world) to offer children genuine emotional warmth. We return, in other words, to the dilemma with which we began.

The forces which drive a man to be creative may have their roots if not in unhappiness, at least in unease. It follows that an education of genuine benevolence may disqualify children from a life of productive thought. If children from progressive schools are to play an active part in the growth of their own culture—in the physical sciences especially—their teachers may have to modify their traditional and entirely laudable concern with their pupils' contentment. Paradoxically, too, it may turn out that the policy of consciously nurturing children's creative potentialities is one which effectively stifles their productivity as adults. Such teachings may have precisely the reverse effect to that intended; it may make children happier and more secure, and thereby reduce their intellectual potentialities rather than increasing them. (The Old Dartingtonian who *is* productive may be so on the strength of an unusually discordant home life rather than of a particularly happy time at school.) On the strength of MacKinnon's evidence about the school careers of great men, it would seem quite unnecessary for the progressive teacher to plunge wholeheartedly into the growing and increasingly rapacious competition for outstanding examination results. What they must acknowledge though is the danger that intellectual excellence in a child may well be sapped both by teachers who are friendly, understanding and considerate and by a harmonious school atmosphere in which all the subtle dangers and savageries of a conventional school are curbed or lacking.

Individual Freedom and the Reform of Teaching
BY DOUGLAS PIDGEON

It is the purpose of this paper to attempt an assessment of the theory and practical application of two very simple and not very novel educational ideas. The first is that, since a major aim of education is the inducement of certain learning in pupils, the emphasis in any educational system should be on learning and not, as at present, on teaching; the second is that this required learning is best achieved when the necessary motivation is inherent in the learning tasks to be performed instead of being imposed from without in the form of some incentive unrelated to the work. If there is a novel element in what follows it is in the implications which arise from considering these two ideas together.

It is generally assumed that in a system of mass education it is necessary to divide children into groups for the purposes of instruction. Thus, almost without exception, every school in every country of the world is designed around the classroom, with the class as the basic unit for teaching purposes. In our own system, where the average staffing ratio is over 20 to 1 and rarely, even in the most privileged schools, drops below 10 to 1, it would seem absurd to question the necessity to form classes and to ask teachers to teach them. At the same time the whole notion of group teaching rests on a number of assumptions which run contrary to the ideals of a child-centred education.

No two children think, act, learn or develop in exactly the same way, and it cannot be supposed, therefore, that anything like perfect communication can be established between a teacher and *all* the pupils in his class. If some pupils understand his explanations there will be others who do not, and it will not always be lack of ability that forms the stumbling block. Thelen's[1] work in the United States has clearly demonstrated how incompatabilities between teacher and taught can slow up, if not prevent, any progress in learning. His idea of forming 'teachability' groups, in which a rapport has been established between pupils and teacher, has much to commend it, but even here many problems remain unsolved, with regard both to forming the groups and to achieving working efficiency once they have been formed.

There are also other difficulties which exist in the group teaching situation. One of these, for example, is the fact that teachers inevitably establish a level of 'expectancy' from the pupils they are given to teach.

Stated in another way, it is contended that the standard or level of achievement reached by any group of pupils will depend, to a very large extent, upon the standard or level expected of them. And, it might be added, it will also depend upon the 'expectancy' of the pupils themselves. In other words, any child's achievement is in large part a function of what is expected of him, and if a collection of essentially different individuals is taught as a group an unwarranted degree of standardization is of necessity imposed upon them.

Most teachers who have taught classes varying across the ability spectrum will agree with the truth of this contention, and evidence from research can, without difficulty, be found to support it. The success of the Higher Horizons programme in New York,[2] in which deliberate attempts were made to change the low expectations of 'deprived' pupils may be cited, as may the figures given in the Early Leaving Report,[3] concerning the proportion of pupils obtaining a 'good' 'O' Level G.C.E. in different parts of the country, compared with the proportion entering Grammar Schools in the same area. No relationship

---

[1] Thelen, H. A., *Classroom Grouping for Teachability,* John Wiley (1967).

[2] *The Evaluation of the Higher Horizons Programme for Under-privileged Children,* by J. W. Wrightstone *et al.,* Bureau of Educational Research, Board of Education of the City of New York.

[3] 'Early Leaving'—Report of the Central Advisory Council for Education, London, H.M.S.O. (1954).

can be found between these two proportions; in England as a whole, for example, with 20 per cent entering Grammar Schools, 12 per cent obtain a 'good' G.C.E., while in Wales, with a near 40 per cent selection, 20 per cent do so. The differences here, and in other parts of the country, are not all explainable by assuming that different standards are adopted by the different examining Boards. Perhaps the surest evidence of the relationship between teacher expectancy and pupil performance comes from the work of Rosenthal and Jacobson in the United States.[1] These investigators have shown that the intellectual performance of so-called 'low' ability children can be raised significantly if their teachers are convinced that they are 'academic spurters'.

This notion of expectancy operates in any kind of situation in which pupils are taught, and it is particularly obvious in schools where grouping or streaming by ability is practised. Thus, for example, the teacher in a streamed school will expect quite a different level of performance from his pupils according to whether they are a 'bright' or a 'dull' group. A relatively high level of performance is expected of bright pupils, and this expectation helps in no small way to ensure whatever success is obtained. At the other end, however, both teachers and pupils of the bottom streams *know* they cannot achieve much, and this knowledge in itself plays a large part in producing low standards from such classes, and preventing them from reaching their full potential. The difference in teachers' expectancy with regard to pupils coming from middle-class and working-class background[2] is, of course, well known; so, too, the examination successes achieved by many independent schools with pupils of relatively low measured ability is not due entirely to the smaller classes in which such pupils may find themselves, or to any superior quality of the teaching, except in so far as the teachers in these schools, coming invariably as they do from middle-class

---

[1] Rosenthal, R., and Jacobson, L., 'Teachers' Expectancies; Determinants of Pupils' I.Q. Gains', *Psychology Reports*, **19**, 115–18 (1966).

[2] Himmelweit, Hilde T., 'Socio-Economic Background and Personality', in *Unesco International Social Science Bulletin*, **7**, No. 1 (1955).

Also Bacchus, M. K., 'A Survey of Secondary Modern Teachers' Concepts of their Pupils' Interests and Abilities in relation to their Social Philosophy and to the Social Class Background of their Pupils', unpublished M.A. Thesis, University of London (1959).

N

background themselves, set their sights at a higher level than their colleagues teaching in Secondary Modern Schools. In other words, it is claimed that the attitudes on the part of both teachers and pupils as to what learning is possible influence to no small extent what is, in fact, learnt.

It is not irrelevant at this point to mention the part that the use of intelligence tests in schools has played in determining pupil expectancy. Not only does the fallacy that school performance is governed almost entirely by a pupil's native ability predominate in many teacher's thinking but the fact that intelligence test scores or I.Q.s do not indicate 'innate ability' any more than a school examination, but are influenced by environmental stimulation (or lack of it), means that in nearly all cases an underestimate is made of a pupil's 'capacity'.

Consideration of factors like these would appear to lead to the postulation that the level of performance which the majority of children are capable of reaching is far higher than that normally expected of them. The point to be made here is that, in a group teaching situation, the standards or levels of achievement required of pupils are inevitably set by an outside authority (by the State, the education authority, the examining board or by the home or the teacher) and the individual child is not given—nor under existing circumstances does he wish to have—the opportunity of deciding what and how much he should learn. It is an hypothesis at least worthy of investigation that if the restrictions were removed and the attitudes of teachers and pupils towards the learning situation changed, then standards would rise.

The only way, of course, by which the above hypothesis could be tested would be to develop a situation in which the restrictions imposed by group teaching were removed. This is not so impossible to achieve, once it is appreciated that the real emphasis in the process of education should be on learning and not, as at present, on teaching.

Learning, after all, is the desired end; teaching only a means to that end. The question raised here is whether it is the best means—whether, in fact, the employment of a teacher to propound his knowledge to a group of often not very willing children, in the hope that some of it will rub off on them, is the most efficient use that can be made of him. While there are, of course, many teachers who attempt something more than just to propound their knowledge, there are, unfortunately, far too many who consider that this is what, in fact, they are paid to do. Even the best teachers will be aware that there are factors inherent in the teaching situation which necessarily impose restrictions on some, if not all, of their pupils. Clearly, for each and every child it is the end—namely learning—that is important, and the real problem, it would seem, is to find more efficient ways both of bringing about this learning and of utilizing a teacher's knowledge.

It requires no deep study of psychology to be aware that little learning takes place without some kind of motivation; the important question, as stated earlier, concerns the kind of motivation which should be involved. At the risk of oversimplifying a very complex problem, it is convenient to regard motivation as being of two basic types—that imposed from without and that inherent in the learning task. The 'imposed' kind is that which, far too often, is employed in schools today—the need to please either the teacher or parents and to avoid their condemnation; the wish to compete successfully in examinations or with classmates, and to avoid being recognized as a 'failure'; or the desire to earn a 'star' or merit point or, indeed, anything that a teacher can think up to induce a competitive spirit to make children learn things they do not really want to. It may be noted, in passing, that motivation of this kind has nothing whatever to do with what is being learned.

Inherent motivation, on the other hand, is that quality in a task which makes children want to do it, and in doing, learn about it. It is that attribute which makes even the most apathetic child say 'Let me have a go' instead of 'Must I?' Note that implicit in the idea of inherent motivation is the active participation in some task. Learning takes place during the activity—in other words, what occurs is learning by discovery; not a very novel idea, but one which has perhaps received a new impetus following the work of Piaget on the learning processes of children.

In Piaget's view[1] intellectual development is a process of

[1] Piaget, M., see his contributions made to the Conference on Cognitive Research and Curriculum Development, reported by Eleanor R. Duckworth in the *Elementary Science Study Newsletter*, June (1964).

equilibration in which the individual plays an active part in regulating his own development. A child must be allowed to do his own learning, because full development will not occur if his role is a passive one. He must be presented with situations in which he can experiment for himself and want to do so; not told, for example, to do a page of sums in a specified way, but presented with material which commands his involvement with it, and which is so structured that learning is a necessary accompaniment; not made to follow the chapters of a dull text-book on geography, nor to listen to the mechanical intoning of an uninspired teacher, but allowed actively to discover about the earth for himself, by exploration and experiment.

From the teacher's point of view, inherent motivation is far more difficult to bring about, especially since it involves a radical change in his own approach to the teaching situation. The task of the teacher would not be to teach so much as to create the situations in which children can learn. As Piaget has said, 'The teacher must provide the instruments which the children can use to decide for themselves. . . . A ready-made truth is only a half-truth.'[1]

The change from imposed to inherent motivation thus involves something much more than a mere change in classroom techniques. Basic attitudes must also change, and the shift in emphasis from teaching to learning must occur in the thinking of pupils as well as of teachers. If a new approach is to be found it is clearly necessary that children learn how to learn, and preferably at an early age.

Learning is something personal and individual—it does not take place automatically as the result of having been present in a classroom while some teaching was going on. What a child learns from any given environmental situation is a result of that child's own involvement in the learning process, and it is necessary that children understand this—understand, in fact, what learning means for them personally. This is largely a matter of approach. Instead of the implicit assumption made by most young children (and by many adults!) that going to school and being 'taught' will result in 'education', children must learn at an early stage that, although the school is the place *where* they can learn and the teacher the person who

[1] Piaget., op. cit.

provides them with the *materials of learning*, the actual learning is something they can only do themselves. The realization of this simple truth comes to many children some time during their school career—usually rather late—but to many others it never comes at all. It would seem essential, however, that if the aim is to allow for the maximum development of all children the school and the teachers within it must make a deliberate effort to ensure that the right 'habits' of learning come at the beginning for all.

It is now necessary to consider the practical implications of what has been said; as has been made clear, it is no minor innovation that is being considered, but a radical change in approach involving a quite different concept of the role of the teacher, in a school which, physically, may need to be constructed on quite different principles from those generally accepted at present.

The essence of this approach, so far as the teacher is concerned, is the placing of each pupil, individually, in an ordered sequence of situations which will enable him to learn most effectively. This implies two things; first, a knowledge of what is the most appropriate sequence in which any particular subject should be presented for learning, and secondly, some appreciation of how children do, in fact, learn, leading to an understanding of what kind of situations need to be provided to ensure that optimal learning takes place.

Progress through a pre-arranged sequence of experiences to the acquisition of some kind of knowledge or skill is one definition of programmed instruction,[1] and the work now going on in this field is relevant to the approach suggested here. It must be made clear, however, that the general use of teaching machines and other such devices is not being put forward, except as they may be seen to be useful adjuncts to the total learning experience at particular stages in a child's development. What is suggested is that all teachers should be familiar with the techniques of programmed learning, so that they are able both to develop their own programmes where necessary and to adapt existing programmes that have been prepared by other experts. The ability, therefore, to write programmes and

[1] See 'Aspects of Programmed Instruction—1, Some Notions and Arguments', J. D. Williams, *Educational Research* **V**, 3, 163–78.

to judge the merits of existing programmes will need to be an integral part of teacher training.

Primarily, however, the need is for each teacher to know in *what order* his subject should be presented for learning. This presupposes that it is possible, in most subjects, to postulate at least the basis of an order of conceptual learning, such that at any point in the learning sequence no major principle or concept is presented for learning which subsumes other concepts not already understood. To illustrate this, two examples will be taken from mathematics. Mathematics has been chosen because it perhaps more readily lends itself to logical structuring, and in fact considerable work along these lines has already been carried out.[1] An order of presentation, however, *is* adopted necessarily by all teachers, and the suggestion here is that far more thought should be given to it in terms of conceptual development. This, of course, is leading into the field of curriculum reform which is at last beginning to receive due attention in this country.

As a first example, the 'simple' sum $13 + 3 = 16$ may be taken. Many young children will be asked to 'do' this sum, without any attempt being made first to ascertain that they are fully operational in the subsumed concepts of number structure, addition and equality. By 'being operational' is meant that they have such understanding that they can generalize to quite different situations and not just obey a rule that they have learnt by heart from following a specific set of examples. In this example 'equality' is a very difficult concept involving, among other things, the notions of conversion and reversibility highlighted by Piaget.

As a second example may be quoted the fact that any multiplication by a number greater than the base of the number system being used (e.g. 37×12 in the decimal system) in fact involves a knowledge of the commutive, associative and distributive laws. It is certainly not suggested that these laws should be learned *as such*, but an understanding of what they imply is not only possible before 'long' multiplication is undertaken but also essential to an understanding of what is really going on when such a process is carried out.

While it may be possible that there is a unique *conceptual*

[1] See *Building at Mathematics*, Z. P. Dienes, Hutchinson (1960).

order of learning (at least in the elementary stages), this does not imply that there is only one way of presenting any given subject. Indeed, the possible variants of the form that a 'learning situation' can take are limited only by the ingenuity of teachers and educational innovators. It is here that the question of motivation becomes important, and as has already been indicated, the key to successful learning is the active participation of the pupil in the learning task.

The nature of this task, however, must vary with the stage of development. In the early stages the emphasis will necessarily be on action involving an element of play, though even here it must be directed towards specific learning. The 'activity' principle has long been recognized in primary education, though unfortunately the purpose of the activity has not always been clear either to teachers or pupils. Activity without purpose may, in fact, be harmful, for it is possible that the wrong kind of learning will take place. It is important therefore that the purpose of any learning task presented to a pupil must be fully understood by the teacher;[1] moreover, although the immediate learning aim, such as the understanding of a particular concept, may not be initially appreciated by the pupil, he should be aware that the activity is directed towards learning. Awareness of this kind becomes increasingly important as the learning progresses, because at some point a stage will be reached when the pursuance of learning for its own sake must provide the necessary motivation. In other words, while a young child will find his motivation in the joy of experimenting and discovering for himself, there must come a stage when he wants to go on learning simply because there is something exciting for him still to learn. This is probably the stage when 'secondary' education has been reached, and clearly it will not come unless the primary stage has been properly structured to this end. Moreover, it will not necessarily come at the same chronological age for all children.

As seen here, the process of education is not one that should be disjointed by administrative necessity, but must be accepted for what it is—a continuous development. It is supposed that a

[1] This is not always the case, unfortunately: many teachers using, for example, the Dienes approach to mathematics learning are unaware of many of the concepts they are presumably expecting their pupils to learn.

continuum of conceptual learning exists along which all children will progress at different rates and at different depths. At any given point in time all pupils of the same chronological age in a school will be dispersed along this continuum[1] for a variety of reasons, only one of which is differing innate ability. In these circumstances a teacher must first ensure correct placement on the continuum for each pupil, and then that progress is made commensurate with the learning achieved. The secondary stage is seen as different from the primary only in that the pupils' view of learning is more mature, and hence the teacher will be directing his activities not so much towards providing appropriate learning situations as towards assisting the pupil with his own learning activities.

The need for the teacher to have both a greater insight into the way children learn and a more detailed knowledge of the logical or conceptual order in which any subject should be presented implies a deeper *subject* awareness at the primary stage of education. Teachers at this stage, as well as at the secondary stage, will require to have some degree of specialization. This idea, again, is not new. Many primary schools at present have specialist teachers for such subjects as music, art and remedial reading, and the utilization of specialist knowledge in other subjects is, of course, one of the basic tenets of team teaching.[2] To know how to develop appropriate learning situations, to know what learning experiences a young child should have and what materials should be presented to him for experimenting with, is *expert* knowledge, and few teachers will be so good that they can be experts in all subjects of the primary school.

The changed role of the teacher, as conceived here, clearly implies a revision of present training procedures. It also implies a rather different conception of school building. The design of such buildings could, of course, take many forms, and much research and experience will be necessary before the problem is solved. The main difference from most existing schools would be complete absence of 'shoe-box' classrooms, and the emphasis in all architectural arrangements for opportunities for learning,

[1] They will, in fact, be dispersed even on the final day of schooling, for differential pre-school learning will have taken place.

[2] See *Team Teaching*, edited by J. T. Shaplin and H. F. Olds (1964).

both individually and in small discussion groups. The decision whether to have primary and secondary education in the same or different buildings is usually made today in favour of the latter, largely for administrative and economic reasons. So far as the proposals in this paper are concerned, either form of organization is possible, with the proviso that, with separate buildings, it would be essential that educational continuity was not disrupted. This would imply a similarity of organization and procedure at the transition stage in both schools.

In the first years of schooling it is clearly important that children develop appropriate social attitudes—how to live and work with others; hence some rooms in which group activities take place are essential. The groups so formed, however, need not be rigid, and they could vary according to the specific needs of the particular exercise. At the same time, provision must be made for individual learning—perhaps a large room equipped with movable partitions that can conveniently be arranged for children to work quietly alone or, if necessary at first, in small groups of two or three. With such an arrangement, it would be part of the process of learning how to learn for the very young children to be introduced slowly to these learning situations. According to the stage of development, however, more and more time would be spent in this way, although group meetings for such activities as games and drama would always be required.

The primary stage of education would have a number of functions, chief among which would be the development of definite and positive attitudes towards future learning and the securing of the foundations of that learning. The progress of the individual would be judged not by the expectations of his teacher or by competition with classmates but by his own achievements. If some pupils learnt at a faster rate, and others absorbed and retained more background to their learning, this would be of little concern where the idea of 'promotion' had no meaning.

The abolition of group teaching, and with it the classroom, requires a different concept of the structure of a school, and the following ideas on how the secondary stage might be arranged are put forward only tentatively, since many other variants are possible.

Students (not children) entering the secondary school would join existing groups containing about twenty-five others whose ages spanned the complete range of the school (e.g. 11–18). Entry to a particular group would depend largely upon the student's wishes, although assessments from the primary school would be used to avoid putting incompatible personalities together and to avoid any suggestion of grouping by ability. Such a group would *not* be for instructional purposes. It would meet in a room which would have facilities for individual learning, possibly in the form of carrels. It would also have provision for keeping the books and other personal belongings of each student, and would have a cloak- and wash-room attached, and possibly even simple cooking facilities, for learning in school need not stop at four o'clock. Physically these 'home' rooms would be grouped around the library, and the rest of the school would branch off from this central area. Each basic group of subjects would occupy a wing of the building— thus there might be separate wings for the physical sciences, the social sciences, languages, arts and crafts, physical education, etc. Each wing would have practical rooms or laboratories, as well as a number of other differently sized rooms for discussion purposes. There would, of course, be a large assembly hall which would be designed for use in a variety of ways, and which would act as the centre of all social activities of the school.

A student's time in school would be shared between individual learning and group activities, the time devoted to each varying with the age and specific need of the student. About a third to a half of his time would be spent in the subject wings of the school, either doing individual experimental work in the practical rooms or participating in small group discussions. Again, about a third to a half of his time would be spent in his home room in individual study, and for the remaining time he would be engaged in large group activities, such as games, music and drama.

A boy (or girl) starting in the school would, for an initial period at least, be put in the care of an older student who would be responsible for showing him the ways of the school and introducing him to the rules and regulations by which, as a school citizen, he would have to abide. Initially, each student would meet his subject teachers, who would discuss with him the course his learning activities would take, and who would arrange for him a suitable time-table. The development of individual time-tables might appear to be an intricate and complex task, but the main necessity would be for each subject teacher to ensure that the practical and discussion rooms were not overcrowded at any given time. As all students would be spending a high proportion of their time in individual study in their home rooms or library, considerable flexibility is possible. Only with such activities as drama and games would it be necessary to structure a 'school' time-table.

One member of staff would have responsibility for the general welfare of students in a home room, though only a small proportion of his time would be spent there. As a subject master and member of a department, he would participate in the work of 'programming' student activities in the practical rooms, and would assume responsibility for supervising the progress of a number of students, each of whom he would meet in small group discussions and, from time to time, individually. He would, of course, spend more time with the younger newer members of his subject group, for the older students would be more able to direct their own studies. In short, present sixth-form attitudes to study would be brought lower down the school and university tutorial methods introduced for older students. Clearly the success of this kind of approach depends upon the right attitudes being implanted at the primary stage.

The problems raised by examinations must, of course, be considered, and the major question would be whether students attending the kind of school described here could perform satisfactorily in an external examination such as the G.C.E. Basically, there is no reason why they should not do so, but it is to be hoped that the form of such examinations would be changed. If examinations must be given, then they should be designed to suit the curriculum and not be, as at present, the determiners of it. More research into the techniques of examining is urgently required, although even now it is possible to devise reliable examinations designed to evaluate specific courses. But are examinations really necessary? If future employers require information on the education of job applicants, are not the student's teachers more qualified to give this than some external examiner who has never seen him? And provided a student has pursued his learning to a recommended point, should he be denied further education in a college or university? Substantial wastage in the form of 'drop-outs' from further education establishments occur under the present system—only research will reveal whether they would increase or decrease under a new system.

Clearly, the practical implications of emphasizing learning in highly self-motivating situations are formidable both in terms of the teacher's role and of school structure. The change in approach by the teacher is the most important and must come first, but effective change can only be truly conceived within a total school reorganization, for, as has been stressed throughout, a complete rethinking of the whole school environment is needed. Just as the traditional concept of teaching limits the full realization of children's learning potential, so the traditional lay-out of the school in class units will inhibit any attempt to put into practice the methods of learning enlarged upon in this paper. The physical design of a school such as that described above will embody in its form the creative attitude towards learning of its teachers and students, and the one cannot exist without the other. No teacher can adequately carry out the ideas put forward here within the traditional classroom structure. Although individual teachers may attempt this—and some in fact are doing so—they will meet with little real success unless their colleagues are themselves participating in these methods, and the whole school organized to accommodate the individual rather than the class.

Such fundamental changes both in the concept of the role of the teacher and in the design of the school will not come quickly. But if they come they will make the school a real centre of creative activity, and result in a fuller and more satisfying life for teachers and students alike.

Progressive Schools and the State
BY MICHAEL YOUNG

'Ending Educational Privilege'

We propose, therefore, to establish under the Minister of Education an Educational Trust. After full consultation as to method and timing, with the local authorities and with the schools themselves, the Trust will recommend the form of integration that will enable each of them to make its best educational contribution. . . . *In making recommendations on how this should be done, the Educational Trust will be required to make special provision for genuine experimental schools.'*

Labour Party, *Signposts for the Sixties*

Special Position of Experimental Schools

So the prospect is that the Government, encouraged (perhaps over-encouraged) by such statements, will rely on the schools to co-operate of their own free will. If that fails to happen compulsory powers may be invoked instead. But even then I doubt whether the progressive schools would be immediately and specifically threatened. This, partly because the Commission's task would be so formidable if it included in its province all independent schools—there are 3,981 of them—and yet unless it did so it would be difficult to justify keeping in the 'progressive schools', which are anyway a category probably difficult to define even in a meeting at Dartington, and impossible in legislation or Orders in Council. But I also think they would be exempt because of the sentiment expressed in the sentence I have italicized in the passage quoted at the beginning of this paper. The Labour Party has never coupled what it calls 'experimental schools', or even independent schools generally, with the Public Schools. It is not all that easy to account for this attitude. The progressive schools are as much confined as the Public Schools to 'those with sufficient means'. But the experimental schools—and I would say the authors of *Signposts* had the progressive schools mainly in mind—have been seen as somehow as much opposed as the Labour Party to the Public Schools, which are the real target of the egalitarians. The adherents of progressive schools and the critics of Public Schools seem, despite all that is said in the next section of this paper, in some vague but nevertheless important way to be on the same side.

What all this adds up to is a prediction that the progressive schools will not be *compelled* to join with the State. But they may be able to join if they wish. Should they? The discussion at Dartington may decide. All I can do in the rest of this paper is to consider what co-operation with the Commission might entail. When we can see the animal we may know whether we like the way he looks.

FREEDOM AND EQUALITY

The first and fundamental question is about freedom—more specifically, whether co-operation with the State would involve a loss of freedom to the schools, and if so how much. Indeed, nearly all the fears of people in the progressive schools revolve around the central issue of freedom. Co-operation with the State might mean that a threefold freedom was lost. Parents would not be free to spend their own money on a school of their choice. Heads and Governors would not then be free to adopt the kind of policy they believe in. The children would not be free in the way that the teachers think is right. The freedoms of parent, of teacher and of child would all be forfeit.

To put it in that somewhat emotive way may seem to answer the question right away. If so many freedoms are at stake who would not go to it for them? Yet apparently the William Temples may be ready to go to the conference chamber instead of the stake. Why the difference? It is worth pausing on this for a moment. I think, as I have already indicated, that the difference is partly to do with religion. In so far as Christianity has stressed 'equality'—we are all, as children of God, equal in the eyes of God—to devout Christians the kind of inequality which is embodied in private fee-paying education is offensive. Children who anyway have the good fortune to be born into wealthy, well-connected families have the added advantage that places are purchased for them at the best schools, which then help to ensure that they will be wealthy and powerful when they become parents in their turn. From this interlocking network of privilege the poor are excluded. Not by any means all the proponents of progressive schools have been as much secularists as Russell and Curry. Neill, I should say, holds a slightly different position, and certainly Badley does. Russell and Curry, not being Christians, were not, perhaps for that reason, egalitarian in predisposition and, not being Christian, they also had not St. Paul's attitude to the sex imprisoned in Roedean. In education their inspiration, along with so many other progressive reformers, has (to deal in vast generalities) come from Greece and the Enlightenment, from Rousseau and Mill rather than from Moses and Tawney. They distrust the State rather than putting their faith in it to correct the human injustice of society.

Both these massive schools of thought are to some degree blended in a democracy, and in the appeal that democracy makes to people who think they do not have it. Men claim equal rights to freedom as much in Smethwick as in Selma. But the gap between those who lean heavily one way rather than another—towards liberty instead of social justice—is still great, and since their premises are different, it is not easy to prop them together again. To those who have a deep-lying distrust of the State, whether democratic or not, or perhaps more if democratic and to some degree subject to the 'popular will', the Commission will make no appeal. Their answer is implicit in their assumptions. It is no use pointing out that the University Grants Committee, though the channel for the transfer of vast amounts of taxpayers' money to the universities, does not control them. The payer does not necessarily call the tune. If anything, it seems, Oxford and Cambridge control the Treasury more than the Treasury controls them. The analogy does not hold up, because no progressive school yet has the prestige of Oxford, or so many ex-pupils in Whitehall. Embark on a financial relationship between big and small, and the small, it is said, would in the end be eaten up.

I take it that at this point in the argument some of the followers of Rousseau at the conference will already have taken up their final stand, and that they will read no more. But on the assumption that some still remain unsure I will descend to a different level of argument. There is another and more practical reason for taking the other side of the question on which so many of the more high-minded (high-minded, that is, in the Christian sense) people in the Public Schools feel vulnerable, that is the restriction of their pupils to the wealthy. A sentence on this has already been quoted from Curry in the preliminary document circulated by Maurice Ash. His attitude was perfectly understandable. If you are conducting an 'experiment' which few of the parents who send their children to State schools would support, then it seems you must somehow strike up a relationship with the one parent in a hundred thousand who agrees with you that the experiment is not so much an experiment as a genuine advance in educational method and approach and is prepared to pay for his beliefs.

It is true that in a general way the Labour Party's scheme does not preclude such particular relationships. Independent schools who enter the fold will, I expect, 'retain their character', and be as entitled to pick the children they want as ever they have been, provided they do not select only those of superior social class or superior academic merit. No doubt some of the best-disposed teachers in the progressive schools will still want to wait and see what the exact terms are. At the same time, I think it is still true that the Commission will jib at paying fees for parents who are in a very small minority, enthusiasts with a handful of others for a doctrine or a practice which to the great majority of the taxpayers (and some of the representatives of the popular will in Parliament) seem extremely odd. No doubt progressive schools are a good deal less odd than they were—they have fallen to some extent under the sway of the institutions which rule the educational system as a whole, the universities, which has made them more like the rest of the schools, while the rest of the schools, at any rate the primary schools, have become a little more like them. But some are more odd than others, and so, irrespective of what the progressive schools wish, some of them would probably not be easily accepted by the Commission. Perhaps others, when observing the shabby treatment reserved for some, might feel that to be counted respectable by the Commission would be too heavy a cross to bear. I dare say the Commissioners, on their fast car trips between Winchester and Curzon Street, Eton and Repton, would not weep to hear on their radio that Summerhill had proudly decided for independence. St. George's, Harpenden, not a progressive school except in being co-educational, has apparently opted for the State and entered into a close relationship with its L.E.A., but St. George's could only do that because it is no Summerhill.

WHAT RELATIONSHIP WITH THE STATE?

But if I have not lost the last supporters by now it may be as well to come back again to the question of what relationship with the State might involve. Progressive, like other independent schools, might have three choices:

(1) *Direct relationship with the Commission.* This is the possibility I was postulating at the beginning of this paper. If the Commission comes into existence it will represent in this sphere the main new departure of the Labour Government. The school prepared to co-operate would probably be required to accept a minority of Governors appointed by the Ministry, and this alone would, of course, be enough to deter some of the existing Boards of Governors. The appointment of Governors would be part of a bargain. The school would have to specify how many and what kind of children, for instance, whether boarding or day, it would do well by, and the Commission would consider whether there was a 'need' on the part of such children sufficient to justify its paying their fees. To decide this it would have to consult with L.E.A.s to determine whether they would co-operate in sending children to the school in question. Each school might be associated with a number of maintained schools from which children would come, either primary or secondary schools. If it turns out that the primary school age is extended to 13 that would probably be the most common age of transfer. Otherwise, in a two-tier secondary system, the age of transfer may be 14.

o

(2) *Relationship with a single L.E.A.* If the Commission is not in the end established, or even if it is, schools that wish might still be able to enter into a treaty with individual L.E.A.s whereby they would take a certain number of children paid for by the L.E.A. concerned. Many L.E.A.s already have their own boarding-schools, or maintain boarding-houses attached to existing Grammar or other day-schools. Some of them might be prepared to increase the number of places they take in independent schools. As already mentioned, St. George's has gone into league with Hertfordshire, and it would not be impossible for others to do the same with their counties. All would depend on whether, again, there was a need on the part of children whose families were unable to give them stability, or where the schools they had been to could not teach the subjects, or teach them in the way they wanted to study.

(3) *Relationship with universities.* The first two possibilities rather envisage that the schools would remain largely as they are, but merely reserve a proportion of places for children from L.E.A. schools. The negotiation would be with individual schools; some would come in, some would stay out when they saw in detail what would be entailed. Another course would be for the progressive schools to get together as a body in whole or part and to take the initiative by presenting to the Commission their own policy for the development of a series of 'experimental' boarding (and perhaps day) schools. The idea is not new. Curry said that 'the school at Dartington is a research station'.

It would be necessary at the very least to submit a series of plans for experiment. Some might incorporate the kind of ventures with new teaching methods for which the State's experimental school at Norkopping has become famous in Sweden. But boarding-schools are not, perhaps, on the whole as well suited as day-schools for classroom experiments, or even for the more daring departures in individual teaching which I hope Mr. Pidgeon will be talking about at the conference. Most of the maintained schools are going to remain day-schools. We are unlikely to follow the Soviet Union in its large-scale move towards boarding education. That being so, the curricular experiments from which most is to be learnt for general application will probably be undertaken in experimental day, rather than boarding, schools. The greatest scope for boarding-schools will be less in classroom reorganization than in the creation of a whole milieu for learning, embracing the entire range of social relationships between children and between children and adults. We still do not know what freedom in all its aspects means for the development of children. To find out means being more deliberate about aims, and about the steps necessary to achieve them. It means being prepared to submit to measurement, that is, to the test of research. The schools would not then just be progressive; they would be experimental, with their results, both positive and negative, garnered as far as that was humanly possible to do.

To mention research is at once to imply the presence of researchers. Where could they come from? The obvious place is the universities. The University Departments and Institutes of Education are showing a new interest in research. The Ministry is at last using public money for the purpose, and the Social Science Research Council, which will probably be set up before the year is out, should bring further funds to their support. The Training Colleges at one time had 'experimental' schools attached to them. The universities could have the same in the future, some of them day, some of them the progressive boarding-schools. Though the Commission would be involved, and would no doubt be called on to find fees for some of the children, the relationship of the schools would be far more with the universities than with the Commission direct, and, stuffy as many of them are at present, the universities might in some ways be preferable.

This is only the barest outline. My only point is that if the progressive schools so decided, they could introduce their own counter-proposal into the debate. They do not need to choose to do either what the State decrees or to stay out completely. There is a third choice. They could take the initiative in determining what their own future should be, and declaring it.

Earlier on I raised the question which I hope will be discussed at this particular session. Should they? What I personally think does not matter. Let me only say, for what it is worth, that I believe a new reconciliation is possible between freedom and equality, and that with some ingenuity it could be a fruitful one.

Co-education and Sex

BY KENNETH BARNES

When we put boys and girls together in a school, especially in a boarding-school, we are producing a sexual situation. This is so obvious that it is difficult now to imagine that teachers ever failed to recognize it. Yet, so I have heard, in the early days of co-educational boarding-schools, if boys and girls fell in love it was regarded as 'silly', and attempts were made to inhibit any such manifestations by the scorn implied in that word. It has been suggested that this policy of repressing sexuality in the co-educational situation produced frigidity in some of the girls involved. I hope there are no co-educational schools in which such a policy persists.

On the other hand, having created a sexual situation, we are responsible for what happens; we must not leave it to take just any course, hoping that an attitude of supposed trust will avoid trouble. This would be to abandon the children concerned not only to impulses within themselves that they are not ready to direct properly but also to powerful external forces over which they have no control.

The sexuality of boys and girls, like every other human drive, needs control and direction—and education. The control must not be by repression, for this may damage their sexuality, as suggested above. It must be through a process that accepts and welcomes sexuality, however great the difficulties it may create. We must accept sexuality, just as we accept the impulse to vigorous physical activity, as an immensely valuable human endowment that can be nourished and educated. This is a wider concept than sublimation, for sublimation too often implies an attempt to side-track the sexual impulse because we are afraid of it and wish it did not exist.

Not that there is no reason for fear. We can give the impulse to violent activity a full outlet in a rugger game or in chopping down a tree with an axe. But the full expression of the sexual impulse, which is actually possible in the early teens, is incompatible with the rest of our educational needs and provisions, and it could bring education to an end. So for practical reasons, if not for ethical or religious reasons, we inevitably distrust sexuality and have to live within a contradiction of fear and acceptance. But a contradiction that is acknowledged need not be harmful; there are inevitably many such contradictions in human life. The harm, if any, is done in the attempt to escape by turning acceptance into repudiation—by wishing away the sexuality of our pupils.

There is no necessary harm in having to live through a conflict. A conflict is not a neurosis; it is through the way the personality deals with conflict that we produce a neurosis or avoid one. The deepest and most penetrative thoughts of mankind have come through having to face a conflict. Man is made for difficulty, not only the difficulty produced by his environment but also the difficulty produced by his ambivalent and turbulent nature. It is in line with this that the most promising of human relationships, the sexual, should offer the most difficulty, that the deepest of experiences should often be prepared for through the most disturbing of initiations.

It is not surprising that the co-educational boarding-schools were pioneers in the early development of sex education. They had to face the situation they had created. In a single-sex school it is possible to forget the need for sex education, or at least to limit it to passing manifestations such as masturbation. But in a co-educational school the whole field of sexual relationships is necessarily opened up, both in relation to the present and the future of the boys and girls under our care. The more progressive co-educational schools have been responsible for the continuing development of sex education chiefly for the reason that, unlike most other schools, they have been primarily concerned with boys and girls as persons developing in relationship rather than as minds to be trained.

The first efforts in sex education were restricted to the giving of anatomical and physiological information, to satisfy justifiable curiosity and to remove ignorance that might be responsible for failure and suffering in the marriage relationship. I began this work early in the thirties when teaching at Bedales, and the open and fearless relationship possible there between children and staff quickly brought other needs to our attention, made it apparent that much more was needed. Even if we assumed that every child would find his or her way safely into the respectability of marriage, we had to recognize that for this, the most demanding of all human adventures, no conscious preparation was given. Why did we assume that we could not produce physicists without a long preparation in mathematics, yet allow people to attempt living for forty or fifty years with another person with no preparation at all?

So sex education had now to include education for marriage, with reference, in passing, to the problems of courtship, to venereal disease—and to pre-marital intercourse as an experience to be avoided. This was a big enough development for its time. It involved a married teacher sharing with his or her pupils some of the fruits of married experience, not only concerning the physical experience but also the intimate relationship of men and women as persons and their problems as parents.

Since the Second World War there has been a further opening up of the facts about sexual relationships and experience; this has shown that yet more is needed. I had already been prepared for this by the results of a questionnaire sent out just before the war to young people after they had left school. This showed that though they were grateful for the information they had been given at school, they still had to cope with bewilderment, frustration and especially the unexpected impact on them of other and very different personalities.

A sex education that assumes that all, or even most, young people can follow the straight and narrow path of morality into the assumed safety of marriage is unimaginative, unrealistic and inadequate. It leaves many injured by the wayside without any Samaritan to attend them. It illustrates the futility of an education primarily concerned with being good and doing the right thing—an education in pharisaism. It fails to recognize that there is often a conflict between warm-heartedness and morality, as Jesus recognized in his encounter with the woman of Bethany. It may be wise for a motorist to plan his journey so that he can avoid rough roads, but when the journey is into the unknown—and life is always like that—it is much more important that his car should be strongly built and well sprung, so that it will not be shattered by the rocks and pot-holes he may unexpectedly meet. Idealism in sex education may leave a young man or woman rigid and brittle, totally unprepared for the real crisis into which life plunges him, unable to adjust to the fact that no man or woman is ever ideal. My own studies over the past few years have made one fact among others abundantly clear. We have always taken it that sex will explode frequently in the lives of the 'worst', but we have now to recognize that it explodes frequently—if unexpectedly and painfully—into the lives of the 'best'.

A co-educational school provides the conditions in which reality can be understood and progressively faced. A single-sex school, it seems to me, simply asks for unreal attitudes, even in spite of the efforts of sensible teachers to the contrary. I had evidence of this in the reaction of a group of girls from a girls' boarding-school who wrote to me about the pamphlet 'Towards a Quaker View of Sex'. Their principal objection seemed to be that it dealt with unpleasant *facts*. I had to reply by referring to the challenging experience of some of my own girl pupils who had subsequently become child-care officers or psychiatric social workers. The difference between the co-educational and the single-sex school is probably more marked in the case of girls than of boys. A boy's sexuality may become distorted in the absence of the other sex, he may become fixed in the homosexual phase; but he remains obviously a sexual being, to himself and to others. A girl's sexuality can be repressed to an extraordinary extent, and she may remain profoundly ignorant of her own nature. She may grow on into adult life without knowing what she is doing; and what she is doing may be to create havoc.

In a co-educational school, though some may not be touched by it at all, boys may pass through the homosexual phase when, for instance, mutual masturbation occurs. Sometimes this becomes a matter of anxious concern when it becomes a cult associated with sadistic bullying, but more usually the boys pass out of it quickly and without anything having to be done about it. Instances of boys growing up in a co-educational boarding-school and remaining homosexual are extremely rare. I have had recently an instance of an 11-year-old boy coming into our bottom form obsessed with masturbation. He called every possible attention to his activities; but his effect on the group was not to create a similar obsession in others. It was to produce a disturbance that quickly brought the matter to my notice. When I had the boy removed—not because of the masturbation but because of associated deeply neurotic tendencies that needed psychiatric treatment—there was general relief. An intrusion into their life had been removed. I would not wish to argue from a single instance of this sort, and I cannot collect enough evidence to be of statistical value; but the instance does fit into a general impression that continued homosexuality is not wanted by boys in a co-educational school, and they are glad to grow out of it.

Under co-educational conditions a girl comes to recognize that she is a sexual being, and she knows what this implies. Further, she is usually content to be her age. She is not drawn into the shocking and dangerous sophistication that is seen in many 13- or 14-year-old girls in the general population. It is generally recognized that a girl's sexuality is diffuse rather than genitally localized, and the sophistication that I have mentioned is an intense hotting-up of this diffuse sexuality—shown in a precocious preoccupation with make-up, stiletto heels, vulgar ornaments, hysterical shrieking and arch manners. Because of its impact on men and boys, this diffuse precocity can plunge the girl suddenly into genital experience—experience for which she is quite unready. Moreover, this condition, once established, seems irremediable. Perhaps other heads have had the experience I have had, of accepting a girl of this age and in this condition, hoping to be able to make a normal and responsible girl of her, but finding that this was not possible: she proves a continuing danger to herself and to boys, and has to leave lest there should be a disastrous result.

It is rare for a girl growing up in a co-educational boarding-school from the pre-puberty stage to become like this. And if a girl comes to the school with this sophistication but before puberty she is likely to drop it and become natural.

Experience in a co-educational boarding-school removes many illusions about girls that are still maintained in middle-class society: the illusion, for instance, that they are naturally modest, fastidious and hygienic. (The recent report on the condition of women's lavatories must have been a shock to those who cherish these illusions!) Those who have believed that women are naturally modest have assumed that no 'nice' woman would appear on the stage of the Windmill Theatre, and they must have been bewildered when unquestionably nice young women appeared in bikinis. The truth of the matter is revealed by the fact that if boys and girls have an opportunity to bathe naked the girls more readily take it—and will do so happily and wholesomely. It is noticeable that the more sophisticated girl, the one who wants to use her sexuality provocatively, is *less* ready to do without a costume.

I suppose most of us are at least a little shocked when we hear girls using four-letter sexual words. Another illusion gone! But it is no use expressing shock; they may have to work their way through and out of this just as boys do. There is sometimes reason, however, to caution girls about accepting whatever a boy-friend says or does, simply because of the female tendency to respond to whatever the male expects. Boys, with their genitally centred interests, can sometimes be appallingly obscene—as is shown by notes picked up from waste-paper baskets or dropping out of pockets—and some of them thrust their obscenity mercilessly on girl-friends. This is an instance of a situation in which girls should be encouraged to be independent and to hold their own standards, if they have any. Indeed, this is necessary throughout the relationship of the sexes.

The fact that in co-education we have to recognize that girls share a basic crudity with the other half of their generation should not be any reason for discouragement. It does not make them any less likeable, and it does show what our real material is and our real task. Aren't we often faced in adult scandals with the challenge to recognize that some young woman whose outer appearance seems to be of impeccable good taste, a model of daintiness and hygiene, has been living a sexual life than can only be described as sleazy? One of the most heartening experiences in school life—more obvious in girls because it happens at an earlier age—is to see a girl achieve a real degree of maturity by the age of 18, a maturity in which she is coming to know herself, to accept her 'earthiness' with all the rest of her and to make it part of her integrity.

I find that young women keep in touch more than do young men, and they are more open about their intimate experiences. The heartening experience I have described is sometimes followed by something even more encouraging; the awareness that they are coping constructively and compassionately with the sexual challenge of the young adult world, meeting the laxities of group life and the urgencies of importunate men, without superiority or prudery, but without losing their own integrity.

It seems to be specially necessary in a co-educational boarding-school to establish a relationship with children at an early stage in which all fear and shame about sexual matters are lifted and their interests and needs become clearly apparent. Perhaps it is a result of many years' experience and of being completely at home in the situation, that I find that after the 11-year-olds have been in the school a month or two it requires only a few remarks, some of them humorous, to put boys and girls in a fearless condition in which questions simply pour out: all the questions that they have been holding back and imperfectly attempting to answer among themselves. It sometimes takes hours to answer simple questions of fact, so many there are. It has to be recognized that, as a result of the greatly increased publicity about sexual matters, there are now many more items of interest and curiosity in the child's mind. We must no longer side-step a question about contraception because the child seems too young (though we may restrict the scope of our reply to what he can reasonably take).

This ease and confidence between adult and child should be maintained as far as possible throughout the latter's school career, for there may soon come a time when you have to discuss with him or her a boy–girl relationship that is warming up. You will not be much use to them if the two regard you as a hostile intruder. You have to get their co-operation and understanding in limiting the degree of sexual expression. You have to be both compassionate and honest; it is useless to act merely with authority, even though at critical moments authority may sometimes be necessary. The two must be able to feel that you are made of the same sexual stuff as they are, and that you can see into their problem precisely for that reason. The question of trust sometimes comes acutely into the situation. I am asked, with evident pain on the face of the questioner, 'Don't you trust us?' Usually I have to reply: 'I trust you just as much as I would trust myself, and that's not very far!' This is not wriggling out; it is the plain truth: that for all of us the avoidance of an action that may prove disastrous depends upon stopping before we reach the steep slope where the skis inevitably take charge of us. Young people usually have too much self-confidence—girls especially, for their bodies do not warn them as soon as does a boy's. I often quote Dr. Marion Hilliard in saying to a girl that 'her best defence is to have no confidence at all in her ability to say nay at the appropriate moment'.

All this has definite implications concerning the size and organization of co-educational boarding-schools. Either the school must be small enough for the Head (or other responsible person) to know the boys and girls and to be accepted by them as a guide or it must be socially subdivided so that there are responsible married adults in contact with groups of manageable size. I would not like a co-educational boarding-school to grow amorphously to a size where contrivances, subtle 'management' or extensive prohibitions have to take the place of personal contact and guidance. Where co-education ceases to demand and provide opportunity for the personal approach to personal problems there is little value left in it. The fundamental justification for co-education is that it can provide the better conditions for the deepening of everything that is intimate and personal.

This should not, however, be taken to imply that our work in this intimate aspect of education can be carried out behind a door that is slammed on the world. We cannot afford to neglect forces that operate on the mass, on every single one of us. This would again be to make the mistake of the idealist, expecting that if you induce the acceptance of the 'right' standards and ideals in your pupils all will be well. We have to assess and direct all our efforts in full awareness of the cultural matrix in which we all move. We must dig out, recognize and criticize the hidden assumptions of our particular society. The characteristics and differences of the sexes as we see them are too often taken as absolute. In the unconscious there operate not only the archetypal forces that are the common inheritance of mankind everywhere but also the habits and assumptions taken in increasingly and imperceptibly from our particular society.

These thoughts lead me to return to the point touched upon earlier concerning the adjustment of sex education to what we expect to be our pupils' future experience. What place should we give to 'morality' in this education?

In recent years many voices have been heard questioning the value of the conventional moral approach: the Quaker pamphlet, its support by social workers and by some distinguished Anglican clergy, the Bishop of Woolwich's criticism of 'packaged morality', similar statements by Anglican writers in Cambridge, the Reith lectures by Professor Carstairs and the even more daring broadcasts by Alex Comfort.

At the time of writing I am having to deal with a problem of two sixth formers—boy and girl—who have established a rapidly warming-up relationship that leads them to break rules right and left (e.g. about bedtimes). They are both thoroughly good people, appreciative, intelligent, devoted to the school. As they themselves admit, when they are together in the evenings all other considerations are swept aside; they become irresponsible. They make no excuses. I could express moral shock at this contradiction in their conduct. But I don't; I've got to work from within the situation, not from outside it. Behind my immediate thoughts is the awareness, sharpened by the research carried out during the activities of the Quaker Committee—that this is precisely the problem of adult life. Unexpected and unintended sexual encounters break into the lives of even the most responsible people and set them adrift for a while on an uncharted sea. That this is not widely recognized is due to the fact that such problems are sometimes lovingly and constructively resolved without any publicity, or the marriage, because it has to be maintained, jogs along reasonably well, or the stronger partner, through sheer generosity of spirit, is able to accept the aberrations of the other. We ought to be glad, not sorry, that in a co-educational school the situation can arise, if only in miniature, that challenges the partners to deal constructively with this disconcerting discovery about their own nature.

There are times when we are bound to be exasperated by teenagers, to lose our tempers, even to be fierce in judgement.

These things can happen without harm and perhaps even with good result, provided the teenagers are not thereby shut out from us, made to feel the mere *objects* of moralizing. I have emphasized the unexpectedness of much sexual experience, and we must hold this in mind in everything we do to prepare our pupils. If I try to put a picture of marriage before them it will probably be that of a marriage between equals, between two independent people who before marriage have achieved a maturity of their own and who after marriage retain the kind of equal-sized independence that lends continued interest to the relationship and the possibility of endless discoveries. I shall want them to be equally intelligent or, if not, at least equally respecting each other's valuations and judgement. I shall probably say that they should have a joint bank account with equal responsibility for signing cheques! Perhaps a pupil will take me seriously enough to say that he or she will be determined to find a partner with whom such a marriage will be possible.

But it remains true that marriage is to some extent a lottery. The impulses that drive people into love and the decision to marry are often irrational. So the erstwhile pupil finds himself not with the woman he dreamed of marrying but a real woman who doesn't fit any dream. The two together have to build a marriage sensitively and tolerantly on what is in fact possible between them, not on what ought to be possible. Some principles may still be important, but persons come before principles.

We may tell our pupils that it is good to avoid pre-marital intercourse, and find excellent reasons for saying this. But we know perfectly well that many of them will not be able to maintain such continence, and not necessarily through any 'fault' that we can discern. Accident and circumstances may prove more powerful than the strongest of intentions. The quality of our preparation of such pupils may make the difference between pre-marital intercourse that is a mere trivial aberration, cheapening their sexuality, and an encounter which, though outside the code, is personal and enriching. I always find that there are some people who are enraged by the suggestion than an encounter outside the conventional code can be enriching. I have little patience with them. They refuse to face facts because they are afraid they may be true. They are our modern pharisees.

No matter how wise our preparation, some of our pupils will make marriages that are so unsatisfactory that divorce is the inevitable end. Are these to be thought of merely as failures? If our only aim was to get pupils safely and permanently married, they are. But an education that is entirely directed towards the hope of success is a misdirected education. Most people experience more failure than success, and an adequate education should help them to assimilate failure, to assimilate their own mistakes and disasters. In other words, it should enable life to be redemptive. Redemption does not mean learning from mistakes in order to achieve ultimate success but taking mistakes and failure humbly into ourselves so that we are deepened and sensitized by them. There is a great difference between a divorce that occurs between people acting in this way and one in which there is only bitterness and despair.

It should be evident that our primary aim should be to encourage in our pupils the development of resilience and compassion, and a fundamentally creative attitude towards difficulty.

It may be observed that I have said much more about sex and co-education in relation to girls than boys. This is because the sexual problem in boys and men remains much as it has always been, whereas in girls and women we have an emerging problem that insistently clamours for attention. It may be true that the future of mankind depends more on the education of girls and on what we expect of women than upon anything else. For woman to achieve her proper place in the world's affairs—a place that need not sacrifice one iota of her womanliness—might be radically to transform the possibilities before mankind, to open up a new era of creative development.

But even if this is accepted, the attitude and education of the boy is just as important as that of the girl, precisely because the girl cannot 'become' unless the boy equally 'becomes' in the relationship. It has been traditionally accepted that the male takes what he can get of sexual experience. The continuation of this tradition is incompatible with what we hope for in the development of girls. I am glad when girls from my school show that they know how to deal with the irresponsible male for whom taking a girl to bed is as casual as lighting a cigarette. But it is a severe criticism of our world and of the education of boys that girls should so often have to face this problem—an uncreative and defensive situation. I think we can claim that boys in a co-educational boarding-school become more imaginative about the nature and needs of girls and women, more aware of what they are doing in a relationship, more responsible for the partner as a person and not likely to treat her as a receptacle.

With the emancipation of women there is the danger that the less-fastidious woman, seeing apparently unlimited freedom ahead of her, will take the right to trivial sexual experience just as men have taken it. This kind of equality will only intensify an evil, and the suicidal attempts of certain young women whose adventures have recently come before the public eye may be the extreme manifestation of an emptiness that a doubled evil is producing.

The Future of Boarding in Modern Society

BY ROYSTON LAMBERT

This is too vast a topic for so small a paper, and must be cut down to manageable size. First to my own dimensions. I imagine I have been asked to write it because I am making an enquiry into boarding-schools—their aims, organization and effects—in this country, and it was thought that the evidence I have gathered would enable me to produce some firm conclusions on which to base an argument as to what might or should happen to our boarding system. If this was the case, then I am going to be disappointing. I fear there are no 'conclusions' as yet to report.

My research, which is planned as an integrated whole, is nearing the end of the first of its two phases of field work, and until both are complete there can obviously be nothing like the balanced evidence from which to derive conclusions. What this paper offers is impressions and arguments only, based on nearly two years of living and researching in boarding-schools of different kinds, but, like all impressions and arguments, subject to drastic revision as the analysis of the material proceeds. That is the first methodological limitation in this paper.

The others are in its scope. I am deliberately not going to question here the value of residential education in itself or to discuss whether it produces desirable or adverse effects, or even any distinct durable effects which cannot be produced by day-school systems. Nor am I setting out to challenge the basic purposes of different kinds of schools. For present purposes, they

are taken for granted. In particular, I am not going to be concerned specially with progressive schools, partly because I
have yet had relatively little to do with them, but mainly
because to concentrate on them would not be to deal with the
future of boarding at all, as it is improbable that their influence
on the majority of schools in the future will be much greater
than in the past. Shrinking my subject still further, I shall, you
will be relieved to hear, not harp on that ancient theme, how
best to integrate the maintained and independent sections of
education, though I shall assume that some integration will
occur.

What I do have to say is both limited and practical; limited
to the predicament in which most boarding-schools find
themselves at the moment, and practical in suggesting a
solution applicable within the next ten years or so. But it
seems to me that if some such solution were applied at the same
time as the overall national structure of our independent
boarding system were being revised, then the very nature of
boarding education would be fundamentally changed. Some
radical alteration is necessary if boarding is to become a more
effective instrument for diverse educational purposes than, in
many cases, it is now.

II

Boarding-schools are, in essence, small social systems
functioning to attain some particular ends. These ends differ
widely from school to school in their context, complexity and
explicitness, but the social systems which serve them have basic
elements in common. They all have a formal structure, economic, academic and social, through which the official aims are to
be realized. Within this there exists an informal social organization which may, or may not, work in the same direction. Every
school, like any other society, is articulated by systems of
authority, status and values both formal and informal. Above
all, like other members of the sociological species of 'total'
institutions to which the boarding-school belongs, such schools
are self-contained communities providing for all the basic
needs of their inmates in one place for twenty-four hours a day
and directing or guiding their activities towards the ends of the

P

institution. The basic similarities of these miniature societies may often be disguised and need to be stressed. The Public School, for example, with its elaborately articulated structure, its published rules and regulations, its carefully graded hierarchy, its manifold sub-systems, its traditional values and modes of expressing them, seems a far cry from a progressive school which expressly repudiates many of the former's aims and methods. But the structural differences between them may not be, in fact, so great. For instance, the absence of elaborate formal organization in the progressive school may derive from the fact that, being a recent creation, it is still under the influence of a Founder and Headmaster whose charismatic attributes enable the society to function without much overt organization or formalized arrangements. Once that individual goes, however, and unless he is replaced by another with the same attributes (a most unlikely occurrence), the school, if it isn't to collapse, will develop a formal bureaucratic organization and will approximate far more to the basic system of a Public School. This is what has happened, for example, at Rendcomb or Bedales and may be happening here. One other reason for apparent difference is that comparison is often made between the elaborate official system and control from above in the one type of school with the seeming lack of either in the other. Important and valid as this difference is, it may not be sociologically so significant. Where the official system in a school may be deliberately undeveloped, it is inherently likely that the informal social system will be performing its functions. Thus one would expect to find that the informal pupils' society of a progressive school contains many of the elements of both the formal and informal system of a Public School. For example, the social controls and limits on freedom may be as great or even greater from being the enforced norms of the informal organization—that is the children—as from being laid down from above by adults as in a Public School.

Few books on progressive schools have described this aspect of their life. But it seems to me that a progressive school is as much a total institution as a Public School, except, as it were, turned upside down.

I have dwelt on this comparison in order to stress the common and inevitable characteristics of boarding-schools as societies in miniature. Most arguments in favour of boarding-schools stem from this latter concept. Basically, such arguments run, boarding offers a protected, selective and controlled society, small enough to provide security yet complete enough to enrich, and through the life of which a child can develop himself individually and equip himself socially for the wider society outside. This latter notion is particularly prevalent among the pupils. As one satisfied customer of 15 put it to me, 'I regard this school as a kind of training centre. I feel that I will benefit from this centre in the years to come.'

But this particular aspect of boarding-schools brings us to their special dilemma and to one of the ways in which they differ from other members of the species of total institutions. Unlike them, unlike, say, a monastery or a mental hospital, with both of which it has some fundamental affinities, the society of the boarding-school is not continuous over time or in place and not self-contained in purpose. Every ten weeks or so when term ends this tiny society disbands. And its educational purpose, which usually includes some variant of the preparation for life, means that it must reflect and be aware of the wider society outside.

III

It is from this situation that the modern predicament of boarding-schools derives. Few relish the microcosmic character imposed by their educational function. Some largely reject the outside society and, cultivating their own values and patterns of life, turn themselves into little citadels from which they hope their pupils will emerge to transform the world around them. 'My school,' wrote one headmaster to me the other day, 'is a society apart, setting different standards of life from the outer community in the hope of exerting some influence upon it.' Most are more open, cultivate a critical awareness of outside life and try to use their own closed society to build up resistance against features they dislike. In both cases the emphasis is on maintaining the identity of the self-contained society of the school to the detriment of fulfilling its microcosmic function, of reflecting or adjusting to the world outside.

Unfortunately for the school, however much it tries it

cannot be self-contained; its pupils are not perpetual inmates, they shuttle back and forth between the two societies. Where they expect to find correspondence, they find contradiction, where they may seek reflection, they find distortion. The one society often repudiates major features of the other. This gap is shown by the extraordinary patterns of their lives which our research is charting. Many of them resent this lack of integration between the life of the school and that of outside society. To them, as the following typical comments from one fairly liberal and unrestrictive school indicate, the school cannot be a microcosm. 'Most emphatically, boarding-school,' writes a sixth former, who started boarding at 13, 'has given me another world to live in. A world which is totally different from the one I used to know all about.' 'I feel the need to get out and see society,' says a boy in the lower sixth. 'In the school one is bricked in literally with permits, slips and the such. . . . One feels so much apart.' 'This place,' notes a 15-year-old, in a phrase which seems to me to sum up the sentiments of a generation of schoolboys, 'this place is like a monastery, except that some old monks want to be cut off from the world, whereas we don't.'

How different the situation was sixty or a hundred years ago! The boarder of those times felt few, if any, of the discrepancies and contradictions between school and outside life which now perplex his descendants. The school consciously acted as a preparation for the wider society and concentrated into its own system the attributes, expectations and values of the classes it served. It was clearly recognized that one of its functions was to train its recruits after the established model of a gentleman and for the position of a governing *élite*. The structure and value system of the school admirably fitted this purpose. Society outside conformed, externally at least, to the tenets and practices of orthodox Christianity; so did the schools. Society relegated women to an inferior place; the schools ignored them altogether. The primary unit of the family was authoritarian in nature and sought in the relationships between sons and parents to establish the self-controlled detachment of adulthood, to play down affection, dependence and the intrinsic quality of childhood. In all this it was faithfully supported by the boarding-school. Microcosm matched macrocosm. Indeed, if you still want to find fragments of Victorian life, customs and values you have only to look among the boarding-schools of England.

Society has changed drastically, but, partly because of the way these changes have occurred and partly because of the in-built resistance of any self-contained society to change, the school has not kept up with it. This is the case, I am beginning to think, with most boarding-schools in England. Not all are Victorian period pieces by any means. But virtually none have so rethought their boarding methods and structure as to base it on what their children experience as the commonplace realities of modern society.

So obvious are some of the disparities between the life of school and society between term and holiday experience that I need only catalogue them here. The role of most independent boarding-schools in training an *élite*, though still defended by some people, has been challenged and undermined. Their proper function in society at large is far less clear than in the nineteenth century. Most schools have religious objectives which they attempt to realize by enforcing observance; in this they are at variance with the habits of the classes they serve, and certainly with the holiday-time life of their pupils. Again, most of them are single-sex schools, often carefully restricting contact with the opposite sex. This is where their life and approach differ most considerably from the home society of their pupils and where the latter find one of the greatest points of strain in their dual existence. The autonomous youth culture which has grown up since the war has infiltrated the life of boarding-schools, but, far more even than day-schools, their reaction has been negative and uncomprehending. The same goes for many other aspects of urban or sub-urban culture. Hence again the large discrepancies we are finding between the values, pattern and style of life of boys in and out of schools.

This and other types of dualism is, of course, experienced and coped with by many children in day-schools. But for boarders, for whom the extremes are greater in any case and for whom the contrasting lives are successive rather than continuous, the situation is far more difficult to manage. Some to whom school life has been the reality find the outside world

daunting, themselves inadequate and their isolation and lack
of friends outside depressing. Here are one or two:

> I find I am left without any social life in the holidays
> so that I have little to do to amuse myself.

> You tend to live in two worlds. It is hard and sometimes
> embarrassing to connect the two.

> It has cut me off from the other sex and I feel rigid and
> socially stiff in their presence. I feel a fear of going out into
> the world merely because I am not prepared socially.

The reaction of others, and a substantial minority, is far
different. Their holiday life is a sort of escapist fantasy, a
frantic period of indulgence, acutely restless, and from which
many confess themselves glad to get back to the secure, orderly
reality of school life. This is not only failure to adjust to the
freer world outside but also the reaction to their lack of roots,
of meaningful social relationships outside the community of
the school. This pattern appears not only among Public School
boys and girls but also among those in maintained boarding-
schools. Here are two expressions of it, typical, I must stress, of
a fair number.

> It has isolated me from most of my friends, made me an
> oddity and a virtual outcast. It makes home more appre-
> ciated, but makes walking down the street, for instance,
> seem what it must seem to a newly released prisoner—a
> breath of fresh air—a taste of freedom—something
> unreal. This is why many boys rebel in the holidays,
> going to the opposite extreme of dress, behaviour and
> respectability often verging on the delinquent. Hatred of
> discipline is something this school has given me. Also a
> desire to go to the opposite extreme from the Victorian
> respectability that reigns here. This school has brushed off
> on me a kind of social sterility and isolation.
> . . . they long to be outside. Boys are often 'tearaways'
> in the holidays. This is just a reaction to being shut in but
> if it can be switched off when you return to school it is all
> right. The thoughts have to be shut from one's mind and
> this is very difficult.

I am not yet in a position to say just how many feel like this and how many act like this, although I hope to be able to do so. Obviously, many adjust pretty well to their two lives. Most also have a very shrewd appreciation of what their schools are positively doing for them—talk of a crisis among the senior boys in boarding-schools grossly over-simplifies the complexity of their situation and practical reactions. But many are bewildered by the disparities of their existence and think them unnecessary. In so far as this is the case, the boarding-school is failing in its microcosmic and preparatory functions.

There is one other, fundamental, way in which the school and the outside world no longer correspond. In the nineteenth century the boarding-school fitted the life, need and assumptions of the middle-class family. This is not true of the present middle-class family (and still less of the working-class one). It is more democratic in character, more openly affectionate and close in relationships and more conscious that childhood and adolescence are distinct and desirable phases of growth. Boarding life as it is practised now in most schools means absence from the family for long periods of time. There is little evidence that in the last century children thought this an undesirable and unnatural thing. It fitted so well the mores of family life. Even if many did feel some strain, the united expectations of both family society and school may have made it easier to bear. But nowadays even children coming from families with a long tradition of boarding, and certainly those who are first-generation boarders, feel deprived of some things on which the family and wider society place great stress, but which no school community can adequately provide: tenderness and love.

The matter is complex. Children are conscious of both gain and loss by living away from home. The gain consists in the new appreciation of their family and of home which the rigours of the school may bring. Many see value in the self-control and respect which distance and infrequency of contact enables them to achieve in their relationships with parents. But many also express a continuing sense of loss—loss of intimacy of intercourse and above all of tenderness and affection which no holiday spasm of excessive mothering and no healthy adult–child relationships in school can really replace. (There is also something very similar in the acute sense of loss of former local friends felt by boys long after they enter the schools from home at 13.) I am not suggesting here any comparison between the family relations of boarders and day pupils. What I am stressing is that boarding children feel they are losing something which many say they need and would like to have, and which the protagonists of boarding, who usually make their case by dwelling on the defects of family life, scarcely seem to recognize. We are back to the central dilemma of boarding-schools again. Self-contained as they may try to be, they can never build into themselves the quality of relationship which it is the prerogative of the modern family to provide.

We have now reached the heart of this paper. Over large and crucial areas of a child's experience, school and outside society fail to correspond or even come into contact. To some considerable degree the society of the boarding-school fails to act as a microcosm, as a means for fulfilling its fundamental educational purpose. Must this be so? Should our boarding system continue at variance with modern urban civilization? Above all, need boarding continue to be at the expense of local ties, a sense of belonging and the irreplaceable strengths of family life? Unless these two questions are properly answered, the schools will fail even more in attaining their objectives as their methods cease to be relevant to modern life. But an answer may soon be imperative. If children from local day-schools and first-generation boarding families are to enter the schools in any numbers the problems of relevance to life, the life they have known and the values and patterns of which they will probably want to keep, may dislocate the society of the school altogether. But this potential hazard could become a constructive opportunity. The entry of these children offers the schools far more than integration into the national structure of education; it gives them the opportunity to render boarding a far more effective educational instrument, by revising our whole conception of what boarding should be.

IV

The answer to the dilemma of boarding-schools is to become 'local' schools. Most of them now pride themselves on being national, whatever that may mean. It means that they claim to have a national stature, though in fact we are finding that the vast majority and even some of the top ten Public Schools are heavily regional in catchment. They are not prepared to admit this in public. This stress on national character is maintained partly for prestige reasons, partly because the schools are business concerns and have to sell themselves in the widest market. What is imposed on most by national necessity is, as with so many other aspects of their life, strongly defended by educational theory. But it is difficult in the mid-1960s, where regional differences are so slight, to see what educational advantages come from this alleged and often spurious national composition. For very few it may provide better academic competition for their scholarships. But for the rest, are children from Wiltshire or Manchester so very different from those from Yorkshire and London?

It is surely far more important educationally, especially if they are all uniformly middle class, for schools to be diverse in the social and occupational background of their children rather than in their geographical distribution. In accepting a local catchment the school would be able to be just this. If integration comes, schools may have to accept a local intake and no longer need to propagate for financial reasons the myth of being national. (Of course, there is no reason why a proportion of their numbers should not come from outside the locality.) Far from being reluctant in their acceptance of local status, the schools should whole-heartedly welcome it, for, if properly used, it offers them at long last the possibility of matching microcosm and macrocosm, of realizing their aims in future through a closer, more interwoven relationship between the miniature and the wider society, rather than seeing them lost, as at present, in the chasm which divides the two. For their pupils life need not be a schism between real and unreal, spasm of withdrawal and spasm of indulgence, but a more satisfying, intelligible and complex whole.

Schools must realize that, whatever their internal richness, however all-embracing their community life, however much they need to maintain their corporate identity, they can never be fully-contained, that their pupils have needs which they as schools cannot really provide. Localism means that more needs can be met and yet the schools can be involved, as never before, in their provision.

How can this be done? Briefly, by bridging the present gulf between school and home existence. If children live locally they can have more continuous contact with their homes. By 'home' I mean not only their immediate family but their local friends and neighbourhood. Though they may still attain the appreciation, self-control and respect for their parents which they now say they have, boarders would not necessarily lose in intimacy or affection or feel that restlessness, that rootless sense of not belonging which so many of them have and which prompts their extreme holiday-time behaviour. This entails that the rigidness of our present-day and boarding patterns should give way to a new flexibility. I am certainly not contending that all schools should be weekly-boarding but that within schools the system should be varied enough to suit the differing needs of individual children and homes. Some might wish to see each other frequently, others rarely or not at all. Apart from one Public School, some more Direct Grant schools and one maintained boarding-school, few schools which set out to be real boarding communities have officially adopted this flexible approach. Though in many more, if they but knew it, their pupils have unofficially done so.

The objections are obvious. As one Housemaster said to me, 'home could become a funk hole', a place to escape from the pressures and responsibilities of community life. Others assert that once the exclusive character of boarding is broken down, the school's sense of community and identity, of being a small distinct society, will disintegrate with it. Still more wish to keep the week-end in particular for the school. But there is plenty of experience and evidence to contradict these arguments. We are finding, for example, that these cherished boarding-school week-ends are, for large numbers of children, tracts of unutterable boredom relieved by bouts of indiscipline, punctuated by compulsory rituals and, for the younger boys, filled with hectic and quite confessedly time-killing activities.

In schools where there is a substantial proportion of local boys a large number go home illegally as it is; after carefully examining them we do not find that they are less integrated, less loyal or less contributive members of their school communities. Those schools which do permit contact with local homes and do have a sense of boarding purpose do not seem to suffer in the vigour, richness and identity of their own corporate life. Even some special schools in which the boarding purpose has a socially therapeutic element permit frequent contact with the home; their internal life is not impoverished and their objects are, indeed, promoted. Contact with home need not sap the strengths of the school, for what those children primarily go home for is just what the school community is not equipped to give them.

Any threat which might possibly emerge to the society of the school would be contained if the school were to try and bring the home into contact with it. One cardinal feature of most schools in this country, whether day or boarding, independent or maintained, is their failure to work through the home as well as the school environment. Boarding-schools are far better placed than the others to draw parents into their life, their values and their work. This opportunity is not being realized at all. Public Schools regard parents as a nuisance, clients to be treated diplomatically, but escorted off the premises as soon as possible. Maintained boarding-schools are not much less welcoming, and are often placed so far away from the localities they serve that parents can only infrequently visit them. Localism offers the chance of drawing the parents and the home into the purpose of the school. In Russia, where the neighbourhood boarding-school has been developed, this is done by the parents doing maintenance and other domestic work. In England it surely ought to be possible to draw parents into the extra-curricular life of the school, as a few schools are pioneering in lonely isolation.

Many of the larger boarding-schools are equipped and function as evening institutes; why cannot parents join them? The L.C.C. Crown Woods School, for example, *is* an Evening Institute, and I have been there when parents from around flock to it; unfortunately, the boarders there are all from abroad. A pioneering opportunity has been missed. Contact in the school between parents and children and staff and parents could be a major way of easing present strains and extending the school's educational influence into an area where it now seldom reaches.

Local catchment also gives the chance for more meaningful involvement with the immediate environment than is at present achieved. Many boarding-schools are disliked locally, regarded as colonies of aliens, and in return keep themselves aloof, or send parties of children to help only the aged and disabled. They very seldom have much contact with other local schools and local children, except on the games field. The children in them rarely think of themselves as belonging to the place as distinct from the school, and a sizeable number regard themselves as not belonging to any place anywhere. One or two Direct Grant and Maintained schools have much interchange with the locality where their children were born, bred and still belong. School and locality interweave far more in their pupils' lives. Skilful deployment of this potential strength at one school, which realized what it could do, at once increased the satisfaction of the pupils and the influence of the school over them.

The moral of this is that schools need to come to terms more with modern society if they are to attain their ends. By rejecting that society, as so many of them do, they are also rejecting one of their educational functions and leaving their pupils largely to fend for themselves in it. The dismissal of the paraphernalia of modern urban life, such as cinemas, coffee bars, theatres, restaurants and shops, the rejection of pop culture, the persecution of modern styles of hair, dress and expressions seem to produce remarkably little effect in the inner life of a school or in the outer life of pupils and divert attention from more significant matters. Half-hearted gestures are often worse than none. The school that permits one dance a term or less usually has more trouble over that isolated, over-exciting, exhibitionism-provoking event than those few schools which allow girl-friends and regular social contact between the sexes inside and outside its bounds. Co-education, in the sense of boys and girls living together on the premises, is not the only answer to single-sex schools, as the satisfactory link-up between some boarding- and day-schools academically and socially shows. Anyway, once the local principle is accepted, the sex problem will become less acute. In all of those single-sex schools with a large local intake (of day boys or boarders) and a fairly tolerant policy there was significantly more contact between the sexes during term and less dissatisfaction on this score. In this and other ways the schools need be less suspicious of modern life and less distrustful of their pupils. The responsibility of senior boys (or others) in most boarding-schools is immense, but the responsibility they are permitted over many of their own most trivial decisions is minute. But to develop that theme would be to digress too far.

One final point. New boarding-schools, especially on the maintained side, are being created. Why are so few of them in towns or suburbs? Why should they be deliberately placed in remote villages or decaying market towns? Why should Coventry's school be lost in rural Shropshire, London's far out in East Anglia, Lancashire's boys' school be in mid-Buckinghamshire? Is remoteness from towns (and home) the indispensable concomitant of boarding? Very few Public or Grammar Schools in towns exploit the opportunities of their position. In future, when new maintained schools are put up, we ought to build on to existing day blocks, or convert adjacent houses or terraces into boarding accommodation. Boarding should not repel the urban environment—or the rural one either. (Some urban schools have lodges or cottages for holidays or courses in the countryside.)

V

This paper has deliberately not discussed whether it is better to board at school than live at home, or questioned the various objectives of schools. Nor have I dwelt on the practical difficulties arising particularly from the preconceptions and extremely limited experience of the staffs of many boarding-schools now. There is a considerable variety in the objectives and in the types of school, but, throughout, an amazing sameness of boarding structure and method. The purposes are manifold, the framework uniform.

I have concluded that boarding-schools are failing in some considerable areas of their purpose (not necessarily all) because they no longer reflect in their structure, practices and values the outside world, of which their inmates are well aware and, regularly, full participants. If they would accept and exploit the position of local schools, diversify their boarding patterns, work with and through the strengths of family and locality they would undoubtedly be more effective in realizing their aims. What is needed now and what the changes of the coming months may well make possible is a fundamental revision in our concept of what boarding should be.

Appendix on Creativity as a Function of the Type of Education

BY ISABEL BOYD CABOT

The following section reports an attempt to test some of the differences between groups of pupils at schools having widely varying educational assumptions. The gap in understanding revealed by the report of the Colloquy makes it important to examine every possible piece of relevant evidence about different educational approaches. Proponents of each approach feel themselves to be right with an almost religious dedication, and although in education, as in religion, there may be as many ways to Heaven as people that want to get there, it is still worth trying to find out the merits of the various ways.

Unfortunately, the instruments surveying the way are still far from efficient—as will be explained later in the report.

The tests used were for the most part those which Dr. Hudson (1966) describes fully in his book about clever schoolboys. Dr. Hudson was most generous in offering the use of these tests, and it is with gratitude we acknowledge the source. The aim of that book was 'to delineate two types of clever schoolboy, the convergers and the divergers'. The former do well in conventional intelligence tests where there is only one possible answer. The latter do well in tests that are known as 'open ended' because there is a very wide range of possible answers. The convergers tend to be science specialists and the divergers arts specialists.

The intention of the present study was not to continue the

investigation of convergers and divergers as belonging to different academic biases but rather to see how, under dissimilar academic environments, divergence (at times equated with creativity) and convergence (at times equated with conformity) might develop. The development of either mode of thinking must, of course, presuppose a body of knowledge, a frame from which the pupil can diverge or to which he can convergently add. This knowledge is mainly acquired in school, but there are many additions which depend on other influences. The literature in this field of investigation has been amply reviewed for some years now. There is also a brief comment on it in Dr. Hudson's paper in this book.

There were certain obstacles which made a completely valid comparison impossible. One was that in each school only one sixth form was tested. Everyone connected in any way with schools knows that there are good groups and difficult groups. Therefore in order to make the testing more complete it would have been necessary to test the sixth forms in each school over a period of years.

Another difficulty lay in the fact that a comparison of the types of school automatically involved a comparison of parental attitudes. Parents who select a boarding-school for their children are usually relatively well-to-do. However, within that group educational expectations will vary. Parents who choose a progressive boarding-school presumably want their children to be considered as persons in their own right and not just dealt with in a kindly but authoritarian way. Parents who choose a more formal school also want the best for their child. To them the best will be a school where the child is in these days reasonably well treated but is in a subservient position to the older pupils and the staff.

The attitudes and affluence of the parents whose children attend a State school may vary widely, but whatever the variation they are all day pupils. This means that presumably the home influence is more direct, although in later adolescence the influence of the peer group is recognized as perhaps stronger. The fact, however, that the student is in the sixth form presupposes support and interest by the parents and also a level of financial stability.

Unfortunately, within the limits of this enquiry it has been impossible to investigate the students' backgrounds more thoroughly.

Lastly there is a much more fundamental difficulty; an attempt is being made to test a social situation when in fact the tests can only discriminate among very personal capacities. Personal capacities can be reduced to general statements about groups of people only if the testing situation is highly structured. As soon as an open-ended test is administered, personal capacities are being tested, and they are not comparable on the same level. They are not in the same field of discourse because each person is unique. When we test people with structured tests—of which many intelligence tests are typical—we are not testing personal qualities; rather, we are testing the capacity to respond in predetermined ways, to fit into the structure of educational society. We can only compare people in relation to certain capacities (e.g. intelligence) in the public sector of their lives and thought. The private sector is where imagination, originality and creativity lie. In this sector no person is like any other, and the nearer we get to genuine creativity, the less we can score. Imagine comparing creativity scores for Beethoven and Mozart!

On a lower level, that of the clever gifted student, it is still difficult to compare the results of open-ended tests. Variety of experience must influence results. In this way even open-ended tests are structured by the tester's choice of words or objects. A bricklayer might well find it difficult to think of many original uses for a brick. So might an aborigine.

Despite these criticisms, interesting observations and comparisons still emerge. In considering the possible value of various educational approaches an examination of the results might at least provoke further speculation and discussion.

Testing

The testing was carried out in the upper and lower sixth forms of four schools. All the students already had a varying number of Ordinary Level passes and were working towards the Advanced Level examinations. More than half of each group was intending to go to University, the rest had a variety of aims involving some form of further training (see Table of Career Choices). The schools were:

1. A boys' Public School which was humanely conventional with a strong religious bias and a tradition of academic success. Forty boys.

2. A girls' progressive boarding-school with a tradition of academic success and a lively interest in the Arts. Thirty-two girls.

3. A co-educational progressive boarding-school with very democratic staff–pupil relationships and a permissive rather than an authoritarian approach. There was also a strong regard for academic success for the able coupled here with much opportunity to work formally and informally in the Arts. Seventeen boys, nineteen girls.

4. A day comprehensive school which most of the students had attended since age 11. The sixth forms were obviously the pride and pleasure of the staff. Relationships were very good. As the school had only been in existence 8 years, there could be no long tradition academically, but there was an excellent record of University entrance. Here, unless the student specialized in the Arts, there was little opportunity to continue to work in this field, except perhaps in the school music or drama societies. Twenty-eight boys, seventeen girls.

The tests used were chosen from the battery of tests described in Appendix B of Dr. Hudson's book (1965). It was thought that, as Dr. Hudson had already used these tests in England in an attempt to discriminate on the basis of academic interests and biases, it would be advisable to use the same tests to try to discriminate between environments and to establish if possible a transferability of concept with Dr. Hudson's results.

Limitations of time in the schools made it impossible to use all the tests, and so the following were selected:

1. *Two tests which attempt to define the divergent type of thinking*

(*a*) '*Uses of objects*'. Here the student is asked for as many uses as possible for the following objects:

A barrel, a paper clip, a tin of boot polish, a brick and a blanket.

This test has been widely used for some years now in America on the grounds that it will distinguish the students capable of fluent, associative and original thought. It also conforms more closely than any other test to the definition of creativity offered by Wallach and Kogan (1965), whose work is mentioned in the discussion of results. The test is scored on both the number and the originality of the replies. The originality is related to the answers given by the whole group tested. This was achieved by listing all the responses given by all 153 students. Any reasonable use suggested once only was scored as unique, and a use suggested by no more than three students was scored as unusual.

(*b*) '*Meanings of words*'. In this test the student is asked for as many different meanings as possible for the following ten words: Bit, bolt, duck, fair, fast, pink, pitch, port, sack, tender. This test has also been in use in America for some time and requires of the student the ability to shift frames of reference within an organized structure. This test was scored by counting the number of different meanings given. Slang was accepted but homophones rejected. This quality is hypothesized to be one of the activities which the divergent thinker finds easy.

II. *A test of verbal and non-verbal reasoning*

This test which was intended to define the convergent thinkers was the A.H.4. It is described by its author, Dr. Heim (1955) as having a variety of biases and principles. The first part of the test has a verbal and numerical bias, while the second part has a diagrammatic basis. Dr. Heim says, 'As in most formal tests of intelligence, the stress is largely on deductive reasoning. In addition, the subject is required in Part I to understand the meaning of everyday words and throughout the test to observe details accurately and to follow simple instructions exactly.' There are norms for a number of different groups, and the pupils tested in this study have been arranged in categories according to the norms for university students. In addition, several other aspects of the students' outlook and interests were explored.

The instruments of this exploration were:

(*i*) *A personal qualities questionnaire.* In this the student is given a list of qualities of which he is asked to approve or disapprove, such as: obedience, independence of parents, highly imaginative, mixing well socially, accepting expert advice, using bad language. Dr. Hudson (1966) compiled it with five characteristics in mind: authoritarianism, rigidity of attitude, social conformity, freedom of emotional expression and defensiveness. Because three groups in the study include girls, the scale to define defensiveness was taken out. As the author of the questionnaire had already discovered that this scale and the one intended to define emotional expressiveness did not differentiate among his divergers and convergers, this omission was unimportant. The scale to define emotional expressiveness was, however, retained to see if this quality would differentiate between the groups in the different schools, although it had failed to distinguish between convergers and divergers.

(*ii*) *Controversial statements.* This consisted of twenty-four statements, some of which were controversial, others of which, although factual, were liable to arouse emotion. The statement that 'A man ought to read just as inclination leads him; for what he reads as a task will do him little good' can be discussed from several points of view. The statement 'The Royal Family costs the British taxpayers some £2,000,000 per annum', although a fact, provoked vigorous comment from many of the students.

The students were asked to comment on any statement that interested them. Most of them responded to almost all the statements. Their comments provided some very interesting insights, and although scoring was difficult, certain statements already isolated by Dr. Hudson were used, as he had used them, to form a liberal–authoritarian scale. It was hoped that the results would add to the information already gathered by the 'Personal qualities' questionnaire.

(*iii*) *A biographical questionnaire.* This asked not only for information about the student's own academic bias and his or her career objectives but also about his or her special interests and hobbies, and affiliation with clubs. Except in the case of outside affiliations, such as a playgoers' group or C.N.D., this was not very revealing, as all the schools appeared to have a wide variety of organizations.

This questionnaire also asked the student for a list of the five people in his form who were most widely read, most interested in technical matters, most interested in painting and music, current affairs, out-of-door activities and who were most persistently hard working. The material in the latter part of this questionnaire would be of more use in a clear division of convergers and divergers and has not been analysed beyond noting the numbers for each student. The first part of the questionnaire forms the basis for the table of careers.

(*iv*) *General knowledge.* This was a factual test involving a knowledge of politics, literature, painting, music, science and the achievements of some famous men. Many questions in this test were similar to those in the tests of culture devised by Richmond (1963). The following are typical examples:

Schizophrenia is: (*a*) part of a Roman Amphitheatre, (*b*) a wild flower, (*c*) mental deficiency, (*d*) the division of states by an invading power, (*e*) part of the body, (*f*) a form of madness, (*g*) dizziness.

Le Corbusier is: (*a*) a wine, (*b*) French slang for a taxi-driver, (*c*) a system of landscape gardening, (*d*) a cooking pot, (*e*) an architect, (*f*) Marie Antoinette's brother, (*g*) a cathedral city.

Continuous Creation is associated with: (*a*) a modern novel, (*b*) origin of the universe, (*c*) salting of the sea, (*d*) atomic reactors, (*e*) evolution, (*f*) original sin, (*g*) none of these.

A few questions were not scored, as they had already become 'dated'.

The ability to answer the questions probably depended more on an attitude of mind than on academic training, despite the fact that the answers to a few of the questions might have been learned while studying.

DISCUSSION OF RESULTS

When considering the following tabulation of the results of the tests it is important to remember all the methodological criticisms raised in the introductory paragraphs. These were: the small size of each group, the testing of only one year, the doubtful validity of the tests devised to isolate convergent and divergent thinking, and the impossibility of measuring either the parents' attitudes or the unique influence of the interaction of each parent with the school in relation to the pupil.

Before going on to consider some of the possible implications of these results it might be useful to clarify the meaning behind the phrase 'levels of significance'. The test of significance is a rough measure of the probability that a result, such as a difference in means (or averages) for different groups, has occurred by chance and does not represent a real difference between the groups. A 1 per cent level of significance means that there is one chance in a hundred that the result has occurred by chance and does not represent a true difference. Obviously, a significance level of 0·01 per cent will indicate a difference that is almost certainly real. The symbol $<$ means less than the number given, and $\ll$ means much less than the number given.

On looking at the table of significances it is immediately obvious that there are few significant differences between the boys and the girls except in the 'Uses of Objects' test. As this is also a test which shows the capacity for associative thinking, now felt by some psychologists to be a more accurate predictor of potential 'creativity', these results are of especial interest. The fact that there are more girls in the progressive group might at first glance be interpreted as meaning that girls were better at such a test, but this initial hypothesis is rendered very doubtful by the fact that high as the significance level is between boys and girls, it is much higher still between the traditional and progressive groups. Thus the results can be interpreted as due to the influence of the progressive approach regardless of the sex of the pupil. It is more probably just a chance association with sex because so many girls happened to be in the progressive schools tested.

The greater imaginative and associative ability shown by the

MEANS SCORES FOR SCHOOLS, SEXES, TYPES OF SCHOOL AND TOTAL SAMPLE

School, etc.	Intelligence	Word association	Uses of objects	Acceptance of authority	Rigidity of attitude	Social conformity	Emotional expressiveness	Liberal opinion	General knowledge
Girls' boarding 32 Students	88·47	28·72	34·31	8·44	7·63	17·00	14·92	20·35	7·97
Co-ed boarding 17 Boys 19 Girls	90·56	28·64	29·28	7·22	8·86	15·03	14·86	19·78	13·56
Comprehensive 17 Girls 28 Boys	94·58	25·80	21·04	8·16	10·24	18·18	14·56	19·44	6·42
Boys' Public 40 boys	92·63	25·55	21·17	8·85	10·38	18·45	13·77	18·08	10·73
All boys 85 students	93·21	26·28	22·30	7·94	9·95	17·41	14·24	19·18	11·06
All girls 68 students	90·13	27·92	30·15	8·47	8·72	17·07	14·85	19·53	7·66
Progressive schools 68 Students	89·57	28·78	31·65	7·74	8·28	15·96	14·91	20·00	10·93
Traditional schools 85 Students	93·66	25·68	21·10	8·48	10·31	18·27	14·19	18·80	8·45
Totals 153 students	91·84	27·02	25·79	8·18	9·40	17·26	14·51	19·33	9·55

In the attitude scales the higher the score, the stronger the characteristic.
When the differences in means were tested by a two-tailed normal distribution test the following significance levels were noted:

	Intelligence	Word association	Uses of objects	Acceptance of authority	Rigidity of attitude	Social conformity	Emotional expressiveness	Liberal opinion	General knowledge
Progressive Traditional Boys and Girls	5 $\quad$ n.s.	<0·1 $\quad$ 1·0	≪0·01 $\quad$ <0·01	(10) $\quad$ n.s.	0·1 $\quad$ (10)	0·2 $\quad$ n.s.	(10) $\quad$ n.s.	5 $\quad$ n.s.	n.s. $\quad$ n.s.

n.s. = no significance.

CAREER CHOICES

School	No. of students	University	Business + Professional	Teaching + Social Services	Arts	Misc.	Don't Know	Subject Biases Arts	Sciences	Mixed
Boys' Public	40	27 66% of school	5	3 doctors, 1 church entered in Univ. column	1	3	4	17	19	4
Girls' boarding	32	19 59%	—	2 doctors entered in Univ. column 3	3	1	6	19	8	5
Co-ed boarding Girls	19	11 58%	1	1 doctor entered in Univ. column	6	1	0	10	6	3
Boys	17	12 70%	—	—	1	1	3	7	8	2
Totals	36	23 64%	1	—	7	2	3	17	14	5
Comprehensive Girls	17	8 47%	1	6	1	—	1	13	4	—
Boys	28	16 57%	2	4 1 doctor entered in Univ. column	3	1	2	6	18	4
Totals	45	24 53%	3	10	4	1	3	19	22	4

Business, etc. = Banking, accountancy, secretarial, computer operator.
Arts = Art school, crafts, drama, architecture.
Misc. = Army, air force (pilot), farming, catering, horses, films.

progressive-schools group on the 'Uses' test may be due to many influences. However, it is not unreasonable to suggest that in an environment relatively free from the more usual authoritarian and examination pressures, surrounded by opportunities for both free and guided work in the arts, given the possibility of informal relationships with adults and given time to follow individual interests undisturbed, such abilities would be fostered.

When scoring the 'Uses' test it was illuminating to see that some suggestions which appeared very original stemmed from activities and experiences within a particular school, e.g.

(1) Posture training with a brick.
(2) Demonstration of magnetism with a paper clip.
(3) Lowering ceiling or roof with a blanket.
(4) Growing seeds in an empty polish tin.
(5) Making a bread board from the base of a barrel.

Each of these answers was given by only one school but in that school by several students. The implication is surely that the wider the range of experience, the more freely people will be able to produce associative thinking.

As there is no other area of testing in which the significances are quite so high, the remaining results will be discussed in the order in which they appear in the table of results.

Verbal and non-verbal reasoning test (Intelligence)

According to the results of this test, the pupils in the traditional schools have a significantly higher score than those in the progressive group. This difference in scores can be seen in another form by studying the grades into which students in each school fell when the norms for College students were applied to the scores. There were eleven A grade results in the conventionally educated group and only four in the progressive group.

The level of significance, although not very high, is sufficient to support the validity of the difference. As the career and educational aims and known examination achievement are all very similar, this difference between the groups could justifiably be taken as further evidence in support of the suggestion made in the introduction that such tests are only testing the students'

Q

capacity to fit into the structure of educational society. In the more conventional schools the pressure to such conformity appears to be stronger. There is more time given to this type of work, with the inevitable consequence of less time to spend on other activities.

STUDENTS' GRADES USING A.H.4 NORMS FOR
UNIVERSITY STUDENTS

Grades	A	B	C	D	E	Number of students
Girls' boarding	1	6	13	8	4	32
Co-ed boarding	3	8	12	7	6	36
Comprehensive	5	8	23	8	1	45
Boys' Public	6	8	12	9	5	40
All boys	10	18	35	14	8	85
All girls	5	12	25	18	8	68
Progressive schools	4	14	25	15	10	68
Traditional schools	11	16	35	17	6	85

Word association test

Again in this test, widely used in the United States as a predictor of latent 'Creative' ability, the differences between the groups is strongly marked, with the progressive schools scoring more highly. This is interesting, as the results of the test itself do not correlate with the results of the 'Uses' test. Presumably, another area of divergent or creative thought is being investigated, but the differences between groups are in the same direction as in the 'Uses' test.

Acceptance of authority

The differences here at the 10 per cent level of significance can hardly be considered important. As Dr. Hudson found that the scale differentiated between his convergers and divergers this has interesting implications. People tend to criticize progressive education as not producing students capable of accepting authority—permanent rebels. Yet according to these results the students under either system differ little. Of course, the results may only mirror a much wider trend in the growing adolescent disregard of authority.

Rigidity

In this scale the difference between the groups was at a highly significant level, with the students from the progressive group showing themselves as much less rigid. To understand the implications of this result it might be best to quote the list of qualities of which the student was supposed to approve or disapprove: (1) highly imaginative; (2) mildly eccentric; (3) having set opinions; (4) accepting expert advice; (5) trying to be original; (6) artistic sensitivity.

Of course the desirability of being more or less rigid depends on the convictions of the adult trying to determine educational standards. Just as many adults will disapprove as will approve of a child being highly imaginative or trying to be original.

Social conformity

The fact that the progressive group is shown to be less socially conforming is rather to be expected. It is probably a reflection of parental attitudes as well as the influence of the school. What is interesting is that this difference should be shown to exist between the groups although the 'acceptance of authority' scale does not distinguish to any degree.

Emotional expressiveness

This scale again fails to differentiate between the groups, as it also failed in Dr. Hudson's experience to show any clear difference between convergers and divergers.

Liberal opinions

The progressive schools group is shown to have more liberal opinions, but the difference between the groups is not nearly so great as in the divergent thinking tests. The questions were marked by two people independently and the results compared, each disagreement being discussed. The overall impression (subjective) of both scorers was of logical thinking being more in evidence in the progressive group. Their answers were very balanced, and a rational streak tended to moderate emotional responses.

Typical of this was the discussion of the statement previously quoted, 'A man should read, etc.' The student said:

> He ought to do both. Much literature is meant to be enjoyed and is not a solemn treatise on various subjects. If he reads only that he wouldn't be very knowledgeable. If he did enjoy reading he probably would not mind being made to read something that was worthwhile. He might forget everything from a stuffy text-book though.

General knowledge

As can be seen from the significance tables, this test failed to differentiate significantly between the groups.

A further analysis of the material suggests many other insights which it is not properly within the province of this report to discuss. One, however, which raises many questions as to attitudes and expectations is the fact that, despite a high Intelligence score, the girls in the Comprehensive school had extremely low scores on the Divergent thinking tests. They are being educated in a society strongly oriented towards masculine succcess, whereas the girls in the Progressive school and even more in the Girls school are much more considered as persons in their own right. The strong pressures of a masculine-oriented society are somewhat mitigated as part of the same process that makes progressive educators see education as concerned with the individual rather than with society. It would need a much larger sample to prove or disprove such a hypothesis, but it has at least a surface plausibility.

These results might, then, with great caution be taken to indicate a possibility that formal education tends to foster more highly structured thinking, while the progressive approach tends to encourage the capacity for the more divergent type of thought.

On a much larger scale evidence in support of this viewpoint is becoming available. Much of this work has been done in America, and it is of interest to note that Professor Torrance

(1965), who has been working in the field of recognition and development of creativity for many years, is now suggesting that the success of divergent thinkers is directly related to the degree of freedom and permissiveness and lack of authoritarian discipline in a school. Again, in America, Wallach and Kogan (1966), having defined creativity as 'the ability to generate or produce within some criterion of relevance many cognitive associates and many that are unique', go on to divide the children they worked with into four groups, the High Creative–High Intelligence, High Creative–Low Intelligence, Low Creative–High Intelligence and Low Creative–Low Intelligence. Having then studied many aspects of behaviour and intellectual functioning in the children, the authors in their final conclusions make a very strong case for the value of a learning situation where as far as possible the 'sense of threat' is removed. This removal of the 'sense of threat' is particularly important for the child with the difficult combination of High Creative–Low Intelligence. These children are often their own worst enemies, disruptive, attention seeking, lacking in confidence, less befriended by their peers and often treated with impatience by their teachers. They are, after all, difficult to manage and often very irritating. This impatience is bound to continue the vicious circle of difficult behaviour. But these children are potentially valuable and need a special kind of tolerance and time to grow.

The authors argue the necessity for understanding in all the different groups, although the one mentioned above is perhaps the most in need. Only in this way, the authors feel, can associative thought be freely and usefully developed.

In England Miss Gardner (1967) makes a similar point in her book *Experiment and Tradition in the Primary Schools*, although she is concerned there with the effects of teaching methods in general rather than the specific fostering of creativity. In a study assessing the results of experimental and orthodox educational methods the children were tested for all the abilities and qualities that critics of a free approach believe cannot be developed without external disciplinary means. The tests were designed to assess concentration, co-operation, honesty, moral judgement, inventiveness and imagination, as well as ordinary academic attainment. In every ability and quality except mechanical and problem arithmetic the children from the free schools were in varying degrees better than those from the more orthodox schools.

Also of interest is the account of a follow-up of ex-pupils of Summerhill School. This was undertaken by Bernstein (1967). He found that generally the former Summerhill students had adapted successfully to society and were particularly well able to cope with authority. The author of the report then goes on to suggest that the more rigid schools could learn much from such an unstructured approach. This less highly structured approach is already accepted as current practice in many elementary schools in Britain.

Of course, the type of educational approach we use ultimately depends on whether we think of education as a device to reinforce the values and ideas of society or as a sufficient good in itself. In a way this is an extension of the difference between the progressive and traditional approaches. The progressives see education as concerned with the individual and the traditionalists see it as concerned with society. In fact, this argument cannot take place, as indeed it failed to do at the Colloquy because, as it were, the two sides are pulling different ropes in the tug of war. There is no dichotomy between the individual and society, because they belong to two different categories. The needs of society cannot be balanced against the needs of the individual, because the two are not the same kind of entity.

At present much of the work in the field of creativity is being carried out because its discovery and nurture are thought to be of value to scientific advance, and hence to society. For years some educators have been concerned for the development of creativity for the child's own sake, hoping that by this means they can encourage the growth of a truly mature personality. To these educators the current emphasis on creativity will hold the danger of doing something good for the wrong reasons. They will realize too that creativity cannot be mass produced on demand.

However, the present interest may cause the contribution of many progressive schools to be more seriously considered. We might end with a quotation from Wallach and Kogan (1966) in their chapter on implications and applications of their findings to education.

'If teachers can be taught to de-emphasize the success–failure aspects of the learning process and to encourage children to approach school assignments in the spirit of associative play much will have been gained.' The progressive schools have essentially been trying to do this for years, and more recently many Infant and Primary schools have started working in this way.

What we now need are schools at the senior levels willing, despite examination pressures, to create an educational atmosphere conducive to the development of the whole person.

Bibliography to Appendix

BERNSTEIN, E., 'Summerhill after 50 years; the first follow up', *New Era*, vol. 48, No. 2, 1967.

GARDNER, D. E. M., *Experiment and Tradition in Primary Schools*, Methuen, 1966.

HEIM, A. W., *Manual for the Group Test of General Intelligence. A.H.4*, National Foundation for Educational Research, 1955.

HUDSON, L., *Contrary Imaginations*, Methuen, 1966.

RICHMOND, K., *Culture and General Education*, Methuen, 1963.

TORRANCE, E. P., Private Communication to Dr. H. J. Butcher, 1965.

WALLACH, M. A., AND KOGAN, N., *Modes of Thinking in Young Children*, New York, Holt, Rinehart & Winston, 1966.

INDEX